John Freely was born in New York in 1926 and joined the US Navy at the age of 17, serving during the last two years of World War II. He has a PhD in physics from New York University and did postdoctoral studies in the history of science at Oxford. He is Professor of Physics at Bosphorus University in Istanbul, where he has taught physics and the history of science since 1960. He has also taught in New York, Boston, London and Athens. He has written more than 40 books, including works in the history of science and travel. His most recent book in the history of science is *Light From the East: How the Science of Medieval Islam Helped to Shape the Western World* (2011). His recent books on history and travel include *The Grand Turk, Storm on Horseback, Children of Achilles, The Cyclades, The Ionian Islands* (all I.B.Tauris), *Crete, The Western Shores of Turkey, Strolling Through Athens, Strolling Through Venice* and the bestselling *Strolling Through Istanbul* (all Tauris Parke Paperbacks).

'This is a magnificent book, covering an extraordinary range of topics and a vast sweep of time. John Freely has lived, written, and taught in Greece, Turkey, and Italy for a lifetime, and this experience has given him the rare ability to tell complex stories in a lucid and engaging manner. This is a book everyone should have.'

– John Camp, Professor of Archaeology,
ASCS, Athens Stavros Niarchos Foundation Professor of Classics,
Randolph-Macon College

THE FLAME OF MILETUS

MILETUS

THE BIRTH OF SCIENCE IN ANCIENT GREECE (AND HOW IT CHANGED THE WORLD)

JOHN FREELY

I.B. TAURIS

LONDON · NEW YORK

FSC
www.fsc.org
MIX
Paper from
responsible sources
FSC® C007584

Published in 2012 by I.B.Tauris & Co Ltd
6 Salem Road, London W2 4BU
175 Fifth Avenue, New York NY 10010
www.ibtauris.com

Distributed in the United States and Canada Exclusively by
Palgrave Macmillan
175 Fifth Avenue, New York NY 10010

ISBN: 978 1 78076 051 3

A full CIP record for this book is available from the British Library
A full CIP record is available from the Library of Congress

Library of Congress Catalog Card Number: available

Printed and bound in Sweden by ScandBook AB

In memory of Olga O'Connor

CONTENTS

List of Plates	viii
Preface	ix
Map	x
1. Ionian Enlightenment	1
2. Harmony and Logos	15
3. The One and the Atom	27
4. The School of Hellas	40
5. The Grove of Apollo	54
6. Aristotle's Successors	66
7. The Geometrization of Nature	77
8. Measuring Heaven and Earth	87
9. Moving the World	95
10. Mathematics, Astronomy and Geography	103
11. Ingenious Devices	114
12. The Art of Healing	124
13. Spheres within Spheres	134
14. Classical Twilight	145
15. From Byzantium and Islam to Western Europe	156
16. The Renaissance: Byzantium to Italy	173
17. The Scientific Revolution: Greek Science Reborn	185
18. Eureka! Greek Science Rediscovered	202
Notes	210
Bibliography	226
Index	236

PLATES

1. Apparent motion of the stars about the celestial pole
2. Use of a gnomon to determine the solstices and equinoxes (above and below)
3. Apparent retrograde motion of a planet (above). Epicycle theory of Apollonius to explain the retrograde motion of the planets (below)
4. The tilt of the earth's axis as the cause of the seasons (above). The equinoxes and solstices shown on the celestial sphere (below)
5. The rotation of the celestial pole about the ecliptic pole due to precession
6. Aristotle's cosmology
7. Measurement of the earth's circumference by Eratosthenes
8. From Aristarchus' *On the Sizes and Distances of the Sun and Moon*; the lunar dichotomy
9. Stellar parallax
10. Hero's inventions: temple doors opened by fire on an altar (above), steam engine (below)
11. Ptolemy's concept of the equant (left). Simplified version of Ptolemy's planetary model (right)
12. Ptolemy's experimental investigation of refraction
13. The Copernican system
14. Tycho Brahe's system (left). Kepler's first two laws of planetary motion (right)
15. Galileo's telescopic view of the moon
16. Projectile in orbit around the earth, from Newton's *Principia*, 1687

PREFACE

This is the story of Greek science from its beginnings in the sixth century BC on the Aegean coast of Asia Minor, through its development in classical Athens and Hellenistic Alexandria, and then its subsequent spread to the wider world. Most histories of Greek science end in late antiquity with the collapse of the Graeco-Roman world. But the present book continues the story to tell of the acquisition of Greek science by Islam and the transmission of Graeco-Islamic science to Western Europe, as well as the preservation of Hellenic culture in Byzantium and its profound influence on the European renaissance. The story is told against the shifting background of the various interconnected cultures involved, an intellectual travelogue that ranges back and forth from East to West with the tides of history, showing how ideas first formulated in the archaic Greek world took wing to survive for two millennia through the rise and fall of empires to inspire the new science that began in Western Europe in the seventeenth century. This is not an academic treatise for specialists, but rather a book written for the general reader with a taste for transcultural history off the beaten track, a fascinating story that is here for the first time told in its entirety.

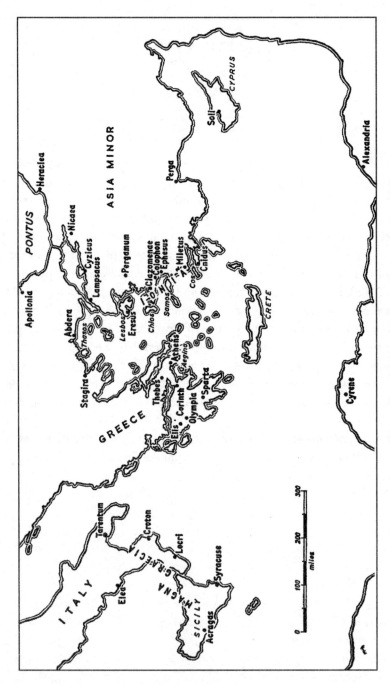

The Greek world in the fifth and fourth centuries BC

CHAPTER 1

IONIAN
ENLIGHTENMENT

The birth of Greek science and philosophy did not occur in what is now Greece itself but in the city of Miletus and other Hellenic colonies on the Aegean coast of Asia Minor, now part of the Republic of Turkey.

I first visited the site of Miletus in April 1962, along with my wife Dolores, travelling there on my spring vacation at Robert College in Istanbul, where I had started teaching physics in the fall of 1960. The first stage of our journey brought us from Istanbul to Izmir on the monthly post boat, after which we boarded a bus to the town of Söke and then a *dolmuş*, or public taxi. This took us out across the delta of the Maeander River to the village of Balat, whose ramshackle houses were built on and from the ruins of ancient Miletus. The name of the village is a corruption of the Greek *palatia*, or palace, from the Turkish legend that the ruins around it had once been the palace of a great king.

We had the archaeological site all to ourselves except for the *bekçi*, or watchman, who was busy looking after his herd of goats, whose tinkling bells were the only sounds that we could hear in the vast expanse of desolate ruins. The best-preserved monument of Miletus is its great Hellenistic theatre, which at the time of our first visit was the only structure of the ancient city that had been restored to any degree, all of its other extant buildings in utter ruins or still covered in silt deposited by the Maeander.

With an old archaeological map to guide us, we made our way to the site of the harbour of Miletus, the famous Lion Port, named for the marble statues of a pair of lions that flanked its fortified entryway. We found that the lions were still there, though almost buried in alluvial earth, marooned

1

miles from the sea that had once been ruled by Miletus. The Greek geographer Strabo notes that 'Many are the achievements of this city, but the greatest is the number of its colonisations, for the Euxine Pontus [Black Sea] has been colonized everywhere by these people, as also the Propontis [Sea of Marmara] and several other regions.' He also says that it was the birthplace of Thales, Anaximander and Anaximenes, the first philosophers of nature, whose ideas took wing and spread to other Greek cities and then, eventually, to the rest of the world.

Miletus and the other Greek cities whose ruins one now sees in western Turkey were founded early in the first millennium BC, when a great migration took the Hellenes eastward across the Aegean to the coast of Asia Minor and its offshore islands. Three Hellenic tribes were involved in this exodus, with the Aeolians settling on the northern Aegean shore of Asia Minor, the Ionians to their south, and the Dorians still farther south, founding colonies extending from the Hellespont to the southwestern-most peninsulas of Anatolia.

Herodotus, describing this population movement in Book I of his *Histories*, writes that the Ionians ended up with the best location in Aegean Asia Minor, for they 'had the good fortune to establish their settlements in a region which enjoys a better climate than any we know of.' The traveller Pausanias says much the same, and goes on to note that 'the wonders of Ionia are numerous, and nor much short of the wonders of Greece itself.'

According to Herodotus, all three groups of Greek colonies formed political confederations, originally twelve cities each of the Aeolians and Ionians and six of the Dorians. These confederations were loosely knit, and the individual city-states were entirely autonomous, as were the other Greek settlements in Asia Minor that never joined any of the three leagues. The Ionian confederation was known as the Dodekapolis, 'the Twelve Cities', ten of them on the Aegean coast of Asia Minor and one each on the islands of Chios and Samos. The cities on the mainland were, from north to south: Phocaea, Clazomenae, Erythrae, Teos, Lebedus, Colophon, Ephesus, Priene, Myus and Miletus. (Smyrna, which had been an Aeolian city, was conquered by Ionians from Colophon in the second half of the eighth century, but it did not become a member of the Dodekapolis until much later.) The Dodekapolis had its common meeting place, the Panionium, on the mainland opposite Samos. The Ionians also met annually on the island of Delos in the Cyclades, the legendary birthplace of Apollo, their patron deity. There they honoured the god in a festival described in the *Homeric Hymn to Delian Apollo*, in which the poet addresses the god himself:

> Yet in Delos do you most delight your heart; for the long-robed Ionians gather in your honour with their children and shy wives. Mindful, they delight you with boxing and dancing and song, so often as they hold their gatherings. A man would say that they were deathless and unaging if he came upon the Ionians so met together. For he would see the graces of them all, and would be pleased at heart gazing at their well-girded women and the men with their swift ships and great renown.

Most of the *Homeric Hymns* date to the archaic period, *ca.* 650–480 BC, whereas authorities now tend to date the composition of the *Odyssey* and the *Iliad* to the period 750–700 BC. A number of the eastern Greek cities, mostly Ionian, claimed to be the birthplace of Homer, which occasioned the Greek epigram: 'Seven wealthy towns contend for Homer dead/Through which the living Homer begged his bread.' The most popular claims were those of Chios, where a guild of rhapsodists called the Homeridai boasted descent from the poet, and Smyrna, whose citizens claimed that he was 'the son of Meles, the river god of their town, by a nymph Creitheis.'

Aeolian Cyme, one of the cities that claimed Homer as a son, was in fact the birthplace of Hesiod's father, Dius. Hesiod, in his *Works and Days*, writes that his father left Cyme and moved to Boeotia, northwest of Attica. One wonders why Dius left the fertile lands and fair weather of the Aeolian coast for the harsh clime of Boeotia, where, as Hesiod writes of his father's life, 'He dwelt near Helicon in Ascre, a village wretched in winter, in summer oppressive, and not pleasant in any season.'

Around 750 BC, the Greek cities began establishing colonies around the farthest reaches of the *oikoumene*, the 'inhabited world' known to the Hellenes. Phocaea and Miletus were by far the most active of the eastern Greek cities in these colonizing expeditions. Phocaea established colonies on Sardinia and Corsica as well as those that developed into the present cities of Marseilles, Nice, Antibes and Seville. Miletus founded more than 30 colonies around the shores of the Black Sea and its approaches in the Hellespont and the Sea of Marmara, including those that became the present Turkish cities of Sinop (Sinope), Samsun (Amisus) and Trabzon (Trebizond). The Milesians also had a privileged position at Naucratis, the great emporium on the Nile delta founded by the Greeks *ca.* 610 BC, in which they established a fortified trading station known as Milesionteichos. The Milesians may also have active in the Greek trading posts on the coast of Syria just north of the Phoenician city-states, which would have put them in contact with Mesopotamia.

Herodotus was the first to suggest that that the Greeks obtained their knowledge of astronomy from Egypt and Mesopotamia. He writes that 'the Egyptians by their study of astronomy discovered the solar year and were the first to divide it into twelve parts – and in my opinion their method of calculation is better than the Greeks.' Herodotus also says that 'knowledge of the sun-dial and the gnomon and the twelve divisions of the day came into Greece from Babylon.'

The gnomon is a rod, usually vertical, used to cast a shadow to indicate the hours on a sundial. It is also used to determine the spring and fall equinoxes, when the sun rises due east and sets due west, as well as the summer and winter solstices, when the noon shadow is shortest and longest, respectively.

The Greek word for star is *aster*, derived from Ishtar, the Mesopotamian fertility goddess, whom they and the Greeks identified with the planet Venus. The Greeks at first failed to distinguish between the morning star they called Eosphoros and the evening star known as Hesperos. They later realized that Eosphoros and Hesperos were the same celestial body, one of the planets, or wandering stars, which they called Aphrodite, the goddess of love, thus perpetuating the cult of Mesopotamian Ishtar. Venus is the only planet mentioned by Homer, who in the *Iliad* calls it Eosphoros when describing the funeral of Patroklos and referring to it as Hesperos when telling of the battle between Achilles and Hektor.

Hesiod's *Works and Days*, written one or two generations after the time of Homer, is essentially a poetic farmer's almanac, marking the various tasks of the agricultural year by the heliacal risings and settings of the various constellations, for instance stars that are on the eastern or western horizons just before sunrise or sunset. The almanac begins with these lines: 'When the Pleiades, daughters of Atlas, are rising, begin your harvest, and your plowing when they are going to set.' In Hesiod's time the Pleiades rose in the east just before sunrise in May, when it was time to harvest winter wheat, the only type grown in antiquity. The Pleiades set in the west just before sunrise in late autumn, when it was time to plow the land and sow the grain. This was the beginning of the agricultural year as Hesiod defined it, whereas in Mesopotamia the beginning of the sidereal year, as measured by the stars, came with the spring equinox.

Hesiod's knowledge of astronomy seems to have come from Mesopotamia, perhaps from the MULAPIN, a Babylonian astronomical text that survives in a number of copies on clay tablets. The MULAPIN is a sidereal calendar of the type known to the Greeks as a *parapegma*, in which the time of the year is marked by the heliacal rising and setting of various constellations, just as in Hesiod's *Works and Days*.

Hesiod was also influenced by other Mesopotamian sources. *Works and Days* resembles Mesopotamian Wisdom Texts, while the *Theogony* shows unmistakable resemblances to the Babylonian creation epic, the *Enamu Elish*, which may have been transmitted to the Greek world from Phoenicia and North Syria.

Homer and Hesiod were the forerunners of the great flowering of Hellenic culture that might be called the Ionian Enlightenment, which began in the archaic period and continued into the early years of the classical era, giving rise to the first philosophers of nature, as well as lyric poets, historians, geographers, architects and city planners.

This extraordinary cultural outburst started in Miletus, which gave birth to the first philosophers of nature, Thales, Anaximander and Anaximenes, whose ideas were debated and developed in turn by Xenophanes of Colophon, Pythagoras of Samos, Heraclitus of Ephesus and Anaxagoras of Clazomenae. Their overlapping careers spanned a period of turmoil in which the Ionian cities lost their freedom, first to the Lydians in the second half of the seventh century BC.

The Persian king Cyrus captured the Lydian capital at Sardis in 546 BC, and the following year his general Harpagus the Mede conquered all the Greek cities in western Asia Minor. Thenceforth the Ionian cities were ruled by a Persian *satrap*, or viceroy, with his capital at Sardis. The Milesians, aided by their Athenian allies, led the Ionian cities in a revolt against Persian rule in 499 BC, burning the capital of the satrapy at Sardis. The Persians finally put down the Ionian revolt in 494 BC in a naval battle off Miletus, which they burned to the ground in retaliation for the burning of Sardis. The Persian advance was finally halted when the forces of King Xerxes were defeated by the Greek allies at the battles of Salamis and Plataea in 480/479 BC, marking the end of the archaic period and the beginning of the classical era.

Xenophanes and Pythagoras left Ionia after the Persian conquest of Asia Minor and moved to Magna Graecia, the Greek colonies in Sicily and southern Italy. They brought with them the Ionian Enlightenment, which continued in Magna Graecia with the natural philosophers Parmenides, Zeno and Empedocles. Anaxagoras, the last of the Ionian philosophers of nature, moved to Athens at the beginning of the classical era, bringing with him his version of the ideas of Thales and his successors, the beginning of the Western tradition of natural philosophy. The Ionian Enlightenment, which involved some of the Aeolian and Doric cities too, included the poets Sappho and Alcaeus and the historian Hellanicus, all of Lesbos; the geographer Hecataeus , the city planner Hippodamus, and the poet Phocylides, all of Miletus; the poets Callinus and Hipponax, both of Ephesus, the poet Mimnermus of Colophon; the architects Rhoecus and Theodorus, both of Samos; and the poet Anacreon of Teos. It also included the historian Herodotus of Halicarnassus, who begins his *Histories* with this line: 'Herodotus of Halicarnassus, his *Researches* are here set down to preserve the astonishing achievement of the past by putting on record the outstanding achievements of our own and other peoples; and more particularly how they came into conflict.'

This cultural flowering was in times past often explained as a manifestation of the 'Greek genius', but more recent scholarship has tried to identify the many factors that might have been involved. These include the political freedom and democratic form of government of the Greek city-states in the crucial period of their development, which with their high level of literacy led them to debate not only their laws and policies but the nature of humanity and the cosmos; their numerous and widespread colonies bringing them into contact with more ancient civilizations in Egypt and Mesopotamia and extending their knowledge of the *oikoumene*, which by the end of the classical era they had explored from the Atlantic through northern Africa and Europe deep into Asia.

All that is known of the thought of the early Greek philosophers, who came to be known as the Pre-Socratics, are fragmentary quotes or paraphrases of their works by later writers of varying reliability. Information about their lives by later writers also varies in reliability, the richest sources being the *Placita* of Aëtius, dating from the first century AD, *Lives of Eminent Philosophers*, written early in the third century AD by Diogenes Laertius, and the *Refutations of All Heresies* by Hippolytus (*ca.* 170–236).

Aristotle refers to the earliest of the Pre-Socratics as *physikoi* (physicists), or sometimes as *physiologoi*, from the Greek *physis*, meaning 'nature' in its widest sense, contrasting them with the earlier *theologoi* (theologians), for they were the first who tried to explain phenomena on natural rather than supernatural grounds. Earthquakes, for example, which both Homer and Hesiod attribute to the action of Poseidon, the 'earth shaker', are explained by Thales as the rocking of the earth while it floated in the all encompassing waters of Oceanus.

Diogenes Laertius says that Ionian philosophy began with Anaximander, but that Thales (*ca.* 624–*ca.* 546 BC), 'a Milesian and therefore an Ionian, instructed Anaximander.' Aristotle considered Thales to be 'the first founder of this kind of philosophy', for example, the thought of those who sought to find what he called the 'material cause' of things.

Herodotus refers to 'Thales of Miletus, a Phoenician by remote descent', but Diogenes in quoting this says that most sources say that he was from a distinguished Milesian family. Thales' mother bore the Greek name Cleobulina; his father was called Examyes, a name used by Carians, the indigenous people of southwestern Anatolia. Herodotus says that when the Ionians settled in Miletus they brought no women with them, but married the wives of the Carians they killed in establishing their colony, and so all of the Milesians had in any event Carian ancestors.

Thales was numbered among the Seven Sages of ancient Greece, and so many discoveries and acts of wisdom were attributed to him as a matter of course. Herodotus says that Thales advised the Ionians to form a common centre of government to deal with the Persian threat, and Diogenes Laertius writes that he persuaded the Milesians not to enter into an alliance with the Lydian king Croesus. Other sources say that Thales was involved in trade and that he cornered the market in olive presses, that he diverted the course of the river Halys for Croesus, and that he predicted the eclipse of the sun visible in central Asia Minor on 28 May 585 BC, which would have been impossible given the state of astronomical knowledge at the time. Another source says that Thales thought that the pointer stars in the Little Bear were a better indicator of the celestial pole than those in the Great Bear, which is particularly interesting, since the Phoenicians sailed by the Little Bear while the Greeks used the Big Bear.

Thales was also supposed to be the first to prove various geometrical theorems, and it was said that he used geometry to measure the heights of the pyramids in Egypt and the distances of ships at sea. The Neoplatonist philosopher Proclus, writing in the fifth century AD, says that Thales learned geometry from the Egyptians and brought the knowledge back to Greece. He writes that Thales 'first went to Egypt and thence introduced this study to Greece. He discovered many propositions himself, and instructed his successors in the principles underlying many others, his method of attack being in some cases more general, in others more empirical.'

The enduring fame of Thales and the other Milesian physicists is their idea that there exists an *arche*, or fundamental substance, which remained the same despite apparent change. Aristotle writes of this in his discussion of what he calls the 'first principle' of Thales:

> Most of the earliest philosophers thought that the principles which were in the nature of matter were the only principles of all things; that of which all things that are consist, and from which they first come to be and into which they are resolved as a final state (the substance remaining but changing in its modifications), and therefore they think that nothing is either created nor destroyed, since this sort of entity is always preserved....
>
> On the number and nature of such principles they do not all agree. Thales, who led the way in this kind of theory, says that the principle is water, and for this reason declared that the earth rests on water.

Aristotle thought that Thales chose water as the *arche* 'from the observation that the nourishment of all creatures is moist, and that warmth itself is generated from moisture and lives by it, and that form from which all things come to be is their first principle. Besides this another reason for his supposition would be that the *semina* of all things have a moist nature, and water is for moist things the origin of their nature.'

A modern physicist would say that Thales chose water as the *arche* because it is normally a liquid but when heated it vaporizes and when frozen it becomes ice, so that the same substance can become any of the three forms of matter: liquid, gas and solid. The idea that the *arche* is neither created nor destroyed appears in modern physics in laws such as the conservation of energy, which states that in a physical process the total energy of the system remains the same, though it may be changed from one form to another, say from potential energy to kinetic energy.

Thales' notion that the earth rests on water is examined more fully by Aristotle in another work, where he writes that 'Others say that [the earth] rests on water. This is the most ancient explanation that has come down to us, and is attributed to Thales of Miletus, namely that the earth is at rest because it can float like wood or similar substances, whose nature it is to rest upon water, though none of them could rest on air.' It has been suggested that the idea of the earth resting on water comes from the Babylonian cosmology of the *Enuma Elish*, in which the earliest stage of the universe is one of watery chaos from which male and female deities emerge to couple and give birth to the gods and then men. This made its way into Greek mythology and thence into the *Iliad*, in the lines where Homer writes of 'Okeanos, whence the gods have risen, and Tethys our mother,' and where he refers to 'Okeanos, whence is risen the seed of all immortals.'

Greek tradition has it that Thales wrote nothing, and that his pupil Anaximander (*ca.* 610–*ca.* 546 BC) was the first to leave a written record of his thoughts. The philosopher and rhetorician Themistius, writing in the fourth century AD, says that Anaximander was 'the first of the Greeks, to our knowledge, who was bold enough to write a book about nature.' The *Suda*, a Byzantine lexicon of *ca.* 1000, lists titles of works by Anaximander, including *On Nature, Description of the Earth, The Fixed Stars* and *Sphere,* though these may represent divisions of a single book recorded in the catalogue of the famous Library of Alexandria.

Anaximander followed Thales in believing that everything in nature was composed of a single fundamental substance which he called the *apeiron,* the 'boundless', which is sometimes translated as 'the infinite', meaning that it not defined or limited by having specific properties. Here he has gone beyond Thales in realizing that the fundamental substance could not be water, which already has form in its perceptible properties, whereas he thought that the *arche* must be absolutely undifferentiated in its original state.

The Aristotelian commentator Simplicius, writing in the sixth century AD, gives his interpretation of what Anaximander meant by the word *apeiron,* which seems to have been coined by him: 'Anaximander named the *arche* and element of existing things "the boundless" (*apeiron*), being the first to use this name for the *arche.* He says that it is neither water nor any of the other so-called elements, but a different substance which is boundless, from which there come into being all the heavens and the worlds within them.'

Anaximander's ideas concerning the origin and nature of the universe are given in three fragments by Aëtius:

> Anaximander of Miletus, son of Praxiades, says that the first principle of existing things is the Boundless; for from this all come into being and into it all perish. Wherefore innumerable worlds are both brought to birth and ... again dissolved into that out of which they came.... According to Anaximander, the sun is essentially a circle twenty-eight times the size of the earth, shaped like a cartwheel. The rim is hollow and full of fire, and at a certain point allows the fire to be seen through an orifice like the nozzle ... of a bellows: this is the sun.... The moon is essentially a circle nineteen times the size of the earth, resembling a cartwheel and full of fire like that of the sun, lying obliquely as does the sun and having a single blowhole like the nozzle of a bellows....

According to Aëtius, Anaximander thought that the shape of the earth 'is similar to the drum of a column,' in that it is cylindrical in form.

Hippolytus says the same, after giving Anaximander's explanation of why the earth is at the centre of the universe: 'The earth hangs freely, not at the compulsion of any force but remaining where it is owing to its equal distance from everything. In shape it is rounded, circular, like the drum of a column; of its surfaces one is that on which we stand, and there is another opposite.'

What Anaximander is saying, according to Hippolytus, is that the earth remains at the centre because there is no reason for it to move in one direction or another, a concept known as the 'principle of the lack of a sufficient reason'. The use of this principle by Anaximander is said to mark the boundary between mythology and science, which always requires an explanation in terms of a sufficient cause.

Anaximander also wrote on the origin of animal and human life, and several sources credit him with a theory of evolution. After describing Anaximander's cosmology, Plutarch writes that 'He says moreover that originally man was born from creatures of a different species, on the grounds that whereas other creatures quickly find food for themselves, man alone needs a long period of suckling; hence if he had been originally what he is now he could never have survived.'

Anaximander seems to have been the first to give naturalistic theories of meteorological phenomena, as evidenced by two fragments from Aëtius, in which he explains the origin of wind and the cause of thunder and lightning: 'Wind is a flow of air, occurring when the finest elements in it are set in motion by the sun. ... When it is imprisoned in thick cloud and forces its way out by reason of its fine texture and lightness, then the tearing makes the noise, and the contrast with the blackness of the cloud produces the flash.'

Anaximander is also credited with astronomical discoveries, and Eusebius of Caesarea (*ca.* 260–340) says that he used a gnomon to determine 'solstices, times, seasons and equinoxes.'

Eratosthenes, who headed the Library of Alexandria in the third century BC, is quoted by Strabo as saying that Anaximander was one of the first to elevate the study of geography to that of philosophy, giving pride of place to Homer: 'Those who followed him were clearly notable men and clearly at home in philosophy, of whom Eratosthenes says that the first after Homer were two, Anaximander the acquaintance and fellow-citizen of Thales, and Hecataeus of Miletus. The one was the first to publish a geographical tablet [map of the earth], whereas Hecataeus left a treatise which is authenticated as his from the rest of his writings.'

Hecataeus, who flourished in the late sixth and early fifth century BC, seems to have belonged to the ruling class of Miletus, and Herodotus mentions him as playing a leading part in the discussions that lead up to the Ionian Revolt of 499–495 BC. He is noted as one of the earliest Greek writers known as logographers, meaning that they wrote in prose as distinct from poets. Thucydides used the term logographer in referring to the pioneers in historical writing who were predecessors and contemporaries of Herodotus. Numerous quotations survive in later writers from the geographical work of Hecataeus, called *Periegesis,* which was in two books, entitled 'Europe' and 'Asia,' the latter including Africa. His work influenced Herodotus, who refers to him at some length, particularly concerning the Ionian Revolt. The *Periegesis* appears to have comprised brief descriptions of the Mediterranean world then known to the Greeks, principally the coastal regions where they had established colonies. Hecataeus also wrote another work generally known as *Genealogiae,* of which the surviving fragments deal with topics in genealogy, mythography, ethnography and chronology.

Anaximenes (fl. 546–526 BC) was a younger contemporary of Anaximander, who is said to have been his mentor. Like Thales and Anaximander, Anaximenes believed that all things in nature are the various forms of one fundamental substance, from which they derive and into which they return. He abandoned the indefinite *apeiron* of Anaximander and held that the *arche* is *pneuma,* meaning 'air' or 'breath,' which through its ceaseless motion changes in density to take on the various forms seen in nature. Anaximenes thus not only identified the *arche,* but also described the physical process by which it takes on one form or another, as Simplicius notes in his commentary:

> Anaximenes of Miletus, son of Eurystratus, the companion of Anaximander, also posits a single infinite underlying substance of things, not, however, indefinite in character like Anaximander's, but determinate, for he calls it 'air' (*pneuma*), and says that it differs in rarity and density according to the different substance. Rarified it becomes fire; condensed it becomes first wind, then cloud, and when condensed still further water, then earth and stones. Everything else is made of these. He too postulated eternal motion.

Cicero, in his *Academica,* gives a somewhat different version of Anaximenes' theory: 'After Anaximander his pupil Anaximenes postulated infinite air, the products of which are however determined. These are earth, water and fire, and from them comes everything else.' This suggests that Anaximenes believed that the genesis of the world took place in two stages, first the

11

formation of earth, water and fire by 'infinite' air, and then the production of 'everything else' in nature, including living beings. This gave rise to the famous theory of the 'four elements' – earth, water, air and fire – first formulated by Empedocles and then adapted by Aristotle, from whom it passed on to the Islamic world and subsequently to Western Europe in the thirteenth century.

According to several sources, Anaximenes thought that the earth was flat and that it floated on the air like a leaf or lid. Aristotle, referring to Anaximenes and others who thought that the flat earth was supported on air, explains their theory:

> It [the earth] does not cleave the air beneath it, but settles on it like a lid, as flat bodies to all appearances do; owing to their resistance they are not easily moved even by the wind. The earth they say, owing to its flatness behaves in the same way in relation to the air immediately underneath it, which, not having sufficient room to change its place, is compressed and stays still owing to the air beneath it, like the water in *klepsydrai* [water clocks]. For this power of the air to bear a great weight when shut up and its motion stopped, they bring forward plenty of evidence.

A fragment by Aëtius draws an analogy between the function of air in the universe and that of the soul in man: 'Anaximenes of Miletus, son of Eurystratus, declared that the origin of existing things was air, for out of it all things come to be and into it they are resolved again. "Just as our soul," he says, "which is air, holds us together, so breath and air surround the whole cosmos." air and breath are used synonymously.'

The poet and philosopher Xenophanes of Colophon (*ca.* 570–*ca.* 478 BC) was a younger contemporary of Anaximenes. He left Ionia after Colophon was conquered by the Persians in 545 BC and moved to Magna Graecia. Diogenes Laertius writes that 'Exiled from his country, he lived in Zancle and Catana', two Greek colonies founded in the eighth century BC. He is also associated with Elea, a colony founded on the Tyrrhenian coast of southern Italy by the Phocaeans after their native city was conquered by the Persians. Late in his life he was in Sicily at the court of King Hieron I (r. 478–467/466 BC) in Syracuse. He lived to a great age, and one source says that he was over 100 when he passed away. One of his extant poems was written at the age of 92, as can be reckoned from the account he gives of his wanderings: 'Seven and sixty years have now been wafting my meditations about the land of Greece, and ere that there were five and twenty years from my birth, if I know how to tell the truth in these things.'

In another of his poems Xenophanes describes life in Colophon before the Persian conquest, when its citizens had become corrupted by the wealth they accumulated under the beneficent rule of the Lydian kings: 'But they learned useless luxuries of the Lydians while they were free of hateful despotism, and went into the marketplace clad in all-purple robes, went no less than a thousand in all, profoundly rejoicing in gold-adorned hair and bedewing their odour with studied anointings; and so demoralized were they by untimely drunkenness that some of them never saw sun rise or set.'

Xenophanes brought the Ionian Enlightenment to Magna Graecia, particularly the idea of the Milesian physicists that all of nature is one. His sense of unity extended even to theology, and he rejected the hierarchical pantheon for a monotheism that identified God with the universe. According to the physician and sceptical philosopher Sextus Empiricus, writing *ca.* AD 200: 'Xenophanes asserted ... that all is one, and god consubstantial with all things, and that he is spherical, impassable, unchanging, and rational.' And as Xenophanes himself says in three of his fragments: 'God is one, greatest among gods and men, in no way like mortals either in body or in mind.... He sees as a whole, perceives as a whole, hears as a whole.... Always he remains in the same place, nor indeed does it befit him to go here and there at different times, but without toil he makes all things shiver by the impulse of his mind.'

Xenophanes objected to the anthropomorphic polytheism of Homer and Hesiod, whom he criticized for having 'ascribed to the gods all deeds that among men are a reproach and a disgrace: thieving, adultery and mutual deception.' He said that men make gods in the image of themselves, so that 'Ethiopians imagine their gods as black and snub-nosed, the Thracians as blue-eyed and red-haired.'

A fragment from Aëtius quotes Xenophanes on atmospheric phenomena: 'Xenophanes says that the original cause of what happens in the upper regions is the heat of the sun. Moisture is drawn up from the sea and the sweet part owing to its texture is drawn out and being thickened into a mist forms the clouds and by vaporization makes winds. For he says explicitly: "Sea is the source of water".'

Two lines by Xenophanes himself give his explanation of the nature of the rainbow, which the Greeks personified as the goddess Iris: 'She whom they call Iris, she too is a cloud, purple and red and yellow to view.'

A famous fragment of Xenophanes states his view concerning the limitations of human knowledge, an anticipation of the Sceptic school of philosophy that would emerge in the fourth century BC: 'Certain truth has no man seen, nor will there ever be a man who knows [from immediate experience] about the gods and about everything of which I speak, for even if he should fully succeed in saying what is true, even if he himself does not *know* it, but in all things there is opinion.'

Although Xenophanes spent the last two-thirds of his life or more in Magna Graecia, he continued to look back to Ionia in his poetry. One of his poems reflects on the good life in Colophon before the Persian army under Harpagus the Mede swept down upon Ionia: 'Such things should be said beside the fire in wintertime when a man reclines full-fed on a soft couch drinking the sweet wine and munching chick peas – such things as Who and whence art thou? and how old art thou, good sir?, and of what age was thou when the Mede came?'

CHAPTER 2

HARMONY AND LOGOS

Pythagoras is one of the most enigmatic figures in the history of Greek science, and the mystery extends to his followers. An eminent historian of the subject has said that, 'The history of Pythagoreanism is perhaps the most controversial subject in all Greek philosophy, and much of it remains obscure.'

Pythagoras was born *ca.* 570 BC on Samos, one of the two Aegean islands that were part of the Panionic League, lying off the coast of Asia Minor northwest of Miletus. According to Strabo, Pythagoras left Samos during the reign of the tyrant Polycrates, who seized power *ca.* 540 BC. He writes that 'It was in his time, as we are told, that Pythagoras, seeing that the tyranny was growing in power, left the city and went off to Egypt and Babylon, to satisfy his fondness for learning; but when he came back and saw that the tyranny still endured, he set sail for Italy and lived there to the end of his life.'

Pythagoras settled in the Greek colony of Croton in southern Italy. There, as Diogenes Laertius writes, he 'laid down a constitution for the Italian Greeks.' He also founded a secret religious society that attracted so many adherents that for a time the Pythagoreans gained control of Croton and most of the other Greek cities in southern Italy. The Neoplatonist philosopher Porphyry (232/3–*ca.* 305) writes of this society in his *Life of Pythagoras*, where he mentions that the Pythagoreans included women as well as men: 'A great reputation grew up around him and he gained many from the city itself as his followers, not only men but also women.'

Around 500 BC a revolt led by a Crotonian named Cylon broke the power of Pythagoras and his followers, and he was forced to flee to Metapontium, where he died *ca.* 490 BC. The Pythagoreans regained some degree of power for a while, but then in the mid-fifth century BC there was a second outbreak which led many of them to leave Magna Graecia for Greece. The Pythagorean society survived as an active sect into the latter half of the fourth century BC, when its demise is noted by the philosopher Aristoxenus, one of its last members: 'They preserved their original ways, and their science, although the sect was dwindling, until, not ignobly, they died out.'

The reputation of Pythagoras began to increase even as his society diminished. Plato, in his *Republic*, has Socrates say that 'Pythagoras was especially loved as a leader of education in the private sphere', and that his followers 'loved him for his teaching and handed on to posterity a certain way of life ... and these latter-day followers even now seem in some way to stand out among others for their manner of life, which they call Pythagorean after him.'

This reverence for Pythagoras eventually gave rise to a movement known as Neopythagoreanism, which began in Rome and Alexandria in the first century BC. The movement reached its peak *ca.* 100 AD with the work of the mathematician Nichomachus of Gerasa, who presents Pythagoras as the founder of Greek mathematics as well as a great philosopher. The Neoplatonist philosopher Iamblichus (fl. *ca.* 160–80) refers to 'the divine Pythagoras,' and Porphyry writes that 'about no one else have greater and more extraordinary things been believed.'

The exaggeration of his reputation in later times makes it difficult to assess the actual thought of Pythagoras, which in any event is obscured by the secrecy of the early Pythagoreans, whose own contributions are often conflated with those of the founder of their movement. Iamblichus wrote an account of Pythagoreanism in ten books, in the first of which he credits Pythagoras with truly superhuman writings: 'This science, therefore, concerning intelligible nature and the Gods, Pythagoras delivers in his writings from a supernal origin. Afterwards he teaches the whole of physics, and unfolds completely ethical philosophy and logic. He likewise delivers all-various disciplines, and the most excellent sciences. And in short there is nothing pertaining to human knowledge which is not actually discussed in these writings.'

Iamblichus gives a list of all Pythagoreans known by name, as well as their native cities. This contains the names of 218 men and 17 women, mostly from Magna Graecia, though there were a number from cities in Greece, including Athens, Corinth, Sparta and Samos. The list of Pythagoreans includes: Parmenides of Elea, in southern Italy, and Empedocles of Acragas in Sicily, two of the great philosophers of nature in the generation following Pythagoras.

Porphyry writes of the doctrines that Pythagoras imparted to his followers, particularly the immortality of the soul and metempsychosis, the transmigration of souls:

> What he said to his disciples no man can tell for certain, since they preserved such an exceptional silence. However, the following facts in particular became universally known: first that he held the soul to be immortal, next that it migrated into other kinds of animal, further that past events repeat themselves in a cyclical process and nothing is new in an absolute sense, and finally that one must regard all living things as kindred. These are the beliefs which Pythagoras is said to have been the first to introduce into Greece.

Xenophanes ridiculed the Pythagorean doctrine of the transmigration of souls. Diogenes Laertius quotes a satirical poem that Xenophanes wrote about Pythagoras; he tells of how Pythagoras saw someone beating a dog and took pity on the animal, shouting to the man: 'Stop! do not beat him; it is the soul of a friend, I recognize his voice.'

The kinship of all living things that Porphyry refers to was part of a broader Pythagorean belief embodied in the word 'cosmos' (Greek *kosmos*), which a modern dictionary defines as an 'orderly, harmonious and systematic universe.' Plato gives the original Greek meaning of the word in a passage from *Meno*, where he appears to be referring to the Pythagoreans. 'The wise men,' he says, 'tell us that heaven and earth, god and men are bound together by kinship and love and orderliness and temperance and justice; and for this reason my friend, they give to the whole the name of *kosmos*, not a name implying disorder or licentiousness.'

The teaching of Pythagoras was apparently on two levels, as Porphyry notes in his account of the Pythagoreans: 'His teaching took two forms, and of his followers some were called *mathematici* and some *acusmatici*. The *mathematici* were those who had mastered the deepest and most fully worked-out parts of his wisdom, and the *acusmatici* those who had only heard summarized precepts from the writings, without full explanation.'

The *mathematici* would appear to have mastered the mathematical philosophy of the Pythagoreans, who believed that everything was based on numbers. According to Aristotle:

> The Pythagoreans, because they saw many of the attributes of numbers belonging to sensible bodies, assumed existing things to be number – not separately existing numbers, but that things actually are composed of numbers. Their reason was that numerical properties are inherent in the musical

scale, in the heavens, and in many other things .... The Pythagoreans say that existing things owe their being to imitation (*mimesis*) of numbers .... Since the nature of everything else seemed to be entirely assimilated to numbers, they assumed the elements of numbers to be the elements of all that exists, and the whole universe to be a *harmonia* and a number.

Iamblichus makes the same distinction as Porphyry, giving a more detailed account of the *acusmatici* and their beliefs and religious practices: 'The philosophy of the *acusmatici* consists of undemonstrated sayings, without argument, enjoining certain courses of action. These and other dicta of Pythagoras they endeavour to preserve as divine revelations, making no claim to say anything of their own. Indeed it would be wrong to do so; those of their number are accounted the wisest who have learned the greater number of *acusmata*.'

The 'undemonstrated sayings' and *acusmata* referred to by Iamblichus were also known as *symbola*. Some were rules of conduct, ceremonial practices or primitive taboos, while others seem to be oracular sayings expressing Pythagorean moral, social or political ideals.

The Neoplatonist Proclus (*ca.* 410–485) says that Pythagoras introduced mathematics into Greek education, and he also credits him with several mathematical discoveries. As he writes, after stating that Thales brought geometry from Egypt to Greece: 'Pythagoras, who came after him, transformed this science into a liberal form of education, examining its principles from the beginning and probing the theorems in an immaterial and intellectual manner. He discovered the theory of proportionals and the construction of cosmic figures.'

The 'cosmic figures' that he refers to are the regular polyhedra, also known as the Platonic solids, in each of which all of the surfaces are equal and equilateral. There are only five regular polyhedra: the tetrahedron, whose surfaces are four equilateral triangles; the cube, with six squares; the octahedron, with eight equilateral triangles; the dodecahedron, with twelve equilateral pentagons; and the icosahedron, with twenty equilateral triangles. Proclus says that Pythagoras himself 'discovered the construction of the five cosmic figures.' But a later source says that only the tetrahedron, cube and dodecahedron came from the Pythagoreans, while the while the mathematician Theatetus, Plato's pupil and friend, discovered the octahedron and icosahedron.

Philolaus of Croton (b. *ca.* 370 BC) was the first Pythagorean to write a book, whose surviving fragments, commented upon by Aristotle and others, are the principal source for the cosmology of Pythagoras and his followers. He is the earliest source to identify the regular polyhedra with the four elements, writing that 'The bodies in the sphere are five: fire, water, earth, and fifthly the hull of the sphere.'

According to Aëtius, Pythagoras associated each of the four elements – earth, water, air and fire – with one of the cosmic figures, while the fifth, the dodecahedron, was inscribed in the enveloping sphere of *ouranos*, the heavens: 'There being five solid figures, called the mathematical solids, Pythagoras says that earth is made from the cube, fire from the pyramid [tetrahedron], air from the octahedron, and water from the icosahedron, and from the dodecahedron is made the sphere of the whole.'

The Pythagoreans apparently used figurate numbers in the form of dots, so that a single dot represented 1, a pair of dots was 2, a triad equaled 3, etc. The dots were arrayed in various ways, so that the number 4 could be displayed as four dots in a straight line, or as two pairs one above the other to give an array in the form of a square, so that four was called a square number. The number ten was formed by an array of dots in the shape of an equilateral triangle, with four dots forming the base, three dots in the first row above, two in the next and one at the vertex. The triangular array was the so-called *tetractys*, the sum of all possible dimensions, for $10 = 1 + 2 + 3 + 4$, where 1 dot represents a geometrical point, 2 points generate a straight line, 3 points not in a straight line determine a plane, and 4 points not all in the same plane form the vertices of a solid.

This version of the Pythagorean notion that numbers were the basis of everything gave rise to the so-called fluxion theory, which is mentioned by the Stoic philosopher Sextus Empiricus in a number of places. One of these references begins with a description of the *tetractys* and goes on to give two versions of the fluxion theory:

> But some say that body is formed from one point. This point by flowing produces a line, the line by flowing makes a surface, and this when moved into depth generates body in three dimensions. But this scheme of the Pythagoreans differs from that of the earlier ones. The earlier created numbers from two principles, the one and the indefinite dyad [the Platonic term for what the Pythagoreans called 'the unlimited'], then from numbers points, lines, plane figures and solids. But these built up everything from a single point.

The *tetractys* became the sacred symbol of the Pythagoreans. According to a number of sources, the Pythagoreans swore an oath to their founder saying 'By him who handed down to us the *tetractys*, source and root of everlasting nature.' This suggests the survival of a more ancient number-mysticism in the beliefs of the Pythagoreans, who acquired the reputation of being magicians and sorcerers. Hippolytus writes of 'magical arts and Pythagorean numbers', and remarks that 'Pythagoras also touched on magic, as they say, and himself discovered an art of physiognomy, laying down as a basis certain numbers and measures.'

Pythagoras is famous for the geometric theorem that bears his name, which states that in a right triangle the square of the hypotenuse equals the sum of the squares of the other two sides. Thus in a right triangle of sides 3, 4 and 5 the sum of the squares of 3 and 4 equals the square of 5. It has been established that the Pythagorean theorem was known to the Babylonians in the first half of the second millennium BC, but as a relationship involving a triplet of numbers rather than a geometrical theorem.

A difficulty arose when figurate numbers were used in applying the Pythagorean theorem to solve such simple problems as comparing the diagonal of a square with its side. Given that the side of a square is 1, the length of the diagonal is the square root of 2, or 1.4142135 ..., an irrational number, in other words, one which cannot be written as the ratio of two integers, and which can be expressed as an infinite decimal with no set of consecutive digits repeating itself. Thus if the side of the square is an integral number of dots, its diagonal will not be an integer, no matter how small a measure is used for the dot, and so the result is irrational, or not reasonable. This is supposed to have caused a crisis among the Pythagoreans, who were sworn to keep the incommensurability of certain numbers secret, or so the story goes.

The Pythagorean notion of the universe as being 'a *harmonia* and a number' seems to stem from their experiments with musical instruments. According to Aristotle, the Pythagoreans 'saw that the modifications and the ratios of the musical scales were expressible in numbers. Therefore, since all other things seemed in their whole nature to be modeled on numbers, and numbers seemed to be the first things in the whole of nature, they supposed the elements of numbers to be the elements of all things, and the whole heaven to be a musical scale and a number.'

Several sources suggest that the numerical relations involved in musical harmony were discovered by Pythagoras himself. According to Porphyry: 'Pythagoras ... discovered that the musical intervals also owe their origin of necessity to number, because they consist in a comparison of one quantity with another. He further investigated in what intervals are concordant or discordant, and in general the origin of all harmony and disharmony.'

The numerical laws governing musical harmony may have been discovered by playing a stringed instrument such as a lyre. When a lyre string is stopped at its midpoint either half gives a note an octave higher than does the full length of the string; if the string is stopped a third of the way from one end, the remaining two-thirds gives a note a fifth higher than the whole string; if the stop is placed a fourth of the way along the remaining three-fourths gives a note a fourth above that of the string's full length. These observations give the numerical ratios 1:2 (octave), 3:2 (fifth), 4:3 (fourth), which represent the relative rates of vibration of the different lengths of the string, the rate being inversely proportional to the length. These ratios involve the numbers 1, 2, 3 and 4, which add up to 10, confirming the Pythagorean belief, quoted by Aristotle, that the number 10, the decad, 'was something perfect and contained in itself the whole nature of number.' Thus the *tetractys* became the sacred symbol of the Pythagoreans, 'the source and root of everlasting nature.'

Alcmaeon of Croton, probably a younger contemporary of Pythagoras, wrote a book on natural science based on his 'theory of opposites.' His work was commented on by Aristotle, who compared his theory to that of the Pythagoreans:

> Alcmaeon says that most human beings go in pairs, but he speaks of the oppositions not, like the Pythagoreans, as limited in number but haphazard, e.g., white-black, sweet-bitter, good-bad, large-small. He threw out indefinite suggestions about the rest, but the Pythagoreans specified how many and what the contraries were. From both therefore we may understand that the opposites are the principle of existing things, but their number, and which they are, we learn only from the Pythagoreans.

The Roman philosopher Boethius (*ca.* 480–524) writes in his *De Arithmetica* of the Pythagorean theory of harmony as the concord of opposites: 'Not without cause is it said that all things, which consist of contraries, are conjoined and composed by a certain harmony. For harmony is the joining together of several things and the consent of contraries.'

The Platonist scholar Theon of Smyrna (fl. 115–140), in a translation by the seventeenth-century poet and historian Thomas Stanley, further develops the theory of opposites to extend it to human affairs:

> The Pythagoreans define Musick an apt composition of contraries, and a union of many, and consent of differences. For it not only co-ordinates rhythms and undulation, but all manner of Systems. Its end is to unite, and

aptly conjoin. God is the reconcilor of things discordant, and this is his chiefest work according to Music and Medicine, to reconcile enmities.

In Musick they say, consists in the agreement of all things, and Aristocracy of the Universe. For, what is harmony in the world, in a City is good government, in a Family Temperance.

According the Philolaus, the Pythagoreans believed that the earth was not stationary but moved in a circle around a central fire called Hestia, the hearth of the cosmos, along with the sun, moon, stars and the five visible planets – Mercury, Venus, Mars, Jupiter and Saturn – as well as another body known as the 'counter-earth.' The central fire and the counter-earth are not visible since the side of the earth on which men live is turned away from them.

Aristotle, in commenting on the cosmology of Philolaus, says that the Pythagoreans introduced the counter-earth to bring the number of moving celestial bodies up to ten, the decad, their sacred number: 'For instance, they regarded the decad as something perfect, and as embracing the whole nature of number, whence they assert that the moving heavenly bodies are also ten; and since there are only nine to be seen, they invent the counter-earth as a tenth.'

Aëtius describes the Philolaic cosmology in detail, giving the order of the various bodies moving about the central fire:

Philolaus teaches that there is fire in the middle lying about the centre, and he calls it the hearth of the whole, the home of Zeus, the mother of the Gods, the altar and sustainer and measure of nature. Moreover there is another fire surrounding the universe at the uppermost limit. The middle is primary in the order of nature, and around it dance ten divine bodies: the heaven [i. e., the stars] and the planets, after them the sun, under it the moon, under that the earth, and under the earth the counter-earth. After all these comes the fire which occupies the position of hearth at the centre.

Aëtius goes on to write of two other astronomers, both of whom flourished in the fourth century BC, who had the earth in motion, not orbiting the central fire as in the Philolaic model, but rotating on its axis: 'Heraclides of Pontus and Ecphantus the Pythagorean make the earth move, not in the sense of changing its location, but turning about an axis like a wheel: it revolves around its centre from West to East.'

Aëtius says that Philolaus and other Pythagoreans believed that the moon was inhabited: 'Some of the Pythagoreans, among whom is Philolaus, explain the earth-like appearance of the moon by saying that it is inhabited like our own, with living creatures and plants that are bigger and fairer than ours. Indeed the animals on it are 15 times as powerful and do not excrete, and the day is correspondingly long.'

The Aristotelian commentator Alexander of Aphrodisias, writing early in the third century AD, comments on Aristotle's statement that the Pythagoreans believed that the universe is a *harmonia* and a number:

> They said too that the whole universe is constructed according to a musical scale ..., because it is both composed of numbers and organized numerically and musically. For the distances between the bodies revolving around the centre are mathematically proportionate; some move faster and some more slowly; the sound made by the slower bodies in their movement is lower in pitch, and that of the faster is higher; hence these separate notes, corresponding to the ratios of the distances, make the resultant sound concordant. Now number, they said, is the source of this harmony, and so they naturally posited number as the principle on which the heaven and the whole universe depended.

Archytas of Tarentum, who flourished in the early fifth century BC, is mentioned by Plutarch in his discussion of the Pythagorean doctrine of celestial harmony. As he writes, in the translation done in 1603 by Philemon Holland: 'Pythagoras, Architas, Plato and all the rest of the old Philosophers doe hold that the motion of the whole world, together with the revolution of the stars, is not performed without Musicke: for they teach that God formed all things by harmonie.'

Aristotle writes of how the Pythagoreans explained why we do not hear this heavenly music: 'To meet the difficulty that none of us is aware of this sound, they account for it by saying the sound is with us right from birth and has thus no contrasting silence to show it up; for voice and silence are perceived by contrast with each other, and so all mankind is undergoing an experience like that of a coppersmith, who becomes by long habit indifferent to the din around him.' Shakespeare makes the same point in *The Merchant of Venice*, where Lorenzo calls Jessica's attention to the harmony of the celestial spheres:

> How sweet the moonlight sleeps upon this bank!
> How will we sit and let the sound of music
> Creep in our ears; soft stillness and the night
> Become the touches of sweet harmony.
> Sit, Jessica. Look how the floor of heaven

Is thick inlaid with patines of bright gold;
There's not the smallest orb which thou behold'st
But in his motion like an angel sings,
Still quiring to the young-ey'd cherubins.
Such harmony is in immortal souls,
But while this muddy vesture of decay
Doth grossly close it in, we cannot hear it.

Heraclitus of Ephesus (b. *ca.* 540 BC) is as enigmatic as Pythagoras, his older contemporary, whom he criticizes along with others who preceded him. He says in one of his fragments: 'Much learning does not teach insight; otherwise it would have taught Hesiod and Pythagoras, and again Xenophanes and Hecataeus.' In other fragments Heraclitus calls Pythagoras 'prince of cheats', and accuses him of having 'made a wisdom of his own, a polymathy, a deceit.'

Heraclitus was known as Skoteinos, the 'Dark' or 'Obscure', because of the enigmatic quality of his oracular statements. One of his fragments says that 'The Lord [Apollo] whose oracle is at Delphi neither speaks nor conceals, but gives a sign.' His contemporaries also called him the *paradoxolog* – a maker of paradoxes – because of his habit of speaking paradoxically and seeing unity in opposites, as in his statement that 'Disease it is that makes health pleasant and good, hunger fullness, weariness rest.'

Diogenes Laertius says that Heraclitus collected his aphorisms in a book that he deposited in the temple of Artemis at Ephesus. A story, probably apocryphal, has it that when Socrates was asked by Euripides what he thought of this book, he replied, 'What I understand was fine, and no doubt also what I didn't understand; but it needs a diver to get to the bottom of it.'

Diogenes also said of Heraclitus that 'He was no man's disciple, but said that he had searched himself and learned everything from himself.' He was acquainted with the thought of his predecessors in Ionia and Magna Graecia and rejected both schools, as is evident in his criticism of Pythagoras, Xenophanes and Hecataeus. Nevertheless he does not criticize Thales, Anaximander or Anaximenes by name.

Heraclitus believed that the enduring reality in nature is not Being, as in the existence of an *arche*, but Becoming, or perpetual change, as expressed in his famous aphorism '*Panta rhei*' (Everything flows). Whereas the Milesian physicists looked for a fundamental substance that remained unchanged in natural phenomena, Heraclitus focused on change itself and the ceaseless flux of nature as in the famous fragment mentioned by Plato: 'Heraclitus somewhere says that all things are in process and that nothing stays still, and likening existing things to the stream of a river he says you could not step twice into the same river.'

The relative stability of nature Heraclitus believed to be due to a balance of what he called the 'strife' or 'tension' of the 'Opposites', which achieve harmony when in equilibrium. As one Heraclitean fragment says: 'They do not grasp how by being at variance it agrees with itself, a backward-turning adjustment like that of the bow or lyre.' Using the example of a tuned lyre whose strings give harmonious sounds when under tension, he says 'Invisible *harmonia* is stronger than visible', and, in another fragment, 'Nature loves concealment'.

Even divinity is a harmonious union of opposites, as Heraclitus says in his aphorism that 'God is day night, winter summer, war peace, satiety hunger; he undergoes alteration in the way that a fire, when it is mixed with spices, is named according to the scent of each of them.'

Heraclitus believed that our senses are deceptive and must be used with caution, for they respond to transitory phenomena and must be interpreted. As he says in another of his aphorisms: 'Evil witnesses are eyes and ears for men, if they do not understand their language.'

The philosophy of Heraclitus is based on his profound belief in what he called Logos, by which he meant Reason, or the intelligible law that governs the universe and all of its elements. One of his fragments speaks of 'the Logos which orders all things', and another says 'everything comes to pass in accordance with the Logos'. But he felt that most people were unable to understand this, as he says at the beginning of the book that he deposited in the temple of Artemis at Ephesus:

> Although this Logos [which I shall describe] exists for ever, men prove as unable to understand it when once they have heard it as before they heard it. For though all things come to pass in accordance with this Logos, men seem as if ignorant when they experience such words and things as I set forth, distinguishing each thing according to its nature and telling how it is. The rest of mankind are unaware of what they do while awake just as they forget what they do while asleep.

Three fragments add to our understanding of what Heraclitus meant by the word Logos, which in later Greek takes on a variety of meanings, such as 'account', 'opinion', 'measure', 'rule' or 'the faculty of reason':

> Listening not to me but to the Logos it is wise to agree that all things are one .... One must follow what is common; but although the Logos is

common, most men live as if they had a private understanding of their own
.... One must speak with intelligence and trust in what is common to all, as
a city in its law and much firmly, for all human laws are nourished by one,
the divine, which extends as far as it will and is sufficient for all and more
than sufficient.

Thus it would seem that the Logos of Heraclitus, as Guthrie puts it, 'is both
human thought and the governing principle of the Universe.... Being universal and all pervading, this Logos – the law by which the world is ordered,
and which can be comprehended in human minds – is of course common
to all.'

Heraclitus in one of his fragments says that the cosmos is a fire which is
constantly being fueled to keep it burning eternally: 'This world-order [kos-
mos], the same for all, none of the gods nor of men is made, but it is always
and ever shall be: an everlasting fire, which is being kindled in measures
and extinguished in measures.'

This particularly enigmatic statement has been the subject of much discussion, but Heraclitus would seem to have meant that the world order is
constantly maintained by the opposing forces such as those in the tuned
lyre. He compared the world order to fire, as Guthrie remarks, quoting
Aristotle:

First, as Aristotle said, fire is the most subtle element, which most nearly
approaches the incorporeal, is itself in motion and imparts motion to other
things. Secondly (a consequence of the first, as Aristotle knew), it is the
same as *psyche*, the vehicle of life. 'Heraclitus says the *arche* is soul, i.e., the
exaltation out of which he composes other things. It is the least corporeal of
substances and is in constant flux.' For soul we may read fire.

Heraclitus says in two other fragments that the soul is 'a spark of the substance of stars', but 'the limits of soul thou wouldst not discover though
thou shouldst travel every road'. A third fragment states that 'A man's character is the immortal and potentially divine part of him.'

These were the oracular aphorisms of Heraclitus, of whom Guthrie
writes thus in conclusion: 'Here we leave this astonishing figure, in his
proud isolation. The thoughts in his mind were ahead of his time and
language. In his own estimation he was a prophet, bearer of the divine law
which the mass of men were incapable of grasping. He could only set it
before them in image and paradox.'

CHAPTER 3

THE ONE
AND THE ATOM

Parmenides was born *ca.* 515 BC at Elea in southern Italy. There is a tradition that he was a pupil of Xenophanes and that he was at some point a Pythagorean. One source for this tradition is Diogenes Laertius, who refers to an otherwise unknown Ameinias: 'Though he was a pupil of Xenophanes he did not follow him. He also associated with Amenias, son of Diochaites, the Pythagorean, whose disciple he became. When he died, Parmenides built a shrine for him, being himself a man of noble birth and wealth, and it was Ameinias, not Xenophanes, who converted him to the quiet life.'

Whereas Heraclitus believed that everything was in a state of flux and nothing was permanent, Parmenides denied absolutely the possibility of any kind of change. His philosophy is set forth in a didactic poem entitled *The Way of Truth*, written in the same hexameter meter of Homer and Hesiod. Only 154 lines of the poem survive, but apparently the entire work was available to Simplicius, who in his commentary on Parmenides quotes from it at length after this introductory statement: 'The lines of Parmenides on the One Being are not many, and I should like to append them to this commentary both as confirmation of what I say and because of the rarity of the work.'

One Parmenidean fragment states that 'Either a thing is or it is not,' meaning that creation or destruction is impossible. Aristotle explains this fragment by saying that 'What is does not come into being, for it is already; and nothing could come into being from what is not.'

A line from *The Way of Truth* says that which is, which we might call the One, is eternal, neither coming into being nor ceasing to exist: 'It was not in the past, nor yet shall it be, since it now is, all together, one and continuous.' Another line states that the One is not only continuous but also indivisible: 'Nor is it divisible, since it all equally is. It does not exist more fully in one direction, which would prevent it from holding together, nor more weakly in another, but all is full of what is. Therefore it is all continuous, for what is is close to what is.' This is equivalent to denying the possibility of the void, or vacuum, that is, empty space is impossible.

Other fragments state that the One is eternal, immutable, immobile and complete into itself and spherical in shape:

> But unmoved, in the grip of mighty bonds, it is without beginning or ceasing, since coming into being and perishing have been driven afar off and true conviction has rejected them. Remaining the same in the same place it rests by itself and so remains firmly where it is; for power-ful Necessity holds it in the bounds of a chain that hems it in all around. Because it is not allowed that what is should be incomplete; for it is not lacking, but by not being it would lack everything .... But since there is no furthest limit, it is complete on every side, like the mass of a well-rounded ball ... .

Parmenides believed that all apparent change, including motion and plu-rality, is an illusion. In one of his fragments he writes of the unreliability of the senses and the need to use reason to pass judgment on what we see and hear, warning that one should not 'let custom, born of much experi-ence, force thee to let wander along this road thy aimless eye, thy echoing tongue, but do thou judge by reason the strife-encountered proof that I have spoken.'

Thus Parmenides, with his concept of the eternal and immutable One, does not admit the existence of motion, multiplicity, change or the void. His cosmos is a full uncreated, indestructible, changeless, motionless, eter-nal and self-contained sphere of being, and all sensory evidence to the contrary is illusory. Echoes of this immutable Parmenidean cosmology reverberated from antiquity down to the European renaissance, as in the last canto of Spenser's *The Faerie Queene*:

> Then gin I thinke on that which Nature sayd,
> Of that same time when no more Change shall be,
> But stedfast rest of all things, firmly stayd
> Upon the pillours of Eternity,
> That is contrayr to Mutabilitie;
> For all that moveth doth in Change delight.

Parmenides was the founder of the Eleatic school of philosophy, which was continued by his pupil Zeno (*ca.* 490–*ca.* 425 BC) of Elea. Zeno, who wrote a treatise presenting a number of paradoxes designed to show that apparent change, including plurality and motion, is illusory, defended the philosophy of Parmenides. Little is known of his life, other than that he was a citizen of his native Elea, where, except for a visit to Athens with Parmenides, he resided all of his life, 'preferring it to the arrogance of Athens.'

Aristotle called Zeno the inventor of dialectic, for his paradoxes start from commonly accepted beliefs with the aim of showing in a dialogue that they lead to contradictions. Most of Zeno's paradoxes involve the notions of plurality and motion. In Plato's dialogue *Parmenides*, Socrates speaks to Parmenides about his philosophy, particularly the notion that the One is not a plurality, and Zeno responds to defend it.

> I see Parmenides, that Zeno's intention is to associate himself with you by means of his treatise no less intimately than by his personal attachment. In a way, his book states the same position as your own; only by varying the form he tries to delude us into thinking that his thesis is a different one. You assert ... that the All is one ....

Yes, Socrates, Zeno replied, but you have not quite seen the real character of my book .... The book is in fact a sort of defence of Parmenides' argument against those who try to make fun of it by showing that his supposition, that there is a One, leads to many absurdities and contradictions. This book, then, is a retort against those who assert a plurality. It pays them back in their own coin with something to spare, and aims at showing that, on a thorough examination, their own supposition that there is a plurality leads to even more absurd consequences than the hypothesis of the One ....

Simplicius, who seems to have had at least a digest of Zeno's work at his disposal, explains the paradox of plurality:

> In his book, in which many arguments are put forward, he shows in each that a man who says that there is a plurality is stating something self-contradictory. One of these arguments is that in which he shows that, if there is a plurality, things are both large and small, so large as to be infinite in magnitude, so small as to have no magnitude at all. And in this argument he show that what has no magnitude nor thickness nor mass does not exist at all ....

Zeno's paradoxes of motion are four in number, the most famous of which is that of the race between Achilles and a tortoise, who is given a head start to compensate for its slowness. Achilles runs to catch up, but to do so he must first reach the point from which the tortoise started, by which time it will have moved farther, and likewise in each diminishing interval that follows. The number of such intervals is infinite, and although the times become increasingly shorter their sum is limitless, according to Zeno. Thus Achilles will never catch up with the tortoise, and the conclusion is that motion is an illusion of the senses. This and other paradoxes of Zeno were not resolved until the nineteenth century, when mathematicians first proved that the sum of an infinite series, such as the time intervals involved in Achilles' race with the tortoise, can be finite.

Some of the profound questions raised by Parmenides were addressed by his younger contemporary Empedocles (ca. 492–ca. 432 BC) of Acragas, a Greek colony in Sicily. Empedocles was the author of two hexameter poems, *On Nature* and *Purifications*, of which a total of 450 lines have survived in the form of quotations by Aristotle and other later writers.

Empedocles was a flamboyant figure, famed as a self-proclaimed miraculous healer and wonder-worker who claimed to be divine. The opening line of *Purifications* is a greeting from Empedocles to his fellow citizens of Acragas, whose acropolis towers over a silt-yellowed river of the same name:

> Friends who inhabit the great town that looks down on yellow Acragas, up on the heights of the citadel, intent on fine works, harbouring with honour the stranger, unacquainted with want, I bid you hail. I an immortal god, no longer a mortal, go about you among all, as is meet, crowned with fillets and blooming garlands. When with these I come to flourishing cities, I am an object of reverence to men and women. They follow me in their thousands, asking whither leads the way to profit, some desiring oracles, whereas others seek to hear the word of healing for every kind of disease, long time transfixed by sore anguish.

Empedocles' poem *On Nature* criticizes those who disagree with the Parmenidean notion that nothing can be created out of nothing or utterly destroyed: 'Fools – for they have no far-reaching thoughts, who suppose that what formerly was not came into being or that anything can die and perish wholly. For there is no means whereby anything could come to be out of what in no way is, and it cannot be brought about or heard of that what is should perish. Wherever one may thrust it, there it will always be.'

He also follows Parmenides in his belief in the denial of the void, as in two of his fragments: 'Nor is any part of the All empty nor yet overflowing .... Of the All, none is empty; whence then can anything enter it?'

Empedocles agreed with Parmenides that sensory evidence is unreliable, but since we are utterly dependent on our senses we should make use of them all with due attention: 'Come now, observe with all thy powers how each thing is clear. Neither holding sight in greater trust with hearing, nor noisy hearing above what the tongue makes plain, nor withhold trust from any of the other limbs [organs, parts of the body], by whatever way there is a channel to understanding, but grasp each thing in the way in which it is clear.'

Empedocles disagreed with the Parmenidean concept of the all-encompassing One, which denied the possibility of plurality, change and motion. Instead he introduced the four elements, earth, water, air and fire – which he called the 'roots of everything' and the 'spring of mortal things.' Instead of the single *arche* of the Milesian physicists, Empedocles now proposes four: 'Fire and water and earth and the immeasurable height of air.' Each of the Empedoclean elements is equal in its own sphere and made up of no more fundamental *arche*; he says that 'all these are equal and coeval, but each is master in a different province and each has its own province.'

Referring to the four elements, Empedocles says that 'from these sprang all things that were and are and shall be, trees and men and women, beasts and birds and water-bred fishes, and the long-lived gods too, mighty in their prerogatives.' He has the four elements intermingling and separating under the influence of two forces that he calls Love and Strife. He says 'the elements are continually subject to an alternate change, at one time mixed together by Love, at another separated by Strife.'

Empedocles thus introduces the concept of force as distinct from matter as the physical cause for the phenomena in nature. Like Heraclitus, he pictured the cosmos as existing in a state of dynamic equilibrium between the opposing forces, with motion taking place when one or the other predominates. Aristotle describes the Empedoclean scheme of nature: 'When the whole is separated into the elements by Strife, fire and each of the others is collected into one; and when under the action of Love they come together into one, it is necessary for the parts from each element to be separated once more.'

Empedocles' identification of earth, water and air as elements corresponds to the modern classification of matter into three states: solid, liquid and gaseous. Fire represented to him not only flames but the phenomena occurring in the heavens, such as lightning and comets, and even the fiery material of which the sun and the stars are made.

The Empedoclean theory of the four elements was one of the most enduring in the history of science, lasting for some two millennia. It left its mark in literature as well as in science, as evidenced by these lines in *The Faerie Queene*, where Spenser writes of how the four elements 'the ground-work bee/Of all the world and of living wights.' He continues:

To thousand sorts of Change we subject see:
Yet are they chang'd (by other wondrous slights)
Into themselves and lose their native mights;
The Fire to Ayre and th' Ayre to Water sheere,
And Water into Earth; yet Water fights
With Fire, and Ayre with Earth, approaching neere:
Yet all are in one body, and as one appeare.

Empedocles was the first to state that light is not transmitted instantaneously but takes time to travel, as Aristotle notes in disagreeing with him: 'Empedocles, and any other who says the same, are wrong in speaking of light as travelling and being at a given moment between the earth and the surrounding sphere.'

Empedocles often used technical similes in explaining his ideas. The most interesting of these is given in his theory of respiration, in which he says that the rhythm of breathing depends on the oscillation of the blood. Here he uses the example of a clepsydra, which Simplicius describes as 'a narrow-necked vessel having a broader base pierced with small holes.' Empedocles uses the simile of a clepsydra in explaining 'the way that all creatures breathe in and out', and in doing so gives the first physical demonstration in the history of physics, showing the effects of air pressure and a partial vacuum:

It is as when a girl plays with a clepsydra of shining bronze. When she puts the opening of the neck against her fair hand, and dips the vessel into the yielding mass of bright water, no liquid enters, but the bulk of air falling from within on the close-set holes prevents it until she uncovers the compressed stream of air. Then as the air gives way, the water duly enters. Similarly when water occupies the interior of the bronze vessel and the opening or passage is stopped by human flesh, the air outside trying to get in keeps back the liquid ... until she releases her hand. Then, the opposite of what happened before, the air rushes in and the water duly rushes out.

> So with breathing, when the blood coursing through the body leaps back to
> the inner recesses, straightway a stream of air comes surging in, but when it
> returns, an equal quantity goes back and is breathed out.

Empedocles claimed to be able to bring the dead back to life, and he is
supposed to have kept a woman alive for 30 days without breath or pulse.
One of the stories told about Empedocles was that he left the world by
jumping into the volcanic crater of Mount Etna, leaving only his sandals
behind, though another legend has him ending his days as an exile in the
Peloponnesos.

Anaxagoras was a slightly older contemporary of Empedocles. He was
born in the Ionian city of Clazomenae *ca.* 500 BC and came to Athens at
the age of 20, probably as a conscript with the army of Xerxes. He was the
first philosopher to live in Athens, where he dwelt for 30 years, becoming
the teacher and friend of Pericles.

According to Diogenes Laertius, Anaxagoras wrote but a single
book, entitled *Physica,* which begins with the statement that 'All things
were together, then Mind (*Nous*) came and set them in order.' By *Nous*
Anaxagoras meant the directing intelligence of the cosmos, as opposed to
inert matter. Plutarch notes in his *Life of Pericles* that Anaxagoras became
so famous for his introduction of *Nous* into philosophy that it became his
nickname:

> But the man who most consorted with Pericles ... was Anaxagoras the
> Clazomenian, whom men of those days used to call '*Nous*' either because
> they admired that comprehension of his, which proved of such surpass-
> ing greatness in the investigation of nature; or because he was the first to
> enthrone in the universe not Chance, nor yet Necessity, but Mind (*Nous*)
> pure and simple, which distinguishes and sets apart, in the midst of an oth-
> erwise chaotic mass, the substances which have like elements.

The views of Anaxagoras on the nature of matter were even more plural-
istic than those of Empedocles, for he postulated the existence of a large
number of elements in his so-called 'seed theory'. 'We must suppose,' he
writes, 'that there are many things of all sorts in things that are aggregated,
seeds of all things, with all sorts of shapes and colours and tastes .... There
is a portion of everything in everything.'

Anaxagoras also postulated an element called the *aither*, which in several places he identifies with fire. He says that 'the sun, the moon and all
the stars are red-hot stones which the rotation of the *aither* carries around

with it.' The *aither* proved to be a very enduring concept, and it reappeared a number of times in cosmological theories up until the early twentieth century.

Anaxagoras combines his concepts of *Nous*, *aither* and the seed theory in his cosmology and theory of matter:

> The rest have a portion of everything, but Mind (*Nous*) is something infinite and independent, and is mixed with no thing, but alone and by itself .... . It is the finest and purest of all things, and has all judgment of everything and greatest power; and everything that has life, both greater and smaller, all these Mind controls; and it controlled the whole revolution, to make it revolve in the beginning. At first it began to revolve for a small part, but now it revolves over a larger field and will include a larger one still. And the things that are being mingled and those that are being separated off and Divided, Mind determined them all. Mind set everything in order, what was to be, what was but is not now, and all that now is and shall be, and this revolution in which revolve the stars, sun, moon, air and fire (*aither*) that are being separated off.

Anaxagoras is credited with several astronomical discoveries, one being that the moon shines by reflecting light from the sun. The source for this is Plato, who writes of 'Anaxagoras' recent assertion that the moon has its light from the sun.' A number of ancient authors write that Anaxagoras described the sun as 'an incandescent stone' and said that it was 'larger than the Peloponnese', perhaps 'many times larger'. He said correctly that solar eclipses take place only at new moon, when the moon gets between the sun and the earth. He also said that the moon has mountains and valleys like the earth.

Around 450 BC the enemies of Pericles indicted Anaxagoras on charges of impiety and medeism – being pro-Persian – but with the aid of Pericles he was able to escape to Lampsacus on the Hellespont. He founded a school in Lampsacus and remained there for the rest of his days. After his death, *ca.* 428 BC, the citizens of Lampsacus erected a monument in his memory, dedicating it to mind and truth, which were at the core of his philosophy. The anniversary of his death was for long afterwards commemorated in Lampsacus, and by his dying request the students were let out of school on that day.

The mathematician Hippocrates of Chios (*ca.* 470–*ca.* 400 BC) was a somewhat younger contemporary of Anaxagoras'. According to the Neoplatonist Proclus (410–485), Hippocrates wrote an *Elements of Geometry*, anticipating by more than a century the famous *Elements* of Euclid. The only surviving fragment of his work contains the following theorem: 'Similar segments of circles are in the same ration as the squares on their bases.' It has been suggested that much of Books III and IV of Euclid's *Elements* came from the work of Hippocrates.

The culmination of pre-Socratic speculation about nature came in the fifth century BC with the atomic theory, first proposed by Leucippus and developed by his pupil Democritus. Their theory holds that the *arche* exists in the form of atoms, the irreducible minima of all substances, which in their ceaseless motion through the void collide and combine with one another to take on all of the various forms in nature.

Little is known about Leucippus, who was a somewhat younger contemporary of Zeno, with whom he may have studied while Parmenides was still alive. It has been suggested that Leucippus was born in Miletus, studied in Elea, and taught at Abdera in Thrace, which had been founded *ca.* 500 BC by refugees from the Ionian city of Teos. His lost work the *Great World-System* apparently originated the atomic theory, which is usually credited to his more famous student Democritus. Democritus presented his atomic theory in a book entitled the *Little World-System*, which he may have so called out of deference to the work of his teacher Leucippus.

Democritus was born in Abdera, where he studied with Leucippus. He writes in the *Little World-System* that he was young in the old age of Anaxagoras, with whom he may have studied, according to some sources. This would mean that Democritus was born *ca.* 460 BC; the date of his death is not known, but he is said to have lived to a great age, possibly more than a hundred.

According to Aristotle, the atomic theory of Leucippus was an attempt to circumvent the impasse created by Parmenides, whose all-encompassing One left no void for motion or any other kind of change and consigned the contrary evidence of the senses to the realm of illusion. He continues:

> But Leucippus thought he had a theory which would agree with the senses and would not abolish coming-to-be or destruction or motion or the plurality of things. So much he conceded to the phenomena, whereas to the proponents of unity he granted that there could not be movement without the void, that the void was 'not being', and nothing of what is is not being; for what, strictly speaking, *is*, is completely full. But such being he claimed, is not a unity. It consists of a plurality of things infinite in number and too small to be seen. They move in the void (for there

is void), and their combination causes coming-to-be, their separation dissolution.

They act and are acted upon as they happen to touch (for in this way they are not one) and generate by coming together and interlocking.

Elsewhere Aristotle gives his interpretation of the atomic theory of Leucippus and Democritus, explaining how they interpret the Parmenidean concepts of 'being' and 'non-being' in connection with atoms and the void, and how the differences in atoms generate the multiplicity in nature:

Leucippus and his associate Democritus name plenum and the void as elements, calling them 'being' and 'not-being': the full and solid is being, the empty and rare is not-being. Hence they say that being exists no more than not being, because void exists no less than body. These are the material causes of things, and just as those who posit a single underlying substance generate everything else by its affections, so they too say that the differences [in the atoms] are responsible for everything else. These according to them are three: shape, arrangement and position.

Aristotle, discussing the atomic theory, says that 'Democritus claims that no elementary particle arises from any other. Nevertheless their common body is the source of everything, differing from part to part in size and shape.' And in another reference he remarks of the Democritian atoms that 'They are differentiated by their shapes, but their substance is one, just as if each were a separate bit of gold.' But for Democritus the atoms of a substance such as gold differ from gold itself in that they are without perceptible qualities, a notion reminiscent of Anaximander's *apeiron*.

There is some question about the range of sizes of the Democritian atoms, which Aristotle says are 'so small as to escape our senses.' Democritus seems to have thought that atoms could have an infinite variety of sizes, but Epicurus later pointed out that this would mean that some could then be visible, or as Aëtius said, could even be as large as the cosmos. There is also a question as to whether the atoms had a minimum size, since Democritus, saying that they were indivisible, ruled out the possibility that they could be infinitely small, contradicting his statement that they could have an infinite variety of sizes. The confusion is probably due to the fact that the concept of infinity was still only vaguely defined.

Aristotle criticizes the atomists for not explaining the cause and nature of atomic motion: 'Leucippus and Democritus, who say that the primary bodies are always in motion in the infinite void, ought to tell us what sort of motion and what is their natural motion.' Elsewhere he is critical of Leucippus for saying, as did Plato, that motion is everlasting: 'but from what cause, or what kind it is, they do not say, nor the reason why it is in this direction or in that.' He also criticizes Democritus for not explaining the cause of the eternal and infinite motion of the atoms: 'They are wrong, and fail to state the causal necessity, who say that things have always happened so and think that this explains their origin. So Democritus of Abdera says that there is no beginning of the infinite, that a cause is an origin and what is everlasting is infinite; therefore to ask "why?" in a case like this is to look for an origin for the infinite.'

What Aristotle is saying is that motion requires a cause, whereas Leucippus and Democritus are stating that motion is the natural state for atoms in an infinite void. This is the modern principle of inertia, in which linear motion at constant speed in a void is a natural state, and only when the velocity changes in magnitude or direction is a cause required in terms of a force.

Leucippus and Democritus had the atoms colliding with one another in their motion through the void, sometimes forming new configurations in the process. Aristotle describes some of the different shapes of the Democritian atoms: 'some are irregular, some hooked, some hollow, others convex, and others have innumerable other differences.' Simplicius, referring to the atomic theory, says that 'These atoms, separate from one another in the void which is infinite, and differing in shape, size, position and order, are in motion in the void, overtake one another and collide. Some rebound at hazard, others become entangled when their shapes, sizes positions and order are favourable, and thus it happens that they bring about generations of composite things ... animals, plants, cosmic systems and in short all perceptible bodies.'

According to Hippolytus, Democritus said that this constant regrouping of the atoms was unlimited in its possibilities, and thus 'there are innumerable worlds of different sizes. In some there is neither sun nor moon, in others they are larger than ours and others have more than one. These worlds are at irregular distances, more in one direction and less in another, and some are flourishing others declining. Here they come into being, there they die, and they are destroyed by collision with one another. Some of the worlds have no animal or vegetable life nor any water.'

Diogenes Laertius is the only source for the cosmogony of Leucippus, who has the atoms forming a vortex in an evolutionary process very much like the modern theory of the formation of stars and galaxies:

> Many bodies [atoms] of all sorts of shape are cut off from the infinite and stream into the great void, and these when collected in a mass produce a single vortex, following the motion of which they collide and revolve in all sorts of ways and begin to be sorted out, like to like .... In this way the earth was formed by the cohesion of the bodies which had moved to the centre. The enclosing membrane in turn is augmented by the influx of atoms from outside; and as it whirls around, it adds to itself those that come in contact with it .... All the stars are ignited by the speed of their motion .... Just as a cosmos is born, so also it grows, declines and perished by some sort of necessity ....

The only fragment of Leucippus that has survived states that 'Nothing occurs at random, but everything for a reason and by necessity.' According to Aristotle, 'Democritus, ignoring the final cause, refers all the operations of nature to necessity.' It would seem that Leucippus and Democritus meant that the atoms 'by necessity' were following the laws of nature governing their motion and collisions, though those laws might be unknown or beyond human reason. These laws completely determined the motion of the atoms, and nothing was random or left to chance.

Democritus agreed with Anaxagoras in saying that the moon resembled the earth, with 'glens and valleys', and he knew that it shone by reflecting light from the sun. Both he and Leucippus retained the older notion that the earth was shaped like a cylinder, though Democritus thought its upper surface was concave rather than flat. Leucippus said that the 'earth was borne rotating about the centre', a motion caused by the swirl of the surrounding vortex.

Both Leucippus and Democritus thought that even the soul, or *psyche*, which distinguishes living beings from non-living objects, was a rarefied material substance which they identified with fire and heat, consisting of small, round atoms. According to Aristotle: 'Democritus says the soul is fire, and hot, for of the infinite shapes and atoms existing he says the spherical are fire and soul .... Similarly Leucippus .... The round ones are soul, because shapes of this kind are best able to slip through anything and to move other things by their own movement.' Elsewhere Aristotle remarks that Democritus said 'that the soul is mortal and perishes along with the body,' its atoms being dispersed, an idea that would be revived by Epicurus.

Democritus travelled widely during his long life, various sources mentioning Egypt, Persia, Babylon and even Ethiopia and India. The early Christian philosopher Clement of Alexandria quotes Democritus as claiming that 'I covered more territory than any man in my time, making the most extensive investigations, and saw more climes and countries and listened to more famous men.' He was a prolific writer, and Diogenes Laertius credits him with more than 60 works, including treatises on philosophy, physics, astronomy, cosmology, mathematics, geography, botany, physiology, medicine, musical theory, linguistics, agriculture and art. All that survives are citations from later writers on his works, the best known of which is the *Little World-System.*

The long lifetime of Democritus spans the period from the last natural philosophers of Ionia and Magna Graecia to the time of Socrates and Plato in the classical era, when Athens became the centre of Greece and the 'school of Hellas'. According to one source Democritus spent several years in Athens, which would have been during the lifetimes of Socrates and Plato. But Plato does not mention Democritus, although he was certainly familiar with his work. According to Diogenes Laertius, Democritus was quoted as saying 'I came to Athens and no one knew me.' This was quite in keeping with the character of Democritus, who in one fragment, paraphrased by Guthrie, says that one should 'avoid all possible disturbances of any kind, mental or emotional. ... This involves taking the least possible action in public affairs or privately, and always keeping well within one's powers.'

Democritus was known as the Laughing Philosopher, largely because of the title of one of his ethical works, *Euthemia,* meaning cheerfulness or contentment, of which one fragment is preserved by Diogenes Laertius: 'The *teleos* [goal] is contentment. It is not the same thing as pleasure, as some have erroneously taken it to be. Rather it is that by which the life of the soul is made calm and stable, undisturbed by fear, superstition or any other emotion. He also calls it well-being, and by many other names.'

CHAPTER 4

THE SCHOOL OF HELLAS

After the defeat of the Persians at Salamis and Plataea in 480–479 BC, Athens, under the leadership of Pericles, became the leading power in the Greek world as well as its intellectual centre. When Pericles delivered his famous funeral oration in 431 BC, honouring the Athenians who fell in the first year of the Peloponnesian War, he reminded his fellow citizens that they were fighting to defend a free and democratic society that was 'open to the world,' one whose 'love of the things of the mind' had made their city 'the school of Hellas'. 'Mighty indeed,' he said, 'are the marks and monuments of our empire which we have left. Future ages will wonder at us, as the present age wonders now.'

Socrates, who fought in the Peloponnesian War, would have heard Pericles' speech. Plato (427–347 BC) was born four years after the death of Pericles, whom he mentions in a number of his dialogues, particularly in the *Phaedrus*. There he has Socrates say that all studies, including rhetoric, require a knowledge of nature: 'This is what Pericles acquired to supplement his natural gifts. In Anaxagoras he found, I think, that kind of man, stored his mind with astronomical lore and learned the nature of mind and thought – matters on which Anaxagoras was continually discoursing – and drew from it what was necessary for the art of speaking.'

According to Aristotle, Plato was acquainted with Socrates 'from his youth'. Plato's dialogue *Phaedo,* known also in antiquity as *On the Soul,* describes the last hours of Socrates in 399 BC before he was forced to commit suicide by drinking hemlock, having been convicted of corrupting the youth of Athens by his subversive ideas.

After the death of Socrates, Plato left Athens and spent some time in Megara. Later, according to Diogenes Laertius, he travelled to the Greek colony of Cyrene in North Africa to study with Theodorus the mathematician, after which he went to Magna Graecia to see the Pythagoreans Philolaus and Eurytus, and thence to Egypt 'to visit the prophets'.

Plato himself, in one of his letters, says that when he was 40, around 387 BC, he 'first came to Italy and Sicily'. In Italy he visited the Pythagorean mathematician and statesman Archytas of Tarentum, after which he crossed to Syracuse in Sicily. There he met the love of his life, Dion, who later ruled Syracuse for three years before his assassination in 354 BC. Even in his old age Plato still mourned for Dion, 'who maddened my soul with love'.

Soon after Plato returned to Athens from Magna Graecia he founded the famous school that came to be called the Academy. The school was about one Attic mile (some 1,200 paces) outside the Dipylon Gate in the Themistoclean walls of ancient Athens along the road known as the Dromos.

The Academy took its name from an ancient shrine of Hekademos, an earth-born hero of Attic mythology, who is supposed to have planted here 12 olive trees that were cuttings from Athena's sacred tree on the Acropolis, her gift to the people of Athens. The *temenos*, or sacred enclosure of the shrine, was vast, judging from the extent of the excavations, with a periphery of about half an Attic mile. The temenos was walled in by Hipparchos (died 514 BC), younger son of Pisastratus, tyrant of Athens. Plutarch says that the grounds were first developed by the Athenian statesman Cimon (*ca.* 512–449 BC), who transformed it 'from a waterless and arid spot into a well-watered grove, with clear running tracks and shady groves.'

There was already a gymnasium here by the time of Aristophanes, as evidenced by a passage in *The Clouds*, produced in 423 BC: 'You will spend your time, sleek and blooming in the gymnasium ... . You will go down to the Academy and run races under the sacred olives with a virtuous comrade, crowned with white reeds and smelling of bindweed and careless ease and the white poplar that sheds its leaves, happy in the springtime when the plane-tree whispers to the elm.'

There were other gymnasia and institutions in and around the *temenos* of Hekademos, but in time the school founded by Plato became so famous that the name Academy came to be applied to it alone. Milton describes it in *Paradise Regained* as 'the olive grove of Academe, Plato's retirement, where the Attic bird trills her thick-warbl'd notes the summer long.'

During its early years the Academy may have been patterned on the educational system described by Plato in the *Republic* and *Laws*, particularly on Book I of the latter, where he writes that 'what we have in mind is education from childhood in virtue, a training which produces a keen desire to become a perfect citizen who knows how to rule and be ruled as justice demands.' Plutarch gives a list of the distinguished statesmen and scholars whom Plato taught at the Academy, 11 in number from all over the Greek world, most notably Aristotle.

The Academy probably corresponded to the colleges of the first European universities, with a community of scholars sharing a common table. Athenaeus of Naucratis (fl. *ca.* AD 200) writes that 'the philosophers make it their business to join with their students in feasting according to set rules.' Plato, in the *Laws*, says that symposia were conducted according to the rules of a master of ceremonies, who must himself remain sober. Antigonus of Carystus (fl. *ca.* 240 BC) writes that Plato did not hold these symposia just for the sake of carousing, 'but that they might manifestly honour the gods and enjoy each other's companionship, and chiefly to refresh themselves with learned discussion.'

Little is known of the Academy's formal organization or curriculum, other than what can be gathered from the writings of Plato, his pupils and his successors. Probably the dialectic method of Socrates was used rather than formal lecturing, and the teaching would not have been intended to impart any specific knowledge other than perhaps logic and mathematics.

Over the entrance of the Academy there is said to have been an inscription stating 'Let no one ignorant of geometry enter here'. This probably derives from Plato's *Republic*, where Socrates says that 'we must require those in our fine city not to neglect geometry in any way, for even its by-products are not insignificant.'

Plato believed that mathematics was a prerequisite for the dialectic process that would give future leaders the philosophical insight necessary for governing a city-state. The mathematical study included arithmetic, plane and solid geometry, harmonics, or the mathematics of music, and astronomy.

Plato may have been converted to mathematics by his friend Archytas of Tarentum, from whom he learned the Pythagorean tradition of number and harmony. When Archytas ruled Tarentum he emphasized the role of mathematics in education. He is credited with designating the four branches of the mathematical quadrivium – arithmetic, geometry, music and astronomy – which, together with the trivium – grammar, rhetoric and dielectics – made up the seven liberal arts.

Archytas is credited with being the first to attempt a three-dimensional solution of the so-called Delian problem. During the plague of 427 BC, when one-fourth of the population of Athens died, the Athenians consulted the oracle at Delphi and were told that the cubical altar of Apollo there must be doubled. The Athenians did so, doubling the length of each side of the altar and thus increasing its volume by a factor of eight. When the plague continued the Athenians realized they should have increased the dimensions of the sides only enough to double the volume, or so the story goes. This was the origin of the Delian problem, also known as the problem of the duplication of the cube: given the edge of a cube, construct with compasses and straight edge a second cube with double the volume of the first. This was one of three famous problems that were current at the time, the others being the squaring of the circle, that is, finding the square that had double the area of a given circle, and trisecting the angle, in both cases using only compasses and a straight age. Only in the nineteenth century did mathematicians prove rigorously that the three problems could not be solved.

Plutarch, in his *Life of Marcellus*, says that Archytas, along with Eudoxus and his pupil Menaechmus, annoyed Pluto by trying to work out problems like the doubling of the cube with mechanical aids, rather than solving them by reasoning alone. Plato considered this to be 'the mere corruption and annihilation of the one good of geometry, which was thus shamefully turning its back upon the unembodied aspects of pure intelligence.' According to the story, Plato warned those who would solve the Delian problem to avoid 'the awkward cylinders of Archytas, the triads which Menaechmus produced by conic section, and the curvilinear shapes of Eudoxus.'

Plato writes of two other mathematician friends of his time in the *Theaetatus*. The dialogue is named for Theaetatus (*ca.* 414–369 BC) of Athens, who studied philosophy at the Academy with Plato and learned mathematics from Theodorus of Cyrene (fl. *ca.* 390 BC), who had also taught Plato. Theodorus is the interlocutor in the dialogue, at the beginning of which he introduces Socrates to Theaetatus, saying 'Well, Socrates, I think you ought to be told, and I think I ought to tell you, about a remarkable boy I met here, one of your fellow countrymen ... His name, Socrates, is Theaetatus.'

Plato says in the *Theaetatus* that Theodorus was the first to prove the irrationality of the non-square integers from 3 through 17. Other ancient writers indicate that Theodorus was the source of a number of theorems in elementary geometry that later were used by Plato in his *Elements*.

As noted earlier, Theaetatus was the first to discover that the octahedron and icosahedrons were regular polyhedra. He is probably the source of the theorem that there are five and only five such perfect solids, which is presented by Euclid in Book XIII of the *Elements*, much of which is believed to come from Theaetatus.

Plato's dialogue *Protagoras* mentions a young man who goes to the Aegean island of Kos to study medicine under Hippocrates the Asclepiad. The renowned physician Hippocrates (460–399 BC) was a contemporary of Socrates. He was known as the Asclepiad because he belonged to one of the families who perpetuated the cult of Asclepios, the god of healing, whose first shrines were founded around 500 BC The most famous of these healing shrines were the Asclepieia at Epidaurus, Athens and Pergamum, besides which there were also celebrated medical schools at Kos and Cnidus. The writings of Hippocrates and his followers, the so-called Hippocratic corpus, comprises some 70 works dating from his time to *ca.* 300 BC. Beside treatises on the various branches of medicine, they include clinical records and notes of lectures given to the general public on medical topics. A treatise on deontology, or medical ethics, contains the famous Hippocratic oath, which is still taken by physicians today. One work in the Hippocratic corpus is entitled *The Sacred Disease*, for the name given to epilepsy, since those suffering from it were believed to be stricken by the gods. The author of this work says that epilepsy, like all other diseases, has a natural cause, and those who first called it sacred were trying to cover up their ignorance. 'I do not believe,' he says, 'that the "Sacred Disease" is any more divine or sacred than any other disease but, on the contrary, has specific characteristics and a definite cause. Nevertheless, because it is completely different from other diseases, it has been regarded as a divine visitation by those who, being only human, regard it with ignorance and astonishment.'

Research on biology and zoology was also carried out at the Academy. Plato's nephew and successor Speusippus has left a number of fragments dealing with zoological classification and nomenclature. A parody by the comic poet Epicrates describes Plato, Speusippus, and Menedemus, who was also associated with the Academy, as setting their students to studying animals, trees and plants so as to assign the pumpkin to its appropriate class.

Plato's attitude toward the study of nature is evident from what he has to say in the *Phaedo*. Here Plato introduces the concept of eternal, unchanging Forms or 'Ideas' and their unstable reflection in the physical, perceptible world of 'becoming'. At one point in the dialogue Socrates talks of how he had been attracted to the ideas of Anaxagoras because of his concept of *Nous,* or Mind, as first cause. But he was ultimately disappointed, for he found that Anaxagoras did not use Mind to explain the phenomena in nature, giving materialistic reasons instead. 'This wonderful hope was dashed as I went on reading,' he says, 'and saw that the man made no use of Mind, nor gave it any responsibility for the management of things, but mentioned as causes air and *aither* and water and many other strange things.'

Socrates was disillusioned with Anaxagoras because he only told him *how* things happened rather than *why*. What Socrates was looking for was a teleological explanation, one involving evidences of design in nature, for he believed that everything in the cosmos was directed towards attaining the best possible end. As he says of his initial attraction for the *Nous* of Anaxagoras: 'I was delighted with this cause and it seemed to me good, in a way, that Mind should be the cause of all. I thought that if this were so, the directing mind would direct everything and arrange each thing in the way that was best. If then one wished to know the cause of each thing, why it comes to be or perishes or exists, one had to find what was the best way for it to be, or to be acted upon.'

Plato also presents his theory of ideal forms in the dialogue *Parmenides*. This is based on a supposed visit that Parmenides of Elea made to Athens in his old age, when he and his pupil Zeno met the young Socrates. The narrator Cephalus of Clazomenae describes the meeting:

Zeno and Parmenides once came to Athens for the Great Panathenaea. Parmenides was already quite venerable, about sixty-five years old, very gray but of distinguished appearance. Zeno was at the time close to forty, a tall handsome man who had been, as rumor had it, the object of Parmenides' affection when he was a boy. Antiphon said that the two of them were staying with Pythadorus, outside the city wall in the Potters' Quarter, and that Socrates had come there along with a number of others, because they were eager to hear Zeno read his book, which he and Parmenides had just brought to Athens for the first time. Socrates was then quite young.

The concept of *Nous* was used by Plato and Aristotle as the foundation of their philosophies of nature, that the notion of 'Mind' or 'Intelligence' controls the operation of the cosmos. The harmony and order of the cosmos do not come about by chance, they believed, but because of the *Nous* that guides it toward the *teleos*, or goal, the end in view. This is the principle of teleology, which holds that the cosmos operates according to a preconceived design, whose end is a perfect universe. When studying nature it is not sufficient to find the physical or material causes, as the Milesian physicists had sought to do; one must look deeper to identify the primary cause, which they believed was the intelligent plan according to which the cosmos was designed. As Plato writes in the *Timaeus*:

> So anyone who is a lover of understanding and knowledge must of necessity pursue as primary causes those that belong to intelligent nature, and as secondary all those belonging to things that are moved by others and that set still others in motion by necessity. We too, surely, must do likewise: we must describe both types of causes, distinguishing those which possess understanding and thus fashion what is beautiful and good, from those which, when deserted by intelligence, produce only haphazard and disorderly effects every time.

Plato's own ideas in science are contained principally in the *Timaeus*, where he presents a detailed cosmology that Timaeus, his protagonist, says is 'along the lines of the likely stories we have been following.' Timaeus introduces a divine creator called the *demiourgos*, or craftsman, who uses the ideal Forms as patterns to shape featureless preexisting matter and steer its chaotic motion so as to give order to the cosmos. But, as Guthrie remarks, the *demiourgos* 'is not in sole and absolute control, but must bend to his will a material that is to some extent recalcitrant. Otherwise, being wholly good himself, he would have made a perfect world.'

Plato used the four elements of Empedocles as the basis for his theory of matter in the *Theaetatus*, having the *demiourgos* (whom he here calls 'the god') mix them together in due proportion: 'Hence the god set water and air between fire and earth, and made them as proportionate to one another as was possible, so what fire is to air, air is to water, and what air is to water, water is to earth. He then bound them together and thus he created the visible and tangible universe ... making it a symphony of proportion.'

Plato adopted the Pythagorean notion of identifying each of the four elements with the cosmic figures, or regular polyhedra: fire with the tetrahedron, air with the octahedron, water with the icosahedron, and earth with the cube, while the fifth solid, the dodecahedron, is mentioned but not associated with an element. He constructed the faces of the four figures identified with the elements using two types of basic triangle, the right-angled isosceles and the half-equilateral. Thus he used six equilateral triangles to construct a square, the face of the cube, and six half-equilaterals to form an equilateral triangle, the face of the tetrahedron, octahedron and icosahedron. By so doing he was able to create a scheme in which the elements can be transformed into one another by a rearrangement of the triangles from which they are constructed, a kind of geometrical atomism.

Plato relates his cosmogony to the presence of mankind, in a luminous passage where Timaeus points out how our sense of number and time comes from our observation of the heavens: 'our ability to see the periods of day and night, of months and of years, of equinoxes and solstices, has led to the invention of number, and has given us the idea of time and opened the path to inquiry into the nature of the universe. These pursuits have given us philosophy, a gift from the gods to the mortal race whose value neither has been or ever will be surpassed.'

Timaeus goes on to point out that speech and hearing were also gifts of the gods, 'given for the same purpose and intended to achieve the same result ... . And harmony, whose movements are akin to the orbits within our souls, is a gift of the Muses.'

Plato's various dialogues reveal that he had a more advanced knowledge of astronomy and cosmology than his predecessors. In the *Phaedo* Socrates says that 'if the earth is a sphere in the middle of the heavens, it has no need of air or any other force to prevent it from falling. The homogeneous nature of the heavens on all sides and the earth's own equipoise are sufficient to hold it, for an object balanced in the middle of something homogeneous will have no tendency to incline more in one direction than any other but will remain unmoved.'

At the end of the last book of the *Republic* Plato relates the tale of Er, a mythical warrior who was killed in battle and then returned to life 12 days later to describe what he had seen of the heavens. The narrator says that on the fourth day of their celestial journey, Er and his companions came to a place where they could look down upon the whole of the universe, which had the form of eight nested whorls rotating about an axis that he calls 'the Spindle of Necessity'. He goes on to say that 'above on the rims of the circles stood a Siren, who accompanied its revolution, uttering a single sound, one note. And the concord of the eight notes produced a single harmony.'

The eight whorls clearly represent the heavenly spheres that carry the sun, the moon, the five visible planets and the fixed stars, and the rate at which each of them rotates is in accordance with the Pythagorean harmony of the celestial orbs. Plato also describes these motions in the *Timaeus*, where he says that god created the celestial bodies so that man could tell time. His description is particularly interesting, for he has the motions of Mercury and Venus tied to that of the Sun, periodically overtaking it and being themselves overtaken.

Such was ... the god's design for the coming to be of time, that he brought into being the Sun, the Moon and five other stars [the visible planets], for the begetting of time. These are called 'wanderers,' and they came to be in order to set limits to and stand guard over the numbers of time. When the god had finished making a body for each of them, he placed them in the orbits traced by the period of the Different – seven bodies in seven orbits.

He set the Moon in the first circle, around the earth, and the Sun in the second, above it. The Dawnbearer (the Morning Star, or Venus) and the star said to be sacred to Hermes (Mercury) he set to run in circles hat equal's the Sun's in speed ... . As a result the Sun, the star of Hermes and the Dawnbearer alike overtake and are overtaken by one another.

The term 'Different', sometimes referred to by Plato as the 'circle of the Different', is the so-called ecliptic, the path of the sun among the fixed stars as plotted on the celestial sphere. The paths of the planets on the celestial sphere are all close to the ecliptic. The poles of the celestial sphere are projections of the earth's axis among the stars. The apparent nightly rotation of the stars around these poles is due to the axial rotation of the earth in the opposite sense. Plato also refers to the 'circle of the Same', by which he means the celestial equator, the projection of the earth's equator on the celestial sphere. These two circles are inclined by an angle of 23.5 degrees because of the tilt of the earth's axis relative to the perpendicular of the plane defined by the ecliptic.

The planets periodically exhibit what is called 'retrograde motion' in other words, for a time they change the direction of their motion along the ecliptic, which occurs whenever the earth overtakes one of the slower outer planets or is passed by one of the swifter planets closer to the sun. All of these features are described by Plato in the *Timaeus*, where the narrator tells of how the planets 'cooperate in producing time':

Some bodies would move in a large circle, others in a smaller one, the latter moving more quickly and the former more slowly. Indeed, because of the movement of the Same, the ones that go around most quickly appear to be overtaken by those going more slowly, even though in fact they are overtaking them. For as it revolves, this movement gives to all these circles a spiral twist [i.e., retrograde motion], because they are moving forward in two contrary directions at once.

The *Timaeus* was translated into Latin late in the fourth century AD by Chalcidius, who accompanied his translation with a commentary on Plato's cosmology. This work survived into the medieval era and was the principal source of knowledge concerning Platonism available in Western Europe up until the twelfth century, when other works of Plato were first translated from Greek into Latin. The *Timaeus* thus had a profound influence on medieval European cosmology, which it retained until it was replaced by the Aristotelian world-picture in the thirteenth century. Nevertheless, it was still a source of inspiration as late as 1597, when Kepler quotes from it regarding the cosmic figures in his *Mysterium Cosmographicum.*

Plato's most enduring influence on science was his advice to approach the study of nature, particularly astronomy, as an exercise in geometry. Through this 'geometrization of nature', applicable only in those disciplines such as mathematical astronomy that could be suitably idealized, one can arrive at relations as 'certain' as those in geometry. As Socrates remarks in the *Republic,* 'let's study astronomy by means of problems, as we do geometry, and leave the things in the sky alone.'

The first recorded astronomical observation in Greece was made in Athens by two contemporaries of Socrates, Meton and Euctemon, who recorded the summer solstice on 27 June 432 BC. Their observation was used by subsequent astronomers to determine a more accurate value for the length of the year.

Meton gave his name to the so-called Metonic cycle, which he had discovered in an attempt to reconcile the solar and lunar calendars. He found that 19 years equalled 235 months almost exactly, meaning that the sun and the moon return to the same places on the ecliptic in that period, so that the moon will be in the same phase on two dates that are 19 years apart. The Babylonians were aware of this cycle, but it is not known whether Meton acquired it from their records or discovered it independently. The Metonic cycle was never adopted by the Athenians, although the *archons* who governed Athens may have used it when faced with the problem of intercalating the lunar and solar calendars. Meton's cycle was used by subsequent astronomers for dating astronomical observations. Callippus of Cyzicus proposed a 76-year cycle as an improvement on Meton's, the first period beginning in 330–329 BC, with each year measuring 325¼ days.

Euctemon is known to have written a *parapegma*, or star-calendar, a version of the Babylonian MULAPIN astronomical text. His *parapegma*, which was accompanied by weather predictions, was designed as a supplement to the civil calendars used by the various Greek cities. Each of these calendars had its own names for the months, and with different beginning dates for the year, making dates used in one city unintelligible to those in another. Thus the *parapegma*, which gave the times of the rising and setting of stars in the twelve signs of the zodiac, could be used as a universal calendar.

According to Simplicius, Plato posed a problem for those studying the heavens: to demonstrate 'on what hypotheses the phenomena concerning the planets [including in that term, as was customary, the sun and moon] could be accounted for by uniform and ordered circular motions.'

The first solution to the problem was given by Eudoxus of Cnidus (*ca.* 400–*ca.* 347 BC), a younger friend of Plato's who may have been associated with the Academy. As a young man he had studied geometry with Archytas of Tarentum, from whom he may have developed his interest in number theory and harmonics. Eudoxus was one of the greatest mathematicians of the classical period, and is credited with some of the theorems that would later appear in the works of Euclid and Archimedes. He was also the leading astronomer of his time and had made careful observations of the celestial bodies from his observatory at Cnidus, the southernmost of the Dorian cities in Asia Minor.

Eudoxus created a model in which the path of each of the celestial bodies – sun, moon and planets – was the resultant of the rotary motions of several interconnected spheres, all of them with the earth as their centre, but with their axes inclined to one another and rotating at different speeds, the planet being attached to the equator on the innermost sphere and the outermost one rotating once daily with the fixed stars. The motions of the sun and moon were accounted for by 3 spheres each, the planets by 4 spheres each, while a single sphere sufficed for the fixed stars, making a total of 27 spheres for the cosmos. Eudoxus was able to explain the retrograde motion of the planets by using appropriate values for the radii and rotational velocities of the planetary spheres. Although the theory gave a plausible physical model of the celestial motions, it had a number of shortcomings, one being its failure to explain the variation in brightness of each of the planets.

Eudoxus' model, known as the theory of homocentric or concentric spheres, was elaborated upon by Callippus, who added two spheres each for the sun and moon, as well as one each for Mercury, Venus and Mars, to make a total of 34. The theory of homocentric spheres was subsequently adopted by Aristotle as the physical model for his geocentric cosmos, using a total of 55 spheres. In this form Eudoxus' theory of the homocentric spheres survived through the medieval era in both Islam and Western Europe, and it was still in use up into the sixteenth century.

Eudoxus wrote a work on astronomy describing the various constellations and the two principal circles on the sphere of the heavens, for instance, the celestial equator and the ecliptic, the path of the sun among the stars. This work did not survive, but it served as a model for Aratus of Soli in Cilicia, who around 275 BC, wrote a long poem entitled *Phaenomena*, the oldest extent description of the constellations in Greek, paraphrasing Eudoxus. The *Phaenomena* was a star-calendar and weather predictor that was extremely popular in the Hellenistic era; it was translated into Latin several times and was widely used in medieval Europe, perpetuating the astronomical work of Eudoxus.

Geminus of Rhodes, writing *ca.* 325 BC, mentions Eudoxus along with Callippus and Euctemon in his own *parapegma*:

> The Sun passes through the Virgin in 30 days. On the 5th day, according to Eudoxus, a great wind blows and it thunders. According to Callippus, the shoulders of the Virgin rise, and the etesian winds cease. On the 10th day, according to Euctemon, the Vintager appears, and the Bird sets at dawn: a storm at sea; south wind. According to Eudoxus, rain, thunder; a great wind blows.

Eudoxus' contributions in mathematics include the famous theory of proportions given by Euclid in Definition 5 of Book V of the *Elements*: 'Magnitudes are said to be in the same ratio, the first to the second and the third to the fourth, when, if any equimultiples whatever be taken of the first and the third, and any equimultiples whatever of the second and the fourth, the former equimultiples alike exceed, are alike equal to, or are alike less than, the latter equimultiples taken in corresponding order.' This theory, which was applied in geometry, arithmetic and music, was revived more than 2,000 years later by Karl Weierstrass (1815–1897) and J. W. R. Dedekind (1831–1916).

Another important advance made by Eudoxus is his theory of infinitesimals, or method of exhaustion, a precursor of the calculus, used by Archimedes to find the areas and volumes of curvilinear figures. The area of a circle can be found by inscribing in it a regular polygon and then increasing the number of sides indefinitely, doubling the number each time. The sum of the small segments left over between the sides of the polygon and the circumference of the circle can be made less than any assigned area, and thus the difference between the area of the circle and that of the polygon, which can readily be computed, becomes vanishingly small. The proposition that formed the basis for the method of exhaustion is stated in Book XI of the *Elements*: 'If from any magnitude there be subtracted a part not less than its half, and if this process of subtraction is continued, ultimately there will remain a magnitude less than any preassigned magnitude of the same kind.'

Archimedes attributed to Eudoxus the proof, using the method of exhaustion, that the volume of a cylinder is one-third the volume of the cylinder having the same base and altitude. Eudoxus is probably the source of Euclidian proofs of theorems concerning areas of circles and volumes of spheres. Euclid's axiomatic method may also have been first systematized by Eudoxus.

Eudoxus also wrote on geography in a work entitled *Ges periodos* (*Tour of the Earth*), of which some 100 fragments survive. His description of the known world includes information on the politics, history and ethnography of the places he covers in his tour, including the customs of the Pythagoreans he visited in Magna Graecia. He also drew up a constitution for his native city of Cnidus, whose ruins can still be seen on the southwesternmost peninsula of Asia Minor, where a sundial has been uncovered that may be from the observatory where Eudoxus surveyed the heavens.

Heraclides Ponticus (*ca.* 390–after 339 BC) studied under Plato at the Academy and later he also attended Aristotle's lectures. His name comes from that of his birthplace, Heraclea on the Pontus Euxinos, or Black Sea, now the Turkish town of Karadeniz Ereğlisi. After the death of Plato's successor Speusippus in 339 BC, Heraclides was one of the candidates to succeed him, but he lost out to Xenocrates by a few votes. He then retired to Heraclea, where he died a few years later.

The titles of 46 dialogues by Heraclides are known, including books on physics, astronomy, music, literature, rhetoric, history and politics, but none of his works have survived except for fragments. He is renowned in modern times for his theory, mentioned earlier, that the apparent nightly circling of the stars around the celestial pole is actually due to the earth's rotation on its axis in the opposite sense every 24 hours. According to Simplicius: 'Heraclides supposed that earth is in the centre and rotates while the heavens is at rest, and he thought by this supposition to save [i.e., account for] the phenomena.' But the theory was not generally accepted, because, it was argued, such a rapid rotation of the earth would produce marked effects which in fact are not observed.

Some nineteenth-century writers, including the Italian astronomer Schiaperelli, credited Heraclides with the theory that Mercury and Venus orbit the sun rather than the earth, an idea that was proposed in the late sixteenth century by the Danish astronomer Tycho Brahe. The only evidence concerning this theory of Heraclides is a passage from the commentary on Plato's *Timaeus* by Chalcidius:

> Finally, Heraclides Ponticus, when he drew the circle of Venus and also the [circle] of the sun, and assigned a single center to both circles, showed that Venus is sometimes above, sometimes below the sun ... . For it is obvious that it is called evening star when it is seen ... following sunset, and morning star when it sets before the sun and rises again before the sun when the night is almost over.

But modern historians of science have concluded that there is no solid basis for crediting Heraclides with the theory that Mercury and Venus orbit the sun. They have also discredited the claim, made by Schiaperelli and other nineteenth-century writers, that Heraclides proposed that the earth orbited the sun along with all of the other planets.

Heraclides did have one other extraordinary idea, which is preserved in a fragment. He believed that the universe is infinite and that each star is itself a whole cosmos, 'containing earth and air in the infinite *aither*'.

These are some of the theories that emerged from Plato's school in the olive grove of Academe, which would continue in existence for more than nine centuries, spreading its ideas throughout the world and shaping mankind's view of the cosmos and thought itself for ages to come.

CHAPTER 5

THE GROVE OF APOLLO

Aristotle was born in 384 BC in the small township of Stagira, near the isthmus of the easternmost of the three peninsulas of the Chalcidice. His father Nicomachus was the personal physician and friend of Amyntas II of Macedon, father of Philip II and grandfather of Alexander the Great. Aristotle may have spent part of his childhood in Pella, the Macedonian capital. Both of his parents died early in his childhood, and he was put in the care of a guardian, Proxenus of Atarnaeus, a city on the northern Aegean coast of Asia Minor.

Around the time of his seventeenth birthday, in 367 BC, Aristotle went to Athens and was enrolled in Plato's Academy. He remained at the Academy until the death of Plato in 347 BC, when he and his colleague Xenocrates left for Assos, a city on the Aegean coast of Asia Minor north of Atarnaeus, birthplace of his guardian Proxenus.

At the time Assos was part of a small principality ruled by Hermias, the Tyrant of Atarneus, who had developed an interest in philosophy through a visit to Plato's Academy. Didymus of Alexandria, writing in the first century BC, describes Hermias as 'a man of taste and culture, and though not a Hellene he studied philosophy with the Platonists.' The Platonists referred to were Erastus and Coriscus, both of Scepsis, a small city north of Assos. Both of them had studied in Plato's academy before returning to Scepsis, after which they became associated with Hermias and introduced him to philosophy. Their influence converted Hermias into an enlightened despot, according to Didymus, who writes that 'He deliberately turned his tyranny into a milder form of government, and thus added to his terrain all the surrounding territory as far as Assos; wherefore he was greatly pleased with the said philosophers, and allotted to them the city of Assos.'

Aristotle remained in Assos for three years, during which time he married Pythias, the niece and adopted daughter of Hermias. After Hermias was killed by the Persians in 344 BC, Aristotle left Assos with Pythias and moved to the nearby island of Lesbos. He probably did so at the suggestion of his younger colleague Theophrastus of Eresus on Lesbos, who had studied under Plato at the Academy. Aristotle remained on Lesbos until 342 BC, when, accompanied by Pythias and Theophrastus, he returned to Macedonia at the invitation of Philip II to tutor prince Alexander.

Aristotle remained in Macedonia until 335 BC, the year after Alexander succeeded to the throne, when he and Pythias and Theophrastus returned to Athens, which then was under the rule of Macedon. Plato's successor Speusippus had died in 339 BC and Xenocrates followed him as head of the Academy. Aristotle and Theophrastus began to teach at the Lyceum, a gymnasium in a grove of trees sacred to Apollo Lykeios, Apollo the Wolf-God, whose site is now the Greek Parliament on Syntagma Square. (Because the wolf can see in the dark, it became associated with Apollo in his role as the morning star, and hence the curious name.)

Hermippus of Smyrna, writing in the third century BC, is quoted by Diogenes Laertius in his description of Aristotle lecturing at the Lyceum, a style that led his followers to be called the Peripatetics: 'he chose a public walk (*peripatos*) in the Lyceum, where he would walk up and down discussing philosophy with his pupils until it was time for their rubbing with oil.'

The buildings of the Lyceum comprised a temple of the Muses, a garden and houses, including a large library and places for scientific research. Aulus Gellius, a Roman who studied at the Academy in the second century AD, gives an interesting account of Aristotle's teaching methods:

> The lectures of the philosopher Aristotle, the teacher of Alexander, and the accomplishments which he imparted to his students, are said to have been of two kinds. Some were called *exoteric*, some *acroatic* [to be listened to]. The name exoteric applied to rhetoric, the cultivation of a quick wit, and education in civics. *Acroatic* on the other hand were works concerned with more arcane and exact philosophy, with the investigation of nature and with dialectical discussion. In the Lyceum he devoted the morning to the acroactic subjects and did not allow anyone to attend without assuring himself of their ability, educational grounding, keenness to learn and willingness to work. The exoteric lectures and speech-classes he held in the same place in the evening, and opened them to any young men without restriction. This he called his 'evening walk', the other the early one, for at both times he walked as he talked. His books also, treatises on all these same subjects, he divided similarly, called some exoteric and some *acroatic*.

Besides his lectures, Aristotle spent considerable time doing biological research, which he probably began in Lesbos with Theophrastus, who continued his own studies in biology at the Lyceum. Aristotle's enthusiasm for the study of living things is evident from a passage in his work *On the Parts of Animals*:

> It remains to treat of the nature of living creatures, omitting nothing (as far as possible), whether of higher or lower dignity. For even in the case of creatures, the composition of which is disagreeable to the sense, Nature, who fashioned them, nevertheless affords an extraordinary pleasure to anyone with a philosophical disposition, capable of understanding cause. We take delight in looking at representations of these things, because we observe at the same time the art of the painter or sculptor who created them; and it would be strange and unreasonable that the contemplation of their works should not yield a still greater satisfaction, when we can make out their causes. In all natural things, there is something to move wonder.

Aristotle's writings are encyclopedic in scope, those that survive including works on logic, metaphysics, rhetoric, theology, politics, economics, literature, ethics, psychology, physics, mechanics, astronomy, meteorology, cosmology, biology, botany, natural history and zoology. Thus Montaigne was led to write of 'Aristotle that hath an oare in every water, and medleth with all things.'

Diogenes Laertius catalogues more than 150 titles by Aristotle, divided into some 550 books. The list is by no means complete, since it omits several major extant works, such as *On the Soul, Parts of Animals* and the *Generation of Animals*. Many works listed in the catalogue have been lost, such as the *Constitutions of 158 States*, of which only that of Athens has survived. The revised Oxford translation comes to 2,383 pages, excluding the fragments, and including a number of works which may not actually be due to Aristotle.

All in all, it is estimated that about a third of Aristotle's works have survived. The extant works are often referred to as 'the lecture manuscripts', which have generally considered to be of two types, one being those from which Aristotle himself lectured, and the other consisting of notes or edited works by a colleague or student.

The lost works include all of what Aristotle called his 'exoteric' or popular writings, which he would have composed to spread his ideas to a wider public. The popular works of Aristotle are frequently mentioned by Greek and Roman writers, and it appears that many of them were dialogues in the tradition of the Platonic dialogues, in which Plato now played the role that Socrates had originally taken.

One of the dominant concepts in Aristotle's philosophy is the principle of teleology, the idea that natural processes are directed toward an end. This is stated most clearly in Book II of the *Physics*, where he draws an analogy between nature and art:

> Now action is for an end; therefore the nature of things also is so. Thus if a house, e. g., had been a thing made by nature, it would have been made in the same way as it is now by art; and if things made by nature were made not only by nature but also by art, they would come to be in the same way as by nature. The one, then is for the sake of the other; and generally art in some cases completes what nature cannot bring to a finish, and in others imitates nature.

Another fundamental characteristic of Aristotle's philosophy is his notion of causation. When looking for the cause of anything we must distinguish between the following four factors, using the names of the various causes as they are given by Aristotle. The material cause of something is known when we identify the material out of which it is formed; the formal cause when we specify the plan or design according to which it is fashioned; the efficient cause when we name the agent that actually made it; the final cause when we give the reason why it was brought into being.

The example which Aristotle gives to illustrate these concepts is that of a sculptor and a statue, bronze or marble. The material cause of the statue is the original mass of bronze or marble from which it is made. The form or concept of the statue that exists in the sculptor's mind is the formal cause. The sculptor himself through his skill and tools is the efficient cause. The final cause is the ultimate purpose or goal (*teleos*) that the sculptor has in mind when he sets out to work.

The first three causes – material, formal and efficient – correspond to the three aspects of existence that can be distinguished as matter, form and actualization of form. But these do not define the course of events in nature, since an acorn, for example, always grows into an oak and never a cypress. The fourth and final form corresponds to the fact that a substance by virtue of its existence not only materializes a form but also implies a purpose. Thus there must be a purpose or design in the acorn such that it always grows into an oak tree. This aspect of existence is indicated by the word entelechy; this means the purpose that guides things to develop in one way rather than another.

Aristotle's notion of the four causes enabled him to put his own work in an historical perspective. According to this view, the Milesian physicists, with their idea of a fundamental substance, had been looking for the material cause of things; the Pythagoreans, with their emphasis on number and harmony, had searched for the formal cause; Empedocles, with his concept of the forces of Love and Conflict, had been concerned with the efficient cause; while Socrates, in seeking the ultimate goal or purpose, had suggested the final cause. According to Aristotle, a complete explanation of nature must recognize the four-fold nature of causation.

Aristotle, in contrast to Plato, had a strong empirical bent, which led the Neoplatonist Proclus to remark that 'he neglected theological principles and spent too much time on physical matters.' This is particularly evident in Aristotle's criticism of Plato's *Timaeus* and his generation of the elements from 'geometrical atoms': 'Those who have spent more time among physical phenomena are better able to posit the kind of principle which can hold together over a wide area, whereas those who through much abstract discussion have lost sight of the facts are more likely to dogmatize on the basis of a few observations.'

Elsewhere he makes the same point, giving as an example the reproduction of bees: 'This then appears to be the manner of reproduction among bees, judging by theory and what appear to be the facts about them. The facts however have not been adequately ascertained. If they ever are, then one must trust the evidence of the senses rather than theory, and theories only if they agree with the phenomena.'

The main outlines of Aristotle's cosmology were inherited from earlier Greek thought. He took from the Milesian physicists the notion that there was one fundamental substance in nature and reconciled this with Empedocles' concept of the four elements: earth, water, air and fire. According to Aristotle, there is a primary substratum in nature, which he calls matter (*hyle*) that underlies and persists through all change. As Aristotle writes in a parenthetical statement in Book I of the *Physics*: 'For my definition of matter is just this – the primary substratum of each thing, from which it comes to be, and persists in the result, not accidentally.'

According to Aristotle, the substratum is completely undifferentiated. It has no qualities whatsoever, being in effect the characteristic raw material out of which the universe is made. Aristotle would describe this process as matter taking on form, matter being the raw material and form all of the qualities that give something its unique character. These two aspects of existence – matter and form – are inseparable, and can only exist in conjunction with one another. Aristotle distinguished between two types of properties, primary and secondary. Primary qualities are those which are inherent in the body itself, such as size, shape and weight, while secondary qualities depend upon the interaction between the body and the observer, as in the case of colour, taste and smell.

Aristotle adopted Empedocles' theory of the four elements – earth, water, air and fire – which, he says, are formed from the basic substratum when they take on a pair of the contrary qualities hot-cold and moist-dry. As he writes in Book II of *On Generation and Corruption*:

> The elements are four, and any four terms can be combined in six couples. Contraries, however, refuse to be coupled, for it is impossible for the same thing to be hot and cold, or moist and dry. Hence it is evident that the couplings of the elements will be four: hot with dry and moist with hot, and again cold with dry and cold with moist. And these four couples have attached themselves to the *apparently* simple bodies (Fire, Air, Water and Earth) in a manner consonant with theory. For Fire is hot and dry, where Air is hot and moist (Air being a sort of vapour); and Water is cold and moist, and Earth is cold and dry. Thus the differences are reasonably distributed among the primary bodies, and the number of the latter is consonant with the theory.

Aristotle then goes on to explain how the elements could be transformed one to another if one of the qualities changed into its contrary, hot to cold, moist to dry, or vice versa in either case:

> Air, for example, will result from Fire if a single quality changes; for Fire, as we saw, is hot and dry while Air is hot and moist, so that there will be Air if the dry be overcome by the moist. Again, Water will result from Air if the hot be overcome by the cold; for Air, as we saw, is hot and moist while Water is cold and moist, so that, if the hot changes, there will be Water. So too, in the same manner, Earth will result from Water and Fire from Earth, since both tally with both. For Water is moist and cold while Earth is cold and dry – so that, if the moist be overcome, there will be Earth; and again, since Fire is dry and hot while Earth is cold and dry, Fire will result from Earth if the cold pass away.

Aristotle's cosmology has the earth as the immovable centre of a finite cosmos divided into two regions, the terrestrial and celestial, which he describes in his work *On the Universe*.

> The Universe then is a system made up of heaven and earth and the natural things that are contained in them .... Of this Universe the centre, which is immovable and fixed, is occupied by the life-bearing earth, the home and mother of diverse creatures. The upper portion of the Universe, a whole with a fixed upper limit everywhere, the home of the gods, is called Heaven.

> Heaven is full of divine bodies, which we usually call stars, and moves with
> an eternal motion, and in one circular orbit revolves in stately measure with
> all the heavenly bodies unceasingly for ever.

Earth, water, air and fire were the basic elements in the terrestrial region,
which itself was divided into two subregions, with the earth at the centre
surrounded by the water of Ocean, and beyond that the air of the atmo-
sphere and fire, the latter consisting of ordinary flames as well as fiery
phenomena such as lightning and meteors. According to Aristotle: 'The
simple bodies, since they are four, fall into two regions, each to each; for
Fire and Air are forms of the body moving towards the [outer] limit, while
Earth and Water are forms of the body which moves toward the centre.'

Aristotle's terrestrial region has the sphere of the earth at the centre,
surrounded by concentric spherical shells of water, air and fire. The four
elements are thus arranged hierarchically, each in its natural place, in
order of decreasing density. The natural motion of each of the four terrestrial elements is toward its natural place, so that if a clod of soil is lifted
from the earth it will naturally fall down once released, while a bubble of
air in water will rise to the surface, and fire on the ground always rises.
The natural motion of bodies in the terrestrial region is temporary, since it
ceases when they reach their natural place.

One of Aristotle's laws of dynamics says that the velocity of a falling body
is directly proportional to its weight, so that a heavy body falls faster than a
light one. As he writes in Book I of *On the Heavens*: 'A given weight moves
a given distance in a given time; a weight which is as great or more moves
the same distance in a less time, the times being in inverse proportion to
the weights. For instance, if one weight is twice another, it will take half as
long over a given movement.

A second law of Aristotelian dynamics, concerning motion through a
resistive medium, can be expressed in modern terms as saying that the
velocity of the object is directly proportional to the motive force and
inversely proportional to the resistance of the medium, provided that the
force is great enough to cause movement. Aristotle pointed out that in a
vacuum the resistance would be zero and so the velocity would be infinite;
this would be impossible in a finite universe, he argued, and thus a void is
impossible.

A third law tries to explain why a projectile continues to move when it is
no longer in contact with its motive force. As Aristotle writes in Book VIII
of the *Physics*: 'If everything that is in motion with the exception of things

that move themselves is moved by something, how is it that some things, e.g., things thrown, continue to be in motion when their mover is no longer in contact with them?' Aristotle's ingenious explanation involves a hypothetical phenomenon called *antiperistasis*, in which the air displaced by the front of the projectile moves into the temporary partial vacuum in its wake and gives it a forward impetus.

These three erroneous theories, that the velocity of a falling body is proportional to its weight, that a void is impossible, and the *antiperistasis* theory of notion, endured up to the late seventeenth century, when they were replaced by the new dynamics of Isaac Newton.

The heavens were a world apart in Aristotelian cosmology, the celestial spheres moved by the so-called Prime Mover, 'a mover that is itself unmoved and eternal'. Since the celestial bodies move eternally in circular paths this must be their natural motion, according to Aristotle, and thus they cannot be made from any of the terrestrial elements, the natural motion of which is linear up or down. Aristotle thus adopted the *aither* of Anaxagoras as the basic element of the heavens, as he writes in Book I of *On the Universe*, going on to describe the motion of the celestial bodies:

Of the stars [including the sun, moon and planets] which are contained in it, some revolve fixedly with the whole heaven, always occupying the same positions. A belt is formed through their midst by the so-called Circle of the Zodiac, which passes crosswise through the tropics, being divided up into twelve regions of the Signs of the Zodiac. Others, which are the planets [including the sun and moon], do not naturally move with the same velocity as those stars of which I have already spoken, nor with the same velocity as one another, but each in a different course, so that one now will be nearer the earth, another higher in the heavens ... the planets fall into seven divisions in seven successive circles, so situated that the highest is always greater than the lower, and the seven circles are successively encompassed by one another and are all surrounded by the sphere of the fixed stars.

Aristotle then goes to describe the terrestrial region below the sphere of the moon, beginning with the upper subregion of fire and air:

After the ethereal and divine nature, which we declare to be orderly and to be, moreover, free from disturbance, change and external influence, there follows immediately an element which is subject throughout to external influence and disturbance and is, in a word, corruptible and perishable. In the first portion of this occurs the substance which is made up of small particles and is fiery, being kindled by the ethereal element owing to its superior size and the rapidity of its movement.

He then describes the lower portion of the terrestrial region, comprising the water of the sea and then the earth itself and its plant and animal life:

> Next to the aerial element the earth and the sea have their fixed position, teeming with plant and animal life and fountains and rivers, either being spent in the earth or discharging their water into the sea. The earth is diversified by countless kinds of verdure and lofty mountains and densely wooded copses and cities, which that intelligent animal man has founded, and islands set in the sea and continents .... This forms the whole of what we call the lower portion of the Universe.

He completes his cosmological description with an overarching view of what came to be known as the Aristotelian world-picture, with its five elements layered hierarchically between the perfect heavens above, dwelling-place of the eternal gods, and the corrupt earth and its mortal inhabitants below:

> Thus the five elements situated in spheres in five regions, the less being in each case surrounded by the greater – namely earth, surrounded by water, water by air, air by fire, and fire by *aither* – make up the whole Universe. All the upper portion represents the dwelling of the gods, the lower the abode of mortal creatures. Of the latter, part is moist, to which we are accustomed to give the names of rivers, springs and seas; while part is dry, which we call land and continents and islands.

Aristotle gives several reasons for holding that the earth is a sphere, rather than flat or a cylinder, as the Milesian physicists had thought. One reason was symmetry, and another was that with earthly bodies falling on it from every direction the ultimate shape could only be a sphere. Still another was that during lunar eclipses the shadow of the earth on the moon is a circular arc. And a fourth reason was that an observer travelling north or south on the earth will see different stars appear or disappear over the horizon. He notes that the latter observation was used by 'those mathematicians who try to calculate the size of the earth's circumference arrive at the figure of 400,000 *stades*.'

Aristotle's value for the circumference of the earth is equivalent to the diameter being about 12,500 miles, compared to the true value of approximately 7,900 miles. He does not identify the mathematicians who did the calculations, but one of them would have been Eudoxus, whose astronomical observations would have enabled him to arrive at such a value.

As noted earlier, Aristotle used Eudoxus' theory of the homocentric spheres to create a physical model of his world picture. He added a number of 'counteracting spheres' to the original theory of Eudoxus and the adaptation by Callippus, so as to unify the motion of all the celestial bodies, bringing the total number of spheres to 55.

Aristotle's hierarchical model of a finite earth-centred universe of nested spheres dominated cosmology for nearly 2,000 years, and it was only abandoned when the scientific revolution in the seventeenth century culminated in the new physics of Newton.

Aristotle's researches in the natural science were in biology and zoology, which comprise more than a fifth of his surviving work. Detailed examination of living creatures gave him the information he was seeking concerning form and final cause to a far greater extent than did the study of inanimate objects. His most important works in this area are his treatises on the *History of Animals, Parts of Animals* and *Generation of Animals*, which are based partly on second-hand information and partly on his own research. He mentions about 500 different kinds of living creatures, of which he personally dissected some 50 types. His method of classification, including the use of terms like genus and species, was used in European science up until the early nineteenth century. As he writes in his treatise on the *Parts of Animals*:

> We have, then, first to describe the common functions, and those which belong to a genus or species. By 'common' I mean those which belong to all animals: by 'to a genus', those of animals whose difference from one another we see to be matters of degree – Bird is a genus. Man is a species, and so is everything not differentiated into subordinate groups. In the first case the common attributes may be called analogous, in the second generic, in the third specific.

Aristotle is at his best when describing marine life, a study that he began in collaboration with Theophrastus when they were on Lesbos. One of the most remarkable of his discoveries concerns what he calls the 'smooth dogfish', a species now known as *Mustelus laevis*, where his description was generally treated with scepticism until it was vindicated in 1843 by Johannes Müller.

Aristotle's classificatory studies led him to recognize a hierarchical continuity in nature from the simplest inanimate objects to the most complex living things, as he notes in Book VIII of the *History of Animals*:

> Nature proceeds little by little from things lifeless to animal life in such a way that it is impossible to determine the exact line of demarcation, nor on which side thereof an intermediate form should be. Thus next after lifeless things comes the plant, and of plants one will differ from another as to its amount of apparent vitality; and, in a word, the whole genus of plants, whilst it is devoid of life as compared with an animal, is endowed with life as compared with other corporeal entities. Indeed, as we just remarked, there is observed in plants a continuous scale of ascent towards the animal. So in the sea there are certain objects concerning which one would be at a loss to determine whether they be animal or vegetable.

Aristotle's writings also included treatises on ethics and politics, which he considered to be continuous parts of what he called 'the philosophy of human nature'. In the closing chapters of the *Nicomachean Ethics* he tries to outline the true nature of happiness, the final goal of human life, which he identifies as philosophic thought, the disinterested pursuit of knowledge for its own sake, an activity that endows us with a spark of divinity:

> If happiness is activity in accordance with excellence, it is reasonable that it should be in accordance with the highest excellence; and this will be that of the best thing in us. Whether it be intellect or something else that is this element which is thought to be our natural ruler and guide and to take thought of things noble and divine, whether it be itself also divine or only the most divine element in us, the activity of this with its proper excellence will be complete happiness.

Aristotle remained at the Lyceum until 322 BC, a year after the death of Alexander the Great, when the changed political situation in Athens made it impossible for him to continue living there. The Athenian assembly decided to revolt against the rule of the Macedonian regent Antipater. Soon afterwards a charge of impiety was made against Aristotle by his enemies, the pretext being his old connection with the pro-Macedonian Hermias. Aristotle thus decided to leave Athens and move to Chalcis, on the channel separating the island of Euboea from the mainland of western Greece, where his mother had left some property A fragment describes his departure from Athens, quoting a remark that he is supposed to made to have made concerning his reason for leaving, referring to the fate of Socrates: 'When the Athenians rose against him, he withdrew to Chalcis, hinting at the reasons: "I will not allow the Athenians to wrong philosophy twice."'

Aristotle died later that year at Chalcis, where his last days must have been bleak, exiled from his beloved school in the grove of Apollo.

CHAPTER 6

ARISTOTLE'S SUCCESSORS

After the death of Aristotle his colleague Theophrastus (*ca.* 371–*ca.* 287 BC) became the dominant figure in Athenian science, directing the Lyceum until his own death around 287 BC, when all of Athens attended his funeral in the garden of his school. Theophrastus may be called the second founder of the Lyceum, which he headed for 35 years, during which he taught some 2,000 students. According to Diogenes Laertius, he added to the school a garden 'that had been obtained for him by Demetrios of Phaleron, who was his friend', and in his last will and testament he bequeathed this and other property jointly to his colleagues at the Lyceum and his relatives:

> The garden and walk and the houses adjoining the garden, I give and bequeath to such of our enrolled friends as wish to study literature and philosophy there in common, since it is not possible for men to be always in residence, on condition that no one alienates the property or devotes it to his private use, but so that they hold it like a temple in joint possession, as is right and proper, on terms of familiarity and friendship.

Theophrastus was almost as prolific and encyclopedic as Aristotle, continuing his master's tradition. Diogenes Laertius credits him with 227 treatises, including works in philosophy, religion, politics, ethics, education, rhetoric, mathematics, astronomy, logic, meteorology and natural history, as well as one on human types, entitled *Characters*. His principal surviving works are two on plants, one on stones, and the *Characters*. The first two works, which have earned him the title of Father of Botany, are the *Enquiry into Plants* and the *Causes of Plants*, in which he deals with some 550 species and varieties of plants, extending from the Mediterranean world as far east as India. His treatise *On Stones* represents the beginning of petrology. One of his shorter works, the *Metaphysics*, sometimes appears in manuscripts together with the longer works by Aristotle on the same subject, giving the erroneous impression that it was a mere appendix to the Aristotelian treatises.

Theophrastus generally follows Aristotle and is deeply indebted to him. nevertheless he can be highly critical of some of his master's theories. Some of these criticisms appear in Theophrastus' *Metaphysics*, where, among other things, he questions the Aristotelian notion that circular motion is natural for the celestial bodies and needs no further explanation. He also expresses reservations about teleology and the Aristotelian doctrine of final cause: 'We must,' he says, 'set certain limits to the final cause and to the tendency towards what is best, and not assume that it exists in absolutely every case. ... For even if this is the desire of nature, yet there is much that does not obey nor receive the good.'

He also wrote a short work *On Fire*, in which he points out the differences between fire and the other three elements, earth, water and air. He says that the most important difference is that earth, water and air are self-subsistent, whereas fire requires a substratum in the form of fuel: 'Everything that burns is always as it were in a process of coming to be and fire is a kind of movement; and it perishes as it comes to be, and as soon as what is combustible is lacking it too perishes ... it seems absurd to call this a primary element and as it were a principle, if it cannot exist without matter.'

The system used by Theophrastus in classifying plants was the same as that which Aristotle had used in many other subjects, including zoology. He describes his system at the beginning of Book I of the *Enquiry into Plants*, where he points out the difficulties involved in making distinctions:

> In considering the distinctive characters of plants and their nature generally one must take into account their parts, their qualities, the ways in which their life originates, and the course which it follows in each case: (conduct and activities we do not find in them as we do in animals). Now the differences in the way in which their life originates, in their qualities and in their life-history are relatively easy to observe and are simpler, while those shewn in their 'parts' present more complexity. Indeed it has not been satisfactorily determined what ought not to be called 'parts,' and some difficulty is involved in making the distinction.

The section on medicinal herbs in Book IX gives some idea of the level of pharmacology and medicine at the time, particularly the interesting description of the famous mandrake root: 'As is said, of some plants the root, fruit and juice are all serviceable, ... such as mandrake; for the leaf of this, they say, used with meal, is useful for wounds, and the root for erysipelas, when scraped and steeped in vinegar, and also for gout, for sleeplessness, and for love-potions. It is administered in wine or vinegar; they cut little balls of it, as or radishes, and making a string of them hang them up in the smoke over must [musk].

The treatise on *Causes of Plants* is divided into six books: 1. Generation and propagation of plants, fructification and maturity of fruits. 2. Things which most help the increase of plants; horticulture and sylviculture. 3. Plantation of shrubs and preparation of the soil; viticulture. 4. Goodness of seeds and their degeneration; culture of legumes. 5. Diseases and other causes of failure. 6. Savours and odours of plants. The section on Grafting and Budding in Book I gives a good idea of the level and character of the treatise:

> It remains to speak of some other of the methods of propagation, such as the matter of grafting and budding. The account is simple and has practically been told before; the ingrafted part uses the other as an ordinary plant uses the ground. 'Budding' also is really a kind of planting; it is not simply a mere mechanical juxtaposition, but it is clear that in this process both the germinating and the supporting force is the vital moisture. The 'eye' having this moisture is suited to the other part, and the part having the nourishment grows the bud as though it were its own.

Theophrastus' work *On Stones*, known in its Latin translation as *De lapidibus*, carries out an investigation suggested by Aristotle in his *Meteorology*, where he distinguishes between metals and 'the kinds of stones that cannot be melted.' Theophrastus begins his treatise by distinguishing between the two types: 'Of the things formed in the ground, some have as their basis water, others earth. Those whose basis is water are the metals, silver, gold and the like; those whose basis is earth are stone, including the rarer species, and also those types of earth itself which are peculiar by reason of their colour, smoothness, density, or some other quality.'

He then on to give a brief description of the ways in which the various kinds of stones are formed so as to give them their distinctive properties:

> All these [stones] must be considered, to put it simply, to be formed from some pure and homogeneous substance. The substance may come into existence by means of a conflux or a percolation, or, as was observed above, may be separated out in some other manner. The stone may be formed in the various cases by any of these means. From these [differences stones get]

their smoothness, density, brightness, transparency and other such properties; and the more uniform and pure each stone is, the more does it have these properties. For, in general, these qualities depend on the perfection of the concretion or coagulation.

Significant fragments survive of two minor works of Theophrastus, *Concerning Odours* and *Concerning Weather Signs*. The first work is a remarkably detailed study of the natural odours of animals and the effect of odours on animals, as well as artificial odours, including the making of perfumes and their use in wine. There is also a section in which Theophrastus writes on the medicinal uses of certain perfumes mixed with spices. 'The effects of plasters and of what some call "poultices" prove what virtues they display, since they disperse tumours and abcesses and produce a distinct effect on various other parts of the body, on its surface, but also on its interior parts: for instance, if one lays a plaster on his abdomen and breast, the patient forthwith produces fragrant odours along with his eructations.'

The second treatise is an equally detailed examination of weather signs, predicting rain and foul or fair spells from clouds, the colour of the sky, the appearance of the sun, and moon, shooting stars, the appearance of the constellations, the timing and intensity of thunder and lightning, the direction and force of the winds, and the erratic behaviour of animals and birds, such as the raven, which if carefully observed would seem to be as good as a barometer for predicting rain, as Theophrastus writes: 'It is a sign if the raven, who is accustomed to make different sounds, repeats one of these twice quickly and makes a whirring sound and shakes his wings. So too if, during a rainy season, he utters many different sounds, or if he searches for lice perched on an olive-tree, and if, whether in fair or wet weather, he imitates, as it were, with his voice falling drops, it is a sign of rain.'

Theophrastus' treatise on *Characters* is a series of satirical sketches of Athenian types who deviated from the accepted norms of behaviour. There are 30 types in all, many of whom would have been recognizable as prominent figures in Athens at the time. The cast of characters is, in the order of their appearance, each known by his defining fault: Dissembling, Flattery, Garrulity, Boorishness, Self-Seeking Affability, Wilful Disreputableness, Loquacity, Newsmaking, Unconscionableness, Penuriousness, Buffoonery, Tactlessness, Officiousness, Stupidity, Surliness, Superstitiousness, Querulousness, Distrustfulness, Nastiness, Ill-Breeding, Petty Pride, Parsimony, Pretentiousness, Arrogance, Cowardice, Oligarchy, Opsimathy or Late-Learning, Backbiting, Friendship with Rascals, Meanness. Despite their faults some of these characters are not without their spurious charm, particularly the Flatterer, as Theophrastus describes him:

> Flattery might be understood to be a sort of converse that is dishonourable, but at the same time profitable to him that flatters; and the Flatterer will say as he walks beside you 'Are you aware how people are looking at you?

> No man in Athens gets such attention'; or this, 'You were the man of the hour yesterday in the Porch; why, although there was more than thirty present, when the talk turned to who was the finest man there, the name that came to every lip both first and last was yours.' And while he says such things as these, he picks a speck from your coat; or if so be a morsel of chaff be blown into your beard, plucks it out and then says with a smile 'D'ye see? Because you and I be not met a whole day, your beard's full of grey hairs – though I own your hair is singularly dark of your age.'

The author himself seems to have been very charming, as evidenced by the account of Athenaeus of Naucratis, from a description written by Hermippus half a century after the death of Theophrastus: 'At a regular hour Theophrastus used to appear in the Garden spruce and gay, and taking his seat proceed to the discourse, indulging as he went along in every pose and gesture imaginable; he once mimicked an epicure by putting out his tongue and licking his lips.'

Athens went through profound changes during the years that Theophrastus headed the Lyceum. At the beginning of the Hellenistic period, in 322 BC, the city came under the harsh rule of the Macedonia regent Antipater, one of the Diadochoi, or Successors, the generals who divided up the empire of Alexander after his death, with Seleucus I Nicator taking Syria and Ptolemy I Soter claiming Egypt, both of them establishing dynasties. Then in 307 BC Athens was captured by Dimitrios I of Macedonia, son of Antigonus I, another of the Diadochoi, who appointed as his governor Dimitrios of Phaleron, a former student of Theophrastus at the Lyceum. This led to a series of civil wars that lasted for nearly half a century, with the government of Athens changing hands seven times.

Theophratus was succeeded as head of the Lyceum by his former student Strato (d. *ca.* 268 BC). Strato was born in Lampsacus on the Asian shore of the Hellespont, where Anaxagoras had founded a school in his latter years, and where the philosopher Epicurus taught before moving to Athens in 306 BC. Strato's interest in philosophy and science may have begun at this school, which he left to study under Theophrastus at the Lyceum in Athens, where he arrived just about the time that Aristotle went into retirement. Around 300 BC, Strato was invited to Alexandria by Ptolemy I Soter to serve as tutor to his son, the future Ptolemy II Philadelphus, and he remained there until he returned to Athens around 287 BC to succeed Theophrastus as director of the Lyceum.

An incomplete list of Strato's works preserved by Diogenes Laertius credits him with more than 40 works, including treatises on logic, ethics, cosmology and meteorology, psychology, physiology and zoology, as well as a book on inventions, all of which are lost. His most important works were considered to be those on physics, which is why later writers called him Strato the Physicist. Diogenes Laertius describes Strato as 'a distinguished man who is generally known as "the physicist", because more than anyone else he devoted himself to the study of nature.'

Since none of Strato's writings survive, knowledge of his work come from later writers, either in fragments where he is quoted or referred to by name, or in passages where he is not named but which can definitely be attributed to him. The most important references of the first type are in the Aristotelian commentaries of Simplicius, while the most significant of the second are in the *Pneumatica* of Hero of Alexandria and works wrongly attributed to Aristotle.

The view of Strato's thought that emerges from a study of these fragments is that he continued in the tradition of Aristotle and Theophrastus, while eliminating from the Aristotelian world picture of anything not subject to the natural laws known to apply in the terrestrial region. Nevertheless, Strato continued to believe that there the terrestrial and celestial regions were subject to different laws, and that there was an Unmoved Mover above and beyond the physical world.

Strato tried to formulate a new cosmology in which the cosmos was explained by natural forces only, and not by transcendental causes. This approach is evident in three fragments attributed to Strato, the first two of them from Cicero and the third from Plutarch: 'Everything that exists is the result of natural weights and movements ... all divine power is contained in nature, which contains in itself the causes of coming-into being, growth and decay, but has no consciousness or shape ... natural processes are governed by what happens spontaneously.' Cicero remarked on the second of these fragments that this 'frees God from his great work and me from fear'.

Strato agreed with Aristotle in believing that the cosmos is unique and finite, but differed with him in saying that a void can exist. These beliefs are evident in a fragment of Strato, in which he says that 'void can exist within the universe, but not outside it.' He seems to have realized that at least a partial vacuum exists through his experiments on pneumatics, or air-pressure, which are referred to by Hero of Alexandria in his *Pneumatica*.

Strato differed from Aristotle in his belief that matter is not continuous, but rather consists of small particles with a void in the interstices where they do not fit together, like grains of sand on a beach.

Strato also rejected Aristotle's theory of the natural motion of the four terrestrial elements, in which heavier bodies naturally move downward and lighter ones go up. Instead he said that the natural motion of all elements is downward, and that a heavier body will displace a lighter one and force it upwards, thus simplifying the theory.

One of Strato's treatises on physics is a lost work entitled *On Motion*, in which, according to Simplicius, he presents demonstrations to show that falling bodies accelerate:

> For in his treatise *On Motion*, after asserting that a body so moving completes the last stage of its trajectory in the shortest time, he adds: 'In the case of bodies moving through the air under the influence of their weight this is clearly what happens. For if one observes water pouring down from a roof and falling from a considerable height, the flow at its top is seen to be continuous, but the water at the bottom falls to the ground in discontinuous parts. This would never happen unless the water traversed each successive space more swiftly.' ... Strato also adduces another argument, as follows: 'If one drops a stone or any other weight from a height of about an inch, the impact made on the ground will not be perceptible, but if one drops the object from a height of one hundred feet or more the impact on the ground will be a powerful one. Now there is no other cause for this powerful impact.... It is merely a case of acceleration.'

Strato or one of his colleagues at the Lyceum may have written the pseudo-Aristotelian treatise entitled *Mechanics*. This contains the earliest extant statement of the law of the lever: that is, if two objects are suspended on either side of a lever, they will balance one another if their distances from the fulcrum are inversely proportional to their weights. But there is no formal mathematical demonstration of the law, such as would later be given by Euclid and Archimedes. The author of the *Mechanics* expresses the law by saying that if a system with two weights on either side of a lever in equilibrium is set in motion about an axis through the fulcrum, the velocities of the objects, in other words, the arcs swept out in equal times, will be in inverse proportion to their weights. The *Mechanics* also applies the law of the lever to three other mechanical devices: the wedge, the pulley and the steelyard, a balance with unequal arm lengths.

Another important concept expressed in the *Mechanics* is the so-called 'parallelogram of velocities.' That is, if a body is moving with constant speed in two dimensions, the components in the two dimensions form the sides of a rectangle whose diagonal represents the resultant velocity. The author of the *Mechanics* also knew, without giving a detailed analysis, that if the two components were not both constant, then the body would not move in a straight line.

Another pseudo-Aristotelian work, a treatise on sound entitled *On Things Heard*, was probably also written by Strato or one of his associates. Aristotle, in his treatise *On The Soul*, states that sound is produced by the collision of bodies with one another and with the surrounding air, which transmits the sound to the ear. The treatise *On Things Heard* gives a clear statement of how sounds are transmitted:

> All sounds, whether articulate or inarticulate, are produced by the meeting of bodies or of the air with bodies ... whether by contraction or expansion or compression, or when it clashes together by an impact from the breath or from the strings of musical instruments. For, when the nearest portion of it is struck by the breath which comes into contact with it, the air is at once driven forcibly on, thrusting forward in like manner the adjoining air, so that the sound travels unaltered in quality as far as the disturbance of the air manages to reach. For though the disturbance originates at a particular point, yet its force is disbursed over an extending area, like breezes which blow from rivers or from the land.

Two other schools of philosophy emerged in Athens late in the fourth century BC These were not formal institutions like the Academy and the Lyceum, but more loosely organized groups that met to discuss philosophy. One of the schools, known as the Garden, was founded by Epicurus of Samos (341–270 BC), while the other, the Porch, was begun by Zeno of Citium (*ca.* 335–270 BC). The name of the first school stemmed from the fact that Epicurus lectured in the garden of his house, while the second was named for the Stoa Poikile, the Painted Porch, in the agora, the meeting place of Zeno and his disciples, who came to be called the Stoics.

Both Epicurus and Zeno created comprehensive philosophical systems that were divided into three parts – ethics, physics and logic – the last two subordinate to the first, since both schools agreed that the principal aim of philosophy was to attain true happiness. As Epicurus wrote in his *Letter to Pythocles*: 'bear in mind that there is no other end to the knowledge of things in the sky ... than peace of mind and firm conviction.'

The physics of Epicurus was based on the atomic theory of Leucippus and Democritus, from which he differed on certain important points. Leucippus and Democritus said that the only basic properties of atoms are their shape, configuration and shape, to which Epicurus added weight, which the early atomists held to be a secondary property that arose when the atoms had come together through their random motion and collisions to form a world. The cosmology of Epicurus pictured the atoms as originally being carried straight downward through the void by their weight, before they suddenly swerve and begin colliding with one another. The great Roman poet Lucretius (*ca.* 94–50 BC) based his superb *De Rerum Natura* (*On the Nature of Things*) on the philosophical system of Epicurus, and in Book II he introduces the all-important 'swerve':

> One further point in this matter I desire you to understand: that while the first bodies [atoms] are being carried downwards through by their own weight in a straight line through the void, at times quite uncertain and uncertain places, they swerve a little from their course, just as much as you might call a change of motion. For if they were not apt to incline, all would fall downwards like raindrops through the profound void, no collision would take place and no blow would be caused amongst the first-beginnings: thus nature would never have produced anything.

Lucretius then goes on to explain how this 'swerve' saves the atomic theory from the absolute determinism that it would otherwise have had, so that it can serve as the basis for his moral philosophy in which humans have free will:

> Again, if all motion is one long chain, and new motion always arises out of the old in order invariable, and if the first-beginnings do not make by swerving a beginning of motion such as to break the decrees of fate, that cause may not follow cause to infinity, whence comes the free will in living creatures all over the earth, whence I say is this free will wrested from the fates by which we proceed whither pleasure takes each, swerving also our motions not at fixed times and fixed places, but just where our mind has taken us?

Zeno of Citium and his followers in the Stoic school rejected the atom and the void, for they looked at nature as a continuum in all of its aspects – space, time and matter – as in the propagation and sequence of physical phenomena. The fundamental Stoic belief was that the cosmos is filled by an all-pervading substance, the *pneuma* of Anaximenes, which, as we have noted can mean 'breath' or 'spirit'.

This idea was further developed by Zeno's follower Chrysippus of Soli (*ca.* 280–207 BC), who held that *pneuma* bound the universe together as one coordinated whole. According to Alexander of Aphrodisias: 'Chrysippus ... supposes the whole of nature is united by the *pneuma* which permeates it and by which the world is kept together and is made coherent and interconnected.' Galen of Pergamum, writing in the second century AD, remarks on the distinction between the *pneuma* and the fundamental substance that it binds together: 'Those who have most expounded the concept of the binding force, like the Stoics, distinguish the binding force from what is bound together by it. The substance of the *pneuma* is the binding agent, while the material substance is what is bound by it.'

The contrast between the atomist and Stoic views can be seen in their conceptions of how phenomena in nature propagate through space. According to the atomists, all effects propagate through the motion of atoms, while the Stoics believed that they are transmitted through the medium of the *pneuma*. The Stoics were the first to use the analogy of water waves to explain the propagation of sound, as Aëtius notes in his account of their wave theory: 'The Stoics say that air is not composed of particles, but that it is a continuum which contains no empty spaces. If it is struck by an impulse it rises in circular waves proceeding in straight sequence to infinity, until all the surrounding air is stirred, just as a pool is stirred by a stone which strikes it. But whereas in the latter case the motion is circular, the air moves spherically.'

The Stoics believed that light as well as sound was propagated through the *pneuma*. This is stated clearly by the Stoic astronomer Cleomedes, writing in the first century AD, where he says that 'Without one binding tension and without the all-permeating pneuma we would not be able to see and hear. For the sense perceptions would be impeded by the intervening empty spaces.' The Stoics believed sight is due to light transmitted through the *pneuma* from the observer's eye to the object observed, a view that was generally held up until the development of modern optics, which has light passing from the object to the eye. Diogenes Laertius credits Chrysippus with having formulated the Stoic theory: 'According to Chrysippus ... sight is due to the light between the observer and the object observed being stretched conically. The cone forms in the eye, with its apex in the eye of the observer and its base in the object observed. In this way the signal is transmitted to the observer by means of the stressed air, just as (by feeling) with a stick.'

The Stoic school, like the Epicurean, was confronted with the problem of reconciling strict causality with free will, since their ethical system was based upon man's responsibility for his actions. Whereas Epicurus took one way out of this dilemma, by introducing the swerve, Chrysippus took another, described by Cicero:

> Chrysippus distinguishes between various kinds of cause in order to evade the necessity of denying free will while preserving fate. He says: 'There are primary and secondary causes. If we say that everything is determined by fate in accordance with preliminary causes, we do not mean the primary determining causes, but the secondary (subsidiary) ones. Even though we have no control of the latter we may still control our instincts.'

The Stoic preoccupation with fate led them to study divination in an attempt to put it on a rational basis. Their method was inductive reasoning, showing how it is possible to foretell a future event through a systematic student of the signs that preceded it, as Cicero notes in his treatise on divination, commentating on the researches of the Stoics:

> The results of these artificial means of divination, by means of entrails, lightning, portents and astrology, have been the subject of observations for a long period of time. But in every field of enquiry great length of time employed in continued observation begets an extraordinary fund of knowledge, which may be acquired without the intervention or inspiration of the gods, since repeated observation makes it clear what effect follows any given cause, and what sign precedes any given event.

Such were some of the conflicting ideas cast up by the two schools of thought that emerged in the generation after Aristotle – the Epicurean atoms in a void versus the continuum of the Stoics – two views that have competed with one another from antiquity to the present, for they seem to represent antithetical ways of looking at nature. Thus even as Athens was giving way to Alexandria as the intellectual centre of the Greek world it continued to be the School of Hellas, with the creation of two new philosophical systems which would take their place beside those of Plato and Aristotle in their influence on Western thought.

CHAPTER 7

THE GEOMETRIZATION OF NATURE

At the beginning of the Hellenistic period the focal point of the Greek world shifted from Athens to Alexandria, the new city that had been founded by Alexander in 331 BC on the Canopic branch of the Nile.

Alexandria emerged as a great cultural centre under Ptolemy I Soter (r. 305–283 BC), who had served with distinction under Alexander and wrote a history of his campaigns. The cultural rise of Alexandria centred on two renowned institutions, the Museum and the Library, both founded by Ptolemy I and further developed by his son and successor Ptolemy II Philadelphus (r. 283–245 BC). The Alexandrian Museum and its associated library were designed as a school of higher studies, patterned on the famous schools of philosophy in Athens, most notably the Academy and the Lyceum.

Strabo, writing in the first quarter of the first century AD, notes that the museum was part of the royal palace complex of the Ptolemies: 'The Museum is also part of the royal palaces: it has a public walk, an exedra with seats, and a large house, in which is the common mess-hall of the men of learning who share the Museum. This group of men not only hold property in common, but also have a priest in charge of the Museum, who formerly was appointed by the kings, but is now appointed by Caesar.'

The Museum was a centre of research in the tradition of the Lyceum of Aristotle and Theophrastus, with an emphasis on science. The scientific character of the museum was probably due to Strato of Lampsacus, who moved to Alexandria around 300 BC, to serve as tutor to the future Ptolemy II Philadelphus, remaining there until he returned to Athens to succeed Theophrastus as director of the Lyceum. The prince developed a deep interest in geography and zoology through his studies with Strato, and this was manifested in the development of the museum when he succeeded his father as king in 283 BC.

The organization of the Library of Alexandria was probably due to Dimitrios of Phaleron, the former governor of Athens, who had been forced to flee from Athens in 307 BC, after which he was given refuge in Alexandria by Ptolemy I. Dimitrios, who had been a student of Theophrastus at the Lyceum, is believed to have been the first chief librarian at the library, a post he held until 284 BC. According to Aristeas Judaeus, a Jewish scholar in the reign of Ptolemy II, Dimitrios 'had at his disposal a large budget in order to collect, if possible, all the books in the world, and by purchases and transcriptions he, to the best of his ability, carried the king's objective into execution.'

This policy continued through the reigns of Ptolemy II and Ptolemy III Euergites (r. 247–221 BC). Athenaeus of Naucratis reports that Ptolemy II bought the books of Aristotle and Theophrastus and transferred them to 'the beautiful city of Alexandria'. By the time of Ptolemy III the library was reputed to have a collection of more than half-a-million parchment rolls, including all the works of Greek writers from Homer onwards.

The third Ptolemy built a new branch of the library within the Serapeum, the temple of Serapis. Ephanius of Salamis, a Christian scholar of the fourth century AD, refers to this addition in writing of the 'first library and another built in the Serapeum, smaller than the first, which was called the daughter of the first'.

Dimitrios was succeeded as chief librarian by Zenodotus of Ephesus, who held the post until 245 BC. His principal assistant was the poet Callimachus of Cyrene (*ca.* 305–*ca.* 240 BC), who classified the 120,000 works in the library according to author and subject, the first time that this had ever been done. His compilation, known as the *Pinakes* (*Tables*), was entitled *Tables of Persons Eminent in Every Branch of Learning Together with a List of Their Writings*, and filled more than 120 books, five times the length of Homer's *Iliad.*

Many of the great mathematicians and scientists of the Hellenistic era were associated with the Museum and Library of Alexandria. The great school of mathematics at Alexandria was founded by Euclid (*ca.* 330–*ca.* 270 BC), whose *Elements* laid the foundations of geometry, for which it served as the basic textbook from antiquity up until modern times. The mathematician Pappus of Alexandria, writing around AD 320, praises Euclid as 'most fair and well disposed toward all who were able in any measure to advance mathematics, careful in no way to give offense, and although an exact scholar not vaunting himself.' Sir Thomas L. Heath, the distinguished historian of ancient Greek mathematics, gives his highest praise to the *Elements*: 'This wonderful book, not withstanding its imperfections, remains the greatest elementary text-book in mathematics that the world is privileged to possess. Scarcely another book except the Bible can have circulated more widely the world over or been more edited and studied.'

Despite Euclid's fame only two facts are known about his life, and even these have been questioned. One is that he was somewhat younger than the pupils of Plato and older than Eratosthenes and Archimedes, and the other is that he taught in Alexandria in the time of Ptolemy I Soter (r. 305–283 BC). Much of this information comes from a summary history of geometry written in the fifth century AD by Proclus:

> Euclid, who was not much younger than Hermotimus and Philippus [two of Plato's pupils], composed *Elements*, putting in order many of the theorems of Eudoxus, perfecting many that had been worked on by Theaetetus, and furnishing with rigorous proofs propositions that had been demonstrated less rigorously. Euclid lived in the time of the first Ptolemy; for Archimedes, whose life overlapped the reign of this Ptolemy too, mentions Euclid.

Euclid's birthplace is unknown, but it is highly probable that he attended Plato's Academy, where he would have become acquainted with the work of Eudoxus and Theaetatus. He was probably invited to Alexandria soon after 300 BC, when Ptolemy I was setting up the library under the direction of Dimitrios of Phaleron, who would have known Euclid in Athens.

The *Elements* established the foundations not only of geometry but also of number theory and geometrical algebra. Aside from the mathematical content of the Elements, its most significant characteristic is its axiomatic method and the logical form in which the theorems are presented. This was to be the model for all subsequent Greek mathematical scientists, for it allowed them to formulate physical laws having the same rigour, self consistency and certainty as relationships in mathematics, or so they believed. Another way of describing this approach, which derives from Plato, is to say that it represents the geometrization of nature. During the Hellenistic period the axiomatic method of Euclid proved highly successful in those fields that lent themselves to geometrization, such as optics, mathematical geography, astronomy, music and mechanics.

The *Elements* is divided into 13 books, which now would be called chapters. The first six books are on elementary plane geometry, the next three on the theory of numbers, the tenth on incommensurables and the last three mostly on solid geometry. Each book (or, in the case of XI–XIII, group of books) is preceded by definitions of the subjects involved. The prefix of Book I also contains five postulates and five common notions. Modern mathematicians refer to these common notions as axioms and see no essential difference between them and the postulates.

The fifth postulate, known as the parallel postulate, has had a very interesting history. A modern abridged version of this postulate can be given as follows: Through a given point P not on a given straight line L, one and only one line can be drawn through P parallel to L. An equivalent statement is that the sum of the angles in a triangle is equal to two right angles. Even in Greek times attempts were made to prove the fifth postulate on the basis of the other four, and these efforts continued in the medieval Arab world, when the *Elements* was translated into Arabic and in Western Europe after the first Latin translations appeared.

Then in the nineteenth century mathematicians began to take a different view, saying that since the fifth postulate cannot be proved let us replace it with another, thus creating a different geometry than that of Euclid. The first to create a non-Euclidian geometry was Nicolai Ivanovitch Lobachevsky (1793–1856). Lobachevsky assumed that, for a point P not on a straight line L, more than one line can be drawn parallel to L. Lobachevsky's postulate was generalized by Janos Bolyai (1802–1860), who assumed that an infinite number of lines can be drawn through P parallel to G.F.B. Riemann (1826–1866), on the other hand, assumed that no lines can be drawn through P parallel to L. Felix Klein (1849–1925) then showed the relationship between Euclidian and non-Euclidian geometry. Euclid's geometry is valid on a plane, which has zero curvature, so that the sum of the angles in a triangle equals two right angles. Lobachevsky's applies to a surface of positive curvature, such as a sphere, on which the angles in a triangle add up to less than two right angles. Reimanian geometry holds on a surface of negative curvature, like a saddle, where the angles in a triangle amount to more than two right angles.

Each of the books in the *Elements* is divided into propositions, which are generally of two types. Those of the first type are concerned with simple problems of geometric construction by straight-edge and compasses, such as 'On a given finite straight line, to construct an equilateral triangle'. The second type are theorems, as, for example, 'in any right-angled triangle the square described on the hypotenuse is equal to the sum of the squares on the other two sides', the famous Pythagorean theorem.

Euclid often makes use of the method called *reduction ad absurdum*, in other words, reduction to the absurd, which Aristotle had introduced in his work on logic. That is, he assumes the contradiction of a theorem to be true and shows that it leads to an impossible result, thus proving the original theorem.

Following the postulates and common notions, Book I deals with the geometry of points, lines, triangle and parallelograms. The propositions fall into three distinct groups. The first, comprising propositions 1–26, is concerned mostly with the construction and properties of triangles. Proposition 5, for example, states that in isosceles triangles the angles at the base are equal to one another, and that, if the equal straight lines are produced, the angles under the base will be equal to one another. Ivor Bulmer-Thomas has pointed out that this proposition 'is interesting historically as having been known (except in France) as the *pons asinorum*; this is usually taken to mean that those who are not going to be good at geometry fail to get past it'.

The second group, propositions 27–32, establishes the theory of parallel lines, concluding with the proposition that the sum of the three angles of any triangle is equal to two right angles. The third, propositions 33–48, deals mostly with triangles, squares and parallelograms with reference to their areas. Proposition 44 is a construction problem: 'to a given straight [line] to apply to a given rectilineal angle a parallelogram equal to a given area and having one of its angles equal to a given angle.' This is Euclid's first use of the so-called 'application of areas,' a powerful method which is the geometrical equivalent of certain algebraic operations. In this proposition it is used to solve a first-degree equation; but Euclid developed it to solve second-degree equations as well.

Proposition 47 is the Pythagorean theorem, where the proof given by Euclid is different than the one given in most modern textbooks. Carl B. Boyer, in *A History of Mathematics*, notes that 'Euclid used instead the beautiful proof with a figure sometimes described as a windmill or as the peacock's tail or as the bride's chair'. As Bulmer-Thomas writes of this proof: 'It is impossible not to admire the ingenuity with which the result is obtained, and not surprising that when Thomas Hobbes first read it he exclaimed, "By God, this is impossible".'

Book II develops the application of areas method, using geometrical form of algebra to solve quadratic equations. For example, the quadratic equation $ax + x^2 = b^2$ is solved through the use of proposition 6: 'If a straight line be bisected and a straight line be added to it in a straight line, the rectangle contained by the whole (with the added straight line) and the added straight line together with the square on the half is equal to the square on the straight line made up of the half and the added straight line.' Propositions 12 and 13 are of interest because they are proofs of what later came to be known in trigonometry as the cosine law, where the former is for acute angles and the latter for obtuse.

Books III is on the geometry of circles, including their intersections and touching. It begins with definitions, the second of which describes a 'tangent' as 'a straight line which meets a circle but, if produced, does not cut it'. Book IV is entirely devoted to problems about circles, particularly concerning rectilineal figures inscribed in, or circumscribed about, a circle.

Book V develops the general theory of proportion, which the Pythagoreans had applied only to commensurable magnitudes, as well as applying it to magnitudes of all kinds, including straight lines, angles, areas and times. Mathematicians have always singled out Book V of the *Elements* for praise, as Bulmer-Thomas notes, quoting Isaac Barrow (1630–1677), who was Newton's mentor, and Arthur Cayley (1821–1895): 'There is no book in the *Elements* that has so won the admiration of mathematicians. Barrow observes: "There is nothing in the whole body of the *Elements* of a more subtile invention, nothing more solidly established and more accurately handled, than the doctrine of proportionals." In like spirit Cayley says, "There is hardly anything in mathematics more beautiful than this wondrous fifth book".'

Book VI uses the general theory of proportions established in Book V to prove theorems related to similar triangles, parallelograms and other polygons. Proposition 31 is noteworthy as being a generalization of the Pythagorean theorem: 'In right-angled triangles the figure on the side subtending the right angle is equal to the similar and similarly described figures on the sides containing the right angle.' Propositions 28 and 29 are a generalization of the method of application of areas.

Books VII, VIII and IX are devoted to the theory of numbers. Book VII begins with definitions, including those of a unit, a number, and the varieties of numbers, as Heath lists them: 'even, odd, even-times even, even-times odd, odd-times odd, prime, prime to one another, composite, plane, solid, cube, similar plane and similar solid numbers, and a perfect number.' Here a plane number is the product of two integers, a solid of three and a cube of four, while a perfect number is 'that which is equal to its own parts', as,for example, $6 = 1 + 2 + 3$. The first two propositions in Book VII constitute what is known as 'Euclid's algorithm' for finding the greatest common divisor of two numbers. The numerical theory of proportion is established in propositions 4–19, 22–32 are concerned with prime numbers, and 33–39 with least common multiples.

Book VIII opens with propositions on numbers 'in continued proportion,' as in geometric progression, and with geometric means. It then deals with some simple properties of squares and cubes.

Book IX begins with some simple propositions such as the following: 'the products of two similar plane numbers is a square (1), and, if the products of two numbers is a square number, the numbers are similar plane numbers (2)'. Proposition 14 states the fundamental theorem in the theory of numbers, which, in modern terminology, says that 'a number can be resolved into prime factors in only one way'.

Book X contains 115 propositions, more than other in the *Elements*, all concerned with a systematic classification of incommensurable line segments. According to Boyer, 'Book X of the *Elements* was, before the advent of early modern algebra, the most admired – and the most feared.' It opens with what Heath describes as 'the famous proposition (X.1) which is the basis of the method of exhaustion used in Book XII, namely that, if from any magnitude there is subtracted more than half (or its half), from the remainder again more than its half (or its half), and so on continually, there will at length remain a magnitude less than any assigned magnitude of the same time.' Euclid used this as a test of incommensurability, which he gives in proposition 2: 'If the lesser of two unequal magnitudes is continually subtracted from the greater, and the remainder never measures that which precedes it, the magnitudes will be incommensurable.'

Books XI–XIII, the last three in the *Elements*, are devoted to geometry in three dimensions. The definitions for these last three books are all in Book XI, where the last four definitions are of four of the five regular solids, the tetrahedron probably excluded because of an earlier definition of a pyramid as 'a solid figure, contained by planes, which is constructed from one plane to any point'. It is interesting to find, as Heath observes, that 'The sphere is defined, not as having all the points on its surface equidistant from the centre, but as the figure comprehended by the revolution of a semicircle about its diameter; this is clearly with an eye to the propositions in Book XIII where the regular solids are to be "comprehended" in a sphere respectively.'

Book XII has eighteen propositions, all of which are concerned with the measurements of figures using the method of exhaustion. Bulmer-Thomas gives a concise summary:

> Book XII applies the method of exhaustion, that is, the inscription of successive figures in the body to be evaluated, in order to prove that circles are to one another as the squares of their diameters, that pyramids of the same height with triangular bases are in the ratio of their bases, that the volume of a cone is one-third of the cylinder which has the same base and equal height, that cones and cylinders having the same height are in the ratio of their bases, that similar cones and cylinders are to one another in the triplicate ratio of the diameters, and that spheres are in the triplicate ratio of their diameters.

The thirteenth and last book is devoted entirely to properties of the five regular solids. The object is to 'comprehend' each of the regular solids in a sphere – that is, to find the ratio of an edge of the solid to the radius of the circumscribed sphere. Propositions 13 through 17 express the ratio of edge to diameter for each of the inscribed regular solids in turn. Finally in Proposition 18, the last in the *Elements*, it is proved that there can be no regular polygon beyond these five.

The transmission of the *Elements* was principally due to an edition and slight emendation done in the fourth century AD by Theon of Alexandria, which furnished the text for every Greek edition of Euclid up until the nineteenth century. The *Elements* were first translated into Arabic in the reign of Caliph Harun al-Rashid (r. 786–809). The first Latin translations of Euclid were made not from the Greek but from the Arabic, the earliest known being those of Adelard of Bath (*ca.* 1080–1152) and Gerard of Cremona (1114–1187). The first printed edition was published at Venice in 1482, a translation from Arabic to Latin done in 1259 by Companus of Novara. This and the first translation of the *Elements* from Greek into Latin, published in 1505 by Bartolomeo Zambeti, formed the basis for most subsequent versions, including those in the vernacular languages of Europe. The first complete English translation, published at London in 1570, was by Sir John Billingsley, later lord mayor of London, with a 'fruitful Praeface' by John Dee, who writes that the book contains 'manifolde additions, Scholies, Annotations and inventions ... gathered out of the most famous and chiefe Mathematicians both of old time and in our age.'

According to Heath, 'The *editio princeps* of the Greek text of the *Elements* contain two Books, XIV and XV, purporting to belong to Euclid's work, but these are not by Euclid. Book XIV is by Hypsicles, the reputed author of an astronomical tract *Anaforikos* (*De ascensioni*) still extant (the earliest surviving Greek work in which we find the division of a circle into 360 degrees), and of works on the harmony of the spheres and on polygonal numbers, which are lost.' Hypsicles flourished in Alexandria in the first half of the second century BC, and his father seems to have been an older contemporary of Apollonius of Perga. The so-called Book XIV that he apparently wrote, like the real Book XIII of the *Elements*, is concerned with the inscription of regular solids in a sphere. Hypsicles' principal claim to fame, the division of the circle into 360 degrees, was almost certainly borrowed from Babylonia. As he describes it in the *Anaforikos*:

> The circle of the zodiac having been divided into 360 equal arcs, let each of the arcs be called a spatial degree, and likewise, if the time taken by the zodiac circle to return from a point to the same point is divided into 360 equal times, let each of the times be called a temporal degree.

Euclid's other extant works include two works in pure geometry, the *Data*, which has survived in Greek, and *On Divisions of Figures*, which has come down in Arabic only. The subject matter of the *Data* is the same as that of Books I–VI of the *Elements*, but in a different form. *On Divisions of Figures*, as its title implies, deals with the division of triangles, parallelograms, circles and other geometric figures by straight lines into two or more parts either equal or in specified ratios.

Pappus of Alexandria says that Euclid wrote a four-book work entitled *Conics*, which has not survived even in quotation. According to Pappus, Apollonius of Perge based the first four books of his own *Conics* on this work, referring to it in Book II, where he says that he extended the developments made by Euclid.

Euclid also wrote several works on applied mathematics, two of which have survived, the *Phenomena* and the *Optica*, the first of which applies geometry to astronomy and the second to the study of light.

The *Phenomena* is a textbook in what the Greeks called *sphaeric*, the geometry of the sphere so far as required for observational astronomy. The preface explains the reasons for thinking that the cosmos is a sphere, and then Euclid goes on to define the special circles on the celestial sphere: the equator, the ecliptic or zodiac, the meridian and the horizon. He is the first to define the latter term, where he says: 'let the name horizon be given to the plane through us passing through the universe and separating off the hemisphere which is visible above the earth.' It has been suggested that Euclid drew on an earlier work on *sphaeric* by Autolycus, and that both of them used a still earlier treatise on the subject by Eudoxus.

The *Optica* is an elementary treatise on perspective, the first Greek work on this subject. The book explains how things *look* from different points of view, as compared with what they actually *are*, as Heath suggests, saying that 'it may have been intended as a corrective of heterodox ideas such as that of the Epicureans, who maintained that the heavenly bodies (e. g. the sun) *are* of the size they *look*.' The first of the definitions, some of which are really postulates, assumes the mistaken Platonic notion that vision is due to rays that go in straight lines from the eye to the object, rather than the other way around. The second and fourth definitions, as Heath paraphrases them, state that 'the figure formed by the visual rays is a cone having its vertex in the eye and its base the extremities of the object; things seen under a greater angle appear greater, those seen under a lesser angle smaller, and those seen under equal angles equal.' Proposition 6 can be used to show that parallel lines appear to meet. Proposition 19 assumes what is now known as the law of reflection, that when a light ray is reflected from a mirror, the angle that the incident and reflected rays make with the perpendicular to the surface are equal.

Proclus attributed to Euclid a treatise on the *Elements of Music*, now lost. Two musical treatises are included in editions of Euclid's works, and it appears that one of them, the *Divisions of the Scale*, may have been extracted from the original *Elements of Music* by a later writer.

Arabic sources attribute to Euclid a treatise on mechanics called the *Book on the Heavy and the Light*, which seems to have survived in the form of three different fragments, one of which is concerned with the balance. The fragments contain the law of the lever and notion of specific gravity, as well as a statement of the Aristotelian dynamics of freely falling bodies. Greek sources make no mention of a Euclidian work on mechanics, and authorities are doubtful about the authorship of the fragments, but Bulmer-Thomas suggests that they are possibly by Euclid. If so, it would have been yet another example of Euclid's pioneering efforts in the geometrization of nature, the beginning of mathematical physics.

CHAPTER 8

MEASURING HEAVEN AND EARTH

Aristarchus of Samos (*ca.* 310–230 BC) is famous for having proposed that the sun is the centre of the cosmos and not the earth, a theory that Copernicus would revive 18 centuries later. The earliest reference to the heliocentric theory of Aristarchus is by Archimedes in his *Sand-Reckoner*, written before 216 BC. The *Sand-Reckoner* is dedicated to King Gelon of Syracuse, whom Archimedes addresses in the introduction:

> Now you are aware that 'universe' is the name given by most astronomers to the sphere whose centre is the centre of the earth and whose radius is equal to the straight line between the centre of the sun and the centre of the earth. This is the common account as you have heard from astronomers. But Aristarchus of Samos brought out a book consisting of some hypotheses in which the premises lead to the result that the universe is many times greater than that now so called. His hypotheses are that the fixed stars and the sun remain unmoved, that the earth revolves around the sun in the circumference of a circle, the sun lying in the middle of the orbit, and that the sphere of the fixed stars, situated about the same centre as the sun, is so great that the circle in which he supposes the earth to revolve bears such a proportion to the distance of the fixed stars as the centre of the sphere bears to its surface.

Aëtius says that Aristarchus was a student of Strato of Lampsacus. This was probably at Alexandria during the years just prior to 287 BC, when Strato returned to Athens to succeed Theophrastus as head of the Lyceum. The astronomer Ptolemy notes in his *Almagest*, written around AD 150, that 'the school of Aristarchus' observed the summer solstice in 279 BC. This is the only contemporary reference to Aristarchus, who had probably passed away before Archimedes wrote *The Sand-Reckoner*.

The heliocentric theory of Aristarchus was not generally accepted in antiquity, principally because it contradicted accepted belief that the earth was the immobile centre of the cosmos. Cleanthes (331–232 BC), who succeeded Zeno of Citium as head of the Stoic school, wrote a tract 'Against Aristarchus', which may have been published during the lifetime of Aristarchus. Plutarch, writing around AD 100, mentions this attack in his brief account of the heliocentric theory, in which he says that Aristarchus had the earth moving around the sun on the ecliptic, while at the same time it was rotating on its axis.

The only ancient astronomer known to have accepted Aristarchus' theory seems to have been Seleucus the Chaldean, who flourished around 150 BC. According to Aëtius, Seleucus put forward a theory of the tides in which 'he too made the earth move', by which he may have meant that it was moving in orbit around the sun as well as rotating on its axis, but the passage is ambiguous. Aside from Seleucus, no other subsequent Greek astronomer mentions the heliocentric theory except to denounce it. Thus the treatise of Aristarchus in which he proposed the heliocentric theory did not survive, and it remained known in later times principally because of the account of it by Archimedes in his *Sand-Reckoner*. The heliocentric theory was revived 18 centuries later by Nicolaus Copernicus, who does not mention Aristarchus in the final version of *De Revolutionibus Orbium Coelestium* (*The Revolutions of the Heavenly Spheres*), published in 1543, though he was almost certainly aware of his predecessor's idea that the planets, including the earth, were orbiting the sun.

The only work of Aristarchus that has survived is his treatise *On the Sizes and Distances of the Sun and Moon.* This is the first attempt to determine astronomical distances and dimensions by mathematical deduction based upon a set of assumptions, thus measuring the heavens by geometricizing nature. Aristarchus makes no mention of his heliocentric theory in this treatise, in which he has the sun and moon are assumed to move in circular orbits around the earth. The Italian astronomer Schiaparelli was the first to suggest that one of the reasons which led Aristarchus to propose the heliocentric theory was that he found that sun was far larger than the earth, and this may have led him to put the larger body at the centre.

Aristarchus' treatise begins with a series of six hypotheses:

1. That the moon receives its light from the sun. 2. That the earth is in the relation of a point and centre to the sphere in which the moon moves. 3. That, when the moon appears to be halved, the great circle which divides the dark and bright portions of the moon is in the direction of our eye. 4. That when the moon appears to be halved, its distance from the sun is less than a quadrant by one-thirtieth of a quadrant. 5. That the breadth of the

(earth's) shadow is (that) of two moons. 6. That the moon subtends one fifteenth part of a sign of the zodiac.

Aristarchus then states that he is in a position to prove three propositions. The trigonometric functions had not yet been formulated, but Aristarchus was able to develop geometric procedure for approximating the sines of small angles between certain limits in expressing his results:

> 1. The distance of the sun from the earth is greater than eighteen times, but less than twenty times, the distance of the moon (from the earth); this follows from the hypothesis about the halved moon. 2. The diameter of the moon has the same ratio (as aforesaid) as the diameter of the moon. 3. The diameter of the sun has to the diameter of the earth a ratio greater than that which 19 has to 3, but less than that which 43 has to 6; this follows from the ratio thus discovered between the distances, the hypothesis about the shadow, and the hypothesis that the moon subtends one fifteenth part of a sign of the zodiac.

The third and fourth hypotheses can be better understood from the first of the three drawings shown in Figure 7, which illustrates the so-called lunar dichotomy. During each lunar cycle, at first quarter and last quarter, the moon is dichotomized, that is, exactly half of its disk is illuminated, with its diameter along the line of sight. Thus angle EMS is 90°, and angle MES, the 'distance from the sun', is 87°, which is 'less than a quadrant (90°) by one-thirtieth of a quadrant,' i.e., 3°. The actual value of angle MES is about 89°50´, so that the ratio of the distances of the sun and moon from the earth should be 18 times larger than the value given by Aristarchus, or about 390.

The second of the three drawings illustrates hypothesis 5, showing the moon halfway through the shadow cone of the earth during a lunar eclipse. Hypothesis 5 says in effect that the shadow cone is twice as wide as the moon when it is occulted during a lunar eclipse, whereas Ptolemy measured the shadow to be 2.6 times the width of the moon.

With regard to hypothesis 6, the 12 signs of the zodiac span 360°, thus each sign takes up 30°, and one-fifteenth of a sign equals 2°, the angle subtended by the moon, according to Aristarchus, whereas the actual value of this angle is about ½°.

Having established the ratio of the distances of the sun and moon, Aristarchus proceeded to determine the ratio of their diameters. He did this in the eighth of the 18 propositions that follow, which states that 'When the sun is totally eclipsed, the sun and moon are then comprehended by one and the same cone which has its vertex at our eye.' This means that the diameters of the sun and moon are in the same proportion as their distance from the earth, since they subtend the same angle, i.e., 2°, according to Aristarchus. It appears he later corrected the value that he gave for this angle from 2° to ½°, for Archimedes writes in the *Sand-Reckoner* that 'Aristarchus discovered that the sun appeared to be 1/720th part of the circle of the zodiac.'

Other dimensions are deduced by Aristarchus in five of the last nine propositions, in which all of the values are greatly underestimated because of the errors in the angles noted above:

> Proposition 10. The sun has to the moon a ratio greater than that which 5832 has to one, but less than that which 8000 has to one ... . Proposition 11. The diameter of the moon is less than 2/45[ths], but greater than 1/30th of the centre of the moon from our eye ... . Proposition 16. The sun has to the earth a ratio greater than that which 6859 has to 27, but less than that which 79507 has to 216 ... . Proposition 17. The diameter of the earth is to the diameter of the moon in a ratio greater than that which 108 has to 43, but less than that which 60 has to 19 ... . Proposition 18. The earth is to the moon in a ratio greater than that which 1259712 has to 79507, but less than that which 216000 has to 6859.

As noted above, the errors that Aristarchus made in measuring angles led to his gross underestimation of the dimensions deduced. James Evans has done a computation to show what would result if Aristarchus had given the correct values for the width of the moon's shadow during a lunar eclipse, and the angle subtended by the sun and moon, as he may have done subsequently. Evans shows that if we substitute these corrected values for the two angles we find:

> Distance of Sun = 1,273 Earth radii; Distance of Moon = 67 Earth radii; Diameter of Moon = 0.292 Earth diameters; Diameter of Sun = 5.55 Earth diameters. The distance and diameter of the moon are now close to the truth. (The actual mean distance of the Moon is about 60 Earth radii. The actual diameter of the Moon is about 0.273 Earth diameters.) But the size and distance of the Sun are still too small by a factor of twenty. ... The problem was hypothesis 4, that the angle between the Sun and the quarter Moon is 87°. This leads to the conclusion that the Sun is 19 times farther from us than the moon is. In fact the Sun is about 389 times farther from us than the Moon is. From this it follows that ... [the angle] is 89°51′ – less than a right angle by only 9′. Even several centuries later, when observational astronomy reached its peak, nobody could measure angles to a precision of 9′. ... The 20-1 ratio between the Sun's and Moon's distance was not called seriously into question until the seventeenth century.

On the Sizes and Distances of the Sun and Moon was translated into Arabic by Qusta ibn Luqa (d. *ca.* 912), and an Arabic recension was done by Nasir al-Din al-Tusi (d. 1274). The first published edition was a Latin translation by George Valla, included in a volume published first in 1488 and again in 1498. It next appeared in a Latin translation done in 1572 by Commandinus, who does not seem to have been aware of the earlier translation by Valla. The first edition of the Greek text was done in 1688 by John Wallis, Savillian professor of geometry at Oxford. The English translation by Thomas Heath was published in 1913. Heath notes that he relied mainly on Wallis' text and the tenth-century manuscript known as *Vaticanus Graecus*, which he says 'seems to be the ultimate source of all the others, and so much superior that the others can practically be left out of account.'

Aëtius says that Aristarchus wrote on vision, light and colours. Heath, quoting Aëtius, writes that 'Aristarchus said that colours are "shapes or forms stamping the air with impressions like themselves as it were", that "colours in darkness have no colouring", and that light is "the colour impinging on a substratum".'

Aëtius also credits Aristarchus with the invention of an improved sundial known as *scaphe*, in which the gnomon, or pointer, is erected vertically in the middle of a hemispherical bowl marked with a grid of lines so that both the height and direction of the sun's shadow could be recorded. This would have been one of the instruments that Aristarchus used in making measurements such as the obliquity of the ecliptic and the length of the solar year, both of which are mentioned by Copernicus in *De Revolutionibus*. Copernicus says that Aristarchus, along with Callippus and Archimedes, 'determined the year as containing a quarter of a day in addition to the 365 whole days – taking the beginning of the year at the summer solstice, after the Athenian manner.'

Heath refers to Censorinus, a Roman grammarian of the third century AD, in saying that Aristarchus added a correction to the value that Callippus had given for the solar year, and that he also gave a value for the so-called Great Year. 'We are told by Censorinus that Aristarchus added 1/1623rd of a year to Callippus' figure of 365¼ days for the solar year, and that he gave 2,484 days as the length of the Great Year, or the period after which the sun, the moon, and the five planets return to the same position in the heavens.' But Heath, after a lengthy analysis of the Great Year, concludes that 'it is difficult to believe that the period of Aristarchus is anything more than a luni-solar cycle.'

The tradition of geometricizing nature was continued by Eratosthenes (*ca.* 276–*ca.* 195 BC), a younger contemporary of Aristarchus, renowned for his measurement of the earth's circumference. Eratosthenes was born in Cyrene, in what is now Libya, and studied in Athens before moving to Alexandria around 235 BC at the invitation of Ptolemy II, who appointed him chief librarian of the library. He also served as the royal tutor and remained in favour at the court for the rest of his days.

Eratosthenes was one of the leading scholars of his day, known as *Pentathlos*, or 'the all-rounder' because of the great range of his writings, which include poetry as well as works in geography, mathematics, music, philosophy, chronology, literary criticism and grammar, of which only fragments remain. He was also called *Beta*, or 'next after the best', since he was reputed to be the second-best in all of his many fields. Strabo, who refers to Eratosthenes' *Geography* frequently, often critically, remarked that Eratosthenes 'was a mathematician among geographers and a geographer among mathematicians.' Nevertheless the *Geography* was a pioneering work in mathematical geography, mapping the *oikoumene* and dividing it into zones, with estimates of distances along a few roughly defined parallels and meridians, along with some description of peoples and places.

According to Strabo, the *Geography* of Eratosthenes was in three books, in the third of which there was a map of the *oikoumene*. As Strabo describes it, the map was divided into two parts by a line drawn parallel to the equator westward from Gibraltar through the Mediterranean and on through Asia as far as India. Perpendicular to this main parallel Eratosthenes drew a meridian line up from Nubia and southern Egypt, passing through Meroë, Syene (modern Aswan), Alexandria, Rhodes, the Bosphorus and the mouth of the Borysthenes (modern Dneiper). These were part of a grid work of imaginary lines, including but not restricted to meridians and parallels of latitude, that Eratosthenes drew through fixed points to establish distances along the lines in absolute terms. One of these was the Tropic of Cancer, the northernmost points where the sun will be overhead at noon. Strabo refers to this as 'the summer tropic', which, he says, 'must pass through Syene, because there, at the time of the summer solstice, the index of the sun-dial does not cast a shadow at noon.' Eratosthenes, in his measurement of the earth's circumference, made use of this observation as well as the fact that he had placed Syene on the same meridian as Alexandria. It is unclear whether this measurement was first published in a separate thesis or in the *Geography*, where in any event it would have been mentioned.

The method that Eratosthenes used to measure the circumference of the earth is described in detail only by the astronomer Cleomedes, who flourished in the latter half of the second century AD. As Cleomedes describes it, the measurement involved simultaneous observations made at Alexandria and Syene, directly to the south on the same meridian. It was observed that at the summer solstice the sun was directly overhead at noon in Syene, while on a sundial at Alexandria it cast a shadow equal to one-fiftieth of a circle. Eratosthenes made the measurement at Alexandria using a *scaphe* sundial, the type that had been invented by Aristarchus, with the gnomon in the middle of a hemispherical bowl.

An idealized version of Eratosthenes' observation is shown in Figure 7, where the lines produced through the vertical gnomons meet at the centre of the earth. The angle of the shadow at Alexandria is equal to the alternate angle subtended by the arc along the meridian between Alexandria and Syene, which Eratosthenes estimated to be 5,000 *stades*. Assuming that the sun is so far away that its rays are at Syene and Alexandria are parallel, Eratosthenes concluded that the north-south distance between the two places is one-fiftieth of the earth's circumference. Thus the circumference of the earth is 50 times the distance between Syene and Alexandria, or 250,000 *stades*, according to Cleomedes. Strabo puts it at 252,000, the number now generally taken to be the value found by Eratosthenes. According to D. R. Dicks: 'On the most probable value of the *stade* Eratosthenes used ..., 252,000 *stades* are equivalent to about 29,000 English miles, which may be compared with the modern figure for the earth's circumference of a little less than 25,000 miles.'

Eratosthenes measured the obliquity of the ecliptic by observing the meridian altitude of the sun at the summer and winter solstices and dividing the difference in the angles by two. The value he obtained was 23°51'20", a value which both Hipparchus and Ptolemy accepted as correct. He divided the globe of the earth into five zones, with a frigid zone around each pole, a torrid zone spanning the equatorial belt between the two tropics, and a temperate zone between each frigid zone and the tropics. Although he was clearly familiar with the concept of the celestial sphere, he does not seem to have done any original work in astronomy other than his measurement of the obliquity of the ecliptic and other measurements made in a geographical context. He is credited by some authorities with a brief tract called *Catasterisms* (Constellations), written as a commentary on, and supplement to, the *Phaenomena* of Aratus. This is essentially a list of constellations and the stories or legends associated with each of them, such as the entry for Cassiopeia:

> Sophocles, the tragic poet, says in his *Andromeda* that this one [Cassiopeia] came to misfortune by contending with the Nereids over beauty, and that Poseidon destroyed the region by sending a sea-monster [Cetus]. This is why her daughter [Andromeda] appropriately lies before the sea-monster. She has a bright star on the head, a dim one on the elbow, one on the hand, one on the knee, one at the end of the foot, a dim one on the breast, a bright one on the left thigh, a bright one on the knee, one on the board, one at each angle of the seat on which she sits; in all thirteen.

Eratosthenes' principal work in mathematics appears to have been the *Platonicus*, which evidently concerned ideas in mathematics connected with Plato's philosophy; this survives only in a few fragments given by Theon of Smyrna, writing in the first half of the second century AD. Here Eratosthenes dealt with the famous Delian problem of doubling the cube, along with such topics as proportion and progression, which he applied to the theory of musical scales. He also invented a method for finding prime numbers called the 'sieve of Eratosthenes', thus described by Boyer: 'With all the natural numbers arranged in order, one simply strikes out every second number following the number two, every third number (in the original sequence) following the number three, every fifth number following the number five, and continue in this manner to strike out every nth number following the number n. The remaining numbers, from two one, will of course be primes.'

Eratosthenes is the first Greek scholar known to have made a scientific study of the dating of historic events, which he wrote about in his *Chronography* and *Olympic Victors*. These were popular works containing anecdotes, some of which were repeated by Plutarch. His datings were considered authoritative in antiquity and some are still in use, such as those of the first Olympiad (777/776 BC), the invasion of Xerxes (480/479 BC), and the beginning of the Peloponnesian War (432/431 BC).

Eratosthenes was renowned in antiquity for his 12-volume treatise in literary criticism, *On the Old Comedy*, now lost except for citations by later writers. He was also highly thought of as a poet, only a few fragments of which survive, most notably a passage copied by Vergil in his *Georgics*. But despite all of these accomplishments Eratosthenes was considered by his peers to be only 'next after the best', such were the standards of excellence in Hellenistic Alexandria.

CHAPTER 9

MOVING THE WORLD

Greek mathematical physics reached its peak with the work of Archimedes (*ca.* 287–212 BC), who was born at Syracuse in Sicily. He mentions in *The Sand Reckoner* that his father was the astronomer Pheidias. Plutarch and the Roman historian Polybius suggest that Archimedes was related to King Hieron II of Syracuse (r. 269–215 BC), to whose son and co-ruler Gelon II he dedicated *The Sand Reckoner*.

Archimedes almost certainly spent some time in Alexandria, where he probably studied with the successors of Euclid. He addressed some of his treatises to scholars who are known to have lived in Alexandria, most notably Eratosthenes. He wrote most of his works in Syracuse, where he died in 212 BC during the siege and capture of the city by the Roman general Marcellus, when he was killed by a Roman soldier while he was drawing a geometrical proposition in the sand, or so the story goes. Plutarch, in his life of Marcellus, writes that Archimedes 'is said to have asked his friends and kinsmen to place on his grave after his death a cylinder circumscribing a sphere, with an inscription giving the ratio by which the included solid exceeds the included.' Cicero found this tombstone when he discovered Archimedes' grave in 75 BC, when he was Quaestor in Sicily. He writes in his *Tusculum Disputations* that he

> ... tracked out his grave ... and found it enclosed all around and covered with brambles and thickets; for I remember certain doggerel lines inscribed, as I had heard, upon his tomb, which stated that a sphere along with a cylinder had been put upon the top of his grave. Accordingly, after taking a good look all around (for there are a great quantity of graves at the Agrigentine Gate), I noticed a small column arising a little above and a cylinder .... Slaves were sent in with sickles ... and when a passage to the place was

opened we approached the pedestal in front of us; the epigram was trace-
able with about half the lines legible, as the latter portion was worn away.

Archimedes was renowned in antiquity as much for his ingenious mechanical inventions as for his mathematical works. He worked for both Hieron
and Gelon as a military engineer, constructing devices such as catapults,
burning mirrors, and a system of compound pulleys for moving large ships
with minimum effort. These devices were used to great advantage by the
Syracusans in resisting the siege of their city in 212 BC by Marcellus.

The weapons that Archimedes is supposed to have invented to use against
the Romans in their siege of Syracuse include the 'burning mirrors' referred
to by Lucian of Samasota, writing in the first century AD. According to
Lucian, Archimedes set up metal mirrors to focus sunlight onto the Roman
triremes to set them on fire. The Greek scientist Ioannis Sakkas verified this
story in a demonstration he arranged in 1975 at the Skaramangas naval base
outside Athens, when he used an array of 70 mirrors to focus sunlight on a
plywood replica of a trireme at a distance of 50 metres and set it afire.

Athenaeus of Naucratis tells the story of another invention of
Archimedes, the *cochlias*, or Archimedean screw. This is a device with a helical screw inside a cylinder; when turned by hand it can transfer water from
a lower to a higher level. According to Athenaeus, Archimedes invented
this device to pump out the bilge water from Hieron's great ship of state,
the *Syracusia*. The *cochlias* was employed in ancient Egypt for irrigation pur-
poses and in Spain for pumping out mines, and it is still in use today.

Archimedes also invented a compound pulley called a *polyspaston*, which
Plutarch writes about in his life of Marcellus. He says that when King Hieron
asked him to demonstrate how a huge weight could be moved by a large
force, Archimedes 'fixed upon a three-masted merchantman of the royal
fleet, which had been dragged ashore by the great labors of many men, and
after putting on board many passenger and the customary freight, he seated
himself at a distance from her, and without any great effort, but quietly setting in motion a system of compound pulleys, drew her towards him smoothly
and evenly, as though she were gliding smoothly through the water.'

Plutarch goes on to quote a supposed remark of Archimedes on this
occasion to the effect that 'if there were another world, and he could go to
it, he could move this one.' The more familiar form of this remark is the one
given by Pappus: 'Give me a place to stand on, and I will move the earth.'

According to Plutarch, Archimedes himself did not have high regard
for his inventions, considering them as being merely the 'diversions of a

geometry at play'. Plutarch goes on to tell of the much higher opinion Archimedes had of his mathematical works, which led him to spurn publication of his mechanical inventions.

> And yet Archimedes possessed such a lofty spirit, so profound a soul, and such a wealth of scientific theory, that though his inventions had won for him a name and fame for superhuman sagacity, he would not consent to leave behind him any treatise on this subject, but regarding the work of an engineer and every art that ministers to the needs of life as ignoble a vulgar. He devoted his earnest efforts only to those studies the subtlety and charm of which were not affected by the claims of necessity. These studies, he though, are not to be compared with any others; in them, the subject vies with the demonstration, the former supplying grandeur and beauty, the latter precision and surpassing power. For it is not possible to find in geometry more profound and difficult questions treated in simpler and purer terms.

The extant mathematical works of Archimedes can be roughly classified in three groups. The first group comprises those works principally concerned with proofs of theorems relating to the areas and volumes of figure bounded by curved lines and surfaces. These treatises are: On the Sphere and the Cylinder, On the Measurement of a Circle, On Conoids and Spheroids, On Spirals, and On the Quadrature of the Parabola, part of which – Propositions 1–17 – also belongs in the second group. The second group is made up of treatises on the geometrical analysis of statical and hydrostatical problems and the application of statics in geometry. These are: On the Equilibrium of Planes, On Floating Bodies, On the *Method of Mechanical Theorems*, which was lost in antiquity and rediscovered early in the twentieth century, and Propositions 1–17 of *On the Quadrature of the Parabola*. The third group consists of miscellaneous mathematical works, including *The Sand-Reckoner, The Cattle Problem* and the fragmentary *Stomachion*.

Other works of Archimedes no longer extant are mentioned by Greek writers. These include the *Elements of Mechanics, On Sphere-making, On Balances, On Uprights, On Polyhedra, On Blocks and Cylinders, The Naming of Numbers* and *Optics*. Other treatises are attributed to Archimedes by Arabic authors and are extant in Arabic manuscripts. These are: The *Lemmata, On Water Clocks, On Touching Circles, On Triangles, On the Properties of the Right Triangle* and *On the Division of the Circle into Seven Equal Parts*. But the *Lemmata* in its present form cannot be by Archimedes, for his name is cited in the proofs. There are two other works attributed to Archimedes by Arabic writers which are now lost: *On Parallel Lines, On Data* and *On the Heptagon in the Circle.*

Archimedes, in the preface to his treatise *On the Method of Mechanical Theorems*, says that he discussed the solution of important problems in quadrature and cubature by a certain mechanical method. The treatise is addressed to Eratosthenes, to whom he explains his method:

> I thought it might be appropriate to write down and set forth for you in this same book a certain method, by means of which you will be able to recognize certain mathematical questions with the aid of mechanics. I am convinced that this is no less useful for finding the proofs of these same theorems. For some things, which first became clear to me by the mechanical method, were afterwards proved geometrically, because their investigation by the said method does not furnish an actual demonstration. For it is easier to supply the proof when we have previously acquired, by the method, some knowledge of the questions than it is to find it without any previous knowledge.

The 'mechanical method' was one in which Archimedes mathematically balanced geometrical figures as if they were weights on a balance, comparing a figure of unknown area with another whose area was already known. The figure whose area was to be determined was divided up into infinitesimal strips, the centre of gravity of each of which was balanced against a strip of the figure of known area. Then, using the law of the lever, the unknown area was determined strip by strip and summed up to give the total area, just as is done in modern integral calculus. The method was extended to three dimensions to determine volumes.

The treatise *On the Sphere and the Cylinder*, addressed to the astronomer Dositheus, is in two books, the first of which begins with definitions. These are followed by five assumptions, the fifth and last of which is known as the Lemma of Archimedes: 'Of unequal magnitudes, the greater exceeds the less by such a magnitude as when added to itself [continually], can be made to exceed any assigned magnitude of the same kind.'

Archimedes then proceeds to determine the areas and volumes of figures using the method of exhaustion, but in a way somewhat different than Euclid. Whereas Euclid had used inscribed figures only, Archimedes used circumscribed figures as well, thus approaching the area or volume to be measured from above and below. Among the results that Archimedes obtained using this and other techniques was the proof that a sphere has two-thirds the volume and surface area of its circumscribing cylinder, which he commemorated with the carving that decorated his tomb.

The treatise *On the Measurement of a Circle* contains only three propositions. Proposition 1 proves that the area of a circle is equal to that of a right-angled triangle having for perpendicular the radius of the circle, and for base its circumference. Proposition 3 proves that the ratio of the circumference of any circle to its diameter, the symbol π, is greater than 223/71 (3.140845 ...) and less than 22/7 (3.1428571 ...), as compared to the true value of 3.145926 ... Archimedes arrived at this result by using his method of exhaustion with a circle and a regular polygon of 96 sides. The treatise also gives an approximate value for the square root of 3, saying that it is greater than 265/153 (1.7320261 ...) and less than 1351/780 (1.7320512 ...), where the true value is 1.7320508 ... .

The treatise *On Conoids and Spheroids*, also addressed to Dositheus, has 32 propositions. Here Archimedes determines the volumes of segments (right or oblique) of paraboloids, hyperboloids and spheroids. The process that Archimedes uses in obtaining these volumes is nearly the same as in modern integral calculus, in which one cuts the figure up into slices of diminishing thickness, so that the difference between the inscribed and circumscribed figures can be made less than any preassigned value.

The treatise *On Spirals*, again addressed to Dositheus, has 26 propositions. This defines what is now called the Archimedean spiral: 'If a straight line one extremity of which remains fixed be made to revolve at a uniform rate in a plane until it returns to the position from which it started, and if, at the same time as the straight line is revolving, a point moving at a uniform rate along the straight line starting from the fixed extremity, the point will describe a spiral in the plane.'

The Archimedean spiral can be used to solve two of the three famous problems of ancient Greek geometry, namely the trisection of any angle and the duplication of the cube, though not with straightedge and compasses.

On the Quadrature of the Parabola, another treatise addressed to Dositheus, contains 24 propositions. Here Archimedes uses two different methods to show that the area enclosed by a parabolic segment is four-thirds the area of a triangle having the same base and equal height. The first method is mechanical and involved the summation of an infinite series and is equivalent to integration. The second method is purely geometrical and simply 'exhausts' the area of the segment by inscribing successive sets in triangles in the usual manner.

The treatise *On the Equilibrium of Planes*, also known as *The Centres of Gravity of Planes*, is in two books. The main problems solved in Book I are the determination of the centres of gravity of a parallelogram, a triangle and a parallel-trapezium. Book II is entirely given over to finding the centres of gravity of any parabolic segment and of a part of it cut off by a chord parallel to the base.

The treatise *On Floating Bodies* demonstrates the famous law of hydrostatics that bears Archimedes' name, it states that a body immersed in a fluid is buoyed up by a force equal to the weight of the fluid it displaces. Archimedes' discovery of this law is the subject of an anecdote told by Vitruvius in *his De architectura*. It seems that King Hieron had commissioned a goldsmith to fashion a golden wreath so that he could consecrate it to the gods out of gratitude for the success of one of his enterprises. When Hieron received the wreath he asked Archimedes to determine whether or not the wreath was of pure gold.

> When Archimedes was turning the problem over, he chanced to come to the place of bathing, and there, as he was sitting down in the tub, he noticed that the amount of water which flowed out of the tub was equal to the amount by which his body was immersed. This indicated to him a method of solving the problem, and he did not delay, but in his joy leapt out of the tub, and rushing naked towards his home, he cried out in a loud voice that he had found what he sought, for as he ran he repeatedly shouted in Greek, *Eurika, eurika* [I have found it!]!

Archimedes weighed the wreath in water and found that it displaced a greater volume of water than the same weight of pure gold. This showed that the wreath was less dense than pure gold, and thus it had been made with an admixture of a lighter metal. Archimedes thus discovered the concept of specific gravity, the weight of a body relative to that of an equivalent volume of water.

The Sand-Reckoner has already been mentioned in connection with the heliocentric theory of Aristarchus. The title of the thesis stems from the fact that in it Archimedes developed a system for expressing the largest numbers imaginable, such as the number of grains of sand in the universe, the latter being defined by the sphere on which the earth moves around the sun in the heliocentric theory.

The Greeks expressed all numbers from 1 to 999 using the letters of the alphabet along with three other signs. Thousands (*chiliades*) were taken as units of a higher order, and above 9,999 came a myriad. This system was very unwieldy, particularly for the expression of very large numbers, and this led Archimedes to create a new system, which he describes in *The Sand Reckoner*.

Archimedes intended *The Sand Reckoner* as a contribution to Greek arithmetic, but its historical interest is based not only on that but of what it reveals of its author's work in astronomy, for which he was renowned in antiquity. He showed his skill as an observational astronomer in this thesis by making a remarkable determination of the apparent diameter of the sun using an instrument called a diopter. Hipparchus mentions Archimedes' determination of the length of the solar year, while the fifth-century Latin writer Macrobius reports on his theory concerning the mutual distances of the sun, moon and planets and their positions in relation to the stellar sphere.

The minor work known as *The Cattle Problem* is contained in an epigram which appears to have been sent by Archimedes to Eratosthenes, with instructions to distribute it to Alexandrian mathematicians. It concerns the mythical Cattle of Helios, which consisted of bulls and cows of each of four colours – white, black, yellow and dappled – and the problem is to count the number of bulls and cows of each colour. The first part of the problem connects the eight unknowns by seven simple equations, and the second part adds two more conditions to which the unknowns are subject. The problem is made more difficult by the ambiguity of the language expressing one of the limiting conditions.

There are two different solutions depending on how the ambiguous limiting condition is interpreted. The solutions to both versions of the problem was given in 1880 by the German mathematician Amthor. The solution to the simpler version gives the total number of cattle as 5,916,837,175,686. The solution to the difficult version gives such gargantuan numbers that Amthor remarked that just to write down all the eight numbers would require a volume of 660 pages! It would thus seem that the simpler version was the one Archimedes proposed, for even he could hardly have solved the more difficult version, given the state of mathematics in his time.

The Stomachion survives in only two fragments, one in Greek and the other in Arabic. Together the two fragments are not enough to understand Archimedes' motive in writing this thesis, which appears to be about a type of geometrical game. The name *Stomachion* means literally 'that which relates to the stomach', and it has been suggested that the game was so called because its difficulties were so great that it could give one a belly-ache. D. J. Dijksterhuis concluded from his study of the ancient sources that the *Stomachion* 'is a kind of game, played with bits of ivory in the form of simple planimetrical figures, the object being to fit these bits together in such a way that the various shapes of human beings, animals or different objects were imitated.' He notes that the game board was apparently known to the Romans as *loculus Archimedius,* or Archimedian box, and that 'it consisted of fourteen bits of ivory of different forms, that these bits together formed a square, that it was possible to compose from them all sorts of figures (a ship, a sword, a tree, a helmet, a dagger, a column), and that this game was considered very instructive for children, because it strengthened the memory.' The *Stomachion* indicates that Archimedes was the first author in a field of mathematics now known as combinatorics, in this case finding the number of possible ways of fitting together the pieces on the game board. A recent analysis has shown that if there are 14 pieces on the board then there are 17,152 ways of arranging them. It is not known whether Archimedes found this solution, but anyone familiar with his work would bet that he did.

Archimedes was the founder of mathematical physics and his work inspired European physicists from Galileo through Newton down to the present day. As David C. Lindberg writes of Archimedes' influence in *The Beginnings of Modern Science*:

> Many scientific problems continued to resist solution by mathematical methods, but Archimedes remained as a symbol of the power of mathematical analysis and a source of inspiration for those who believed that mathematics was capable of ever increasing triumphs. His works had limited influence during the Middle Ages, but in the Renaissance they became the basis of a powerful tradition of mathematical science.

CHAPTER 10

MATHEMATICS, ASTRONOMY AND GEOGRAPHY

The third of the three great Hellenistic mathematicians, after Euclid and Archimedes, is Apollonius of Perge, known in antiquity as the Great Geometer, renowned for his treatise on *Conics*. As Carl B. Boyer writes in his history of mathematics, these 'three mathematicians stood head and shoulders above all others of the time, as well as above most of their predecessors and successors ... it is their work that leads to the designation of the period from about 300 to 200 BC as the "Golden Age" of Greek mathematics.'

Little is known about the life of Apollonius. According to the mathematician Eutocius of Ascalon, writing early in the fifth century AD, Apollonius was born in the city of Perge on the Mediterranean coast of Asia Minor during the reign of the Egyptian king Ptolemy III Eurgetes (r. 246–221 BC). Other chronological evidence indicates that his date of birth was around 240 BC, and that at one time or another he lived for some time in Alexandria and visited Ephesus and Pergamum.

The conic sections had been studied in the Greek world as early as the mid-fourth century BC, and by the beginning of the following century there are references to two textbooks on the subject, one by Euclid and the other by his somewhat older contemporary Aristaeus, both now lost. According to Heath, Apollonius was the first to give the names parabola, hyperbola and ellipse to the three conic sections.

Apollonius differed from his predecessors by replacing the single-napped cone with a double-napped cone, so that the vertices coincide and the axes are in a straight line. His definition of a circular cone is the same as that used today: 'If a straight line, indefinite in length and passing always through a fixed point is made to move around the circumference of a circle which is not in the same plane so as to pass successively through every point of that circumference, the moving straight line will trace out the surface of a cone.'

Apollonius generates all three conic sections by cutting the double oblique circular cone with a plane at right angles to the so-called axial triangle, which is any triangle through the axis. There are three non-trivial possibilities, each of which gives one of the conic sections. The first is that the line of intersection of the two planes intersects only one of the two sides of the axial triangle, in other words, it is parallel to the other side. The second is that the line of intersection intersects one side of the axial triangle below the vertex and the extension of the other side above the vertex. The third is that the line of intersection intersects both sides of the axial triangle below the vertex. The first of these sections is a parabola, the second a hyperbola, and the third an ellipse, of which the circle is a special case when the cutting plane is parallel to the base of the cone.

The treatise on *Conics* was originally in eight books, of which Books I–IV survive in the original Greek, VI–VII only in Arabic translation. Book VIII is lost, but some notion of what it contained can be surmised from the lemmas of Pappus. The contents of the *Conics* are outlined by Apollonius in the Preface to Book I:

> The first four books constitute an elementary introduction. The first contains the methods of generating the three sections and their basic properties, developed more fully and more generally than in the writings of others; the second contains the properties of the diameter and axes of the second, the asymptotes, and other things ...; the third contains many surprising theorems useful for the syntheses of solid loci and for determinations of the possibilities of solutions; of the latter the greater part and the most beautiful are new. ... The remaining books are particular extensions; one of them [V] deals somewhat fully with maxima and minima, another [VI] with equal and similar conic sections, another [VII] with theorems concerning determinations, another [VIII] with determinate conic problems.

Pappus, in his *Treasury of Analysis*, includes summaries of and lemmas to six other works of Apollonius beside the *Conics*, only one of which have survived. According to G. J. Toomer, 'All belong to "higher geometry," and all consisted of exhaustive discussion of a few general problems.' He goes on to say that many of the problems in these six works 'can be reduced to problems in conics.'

The treatise *De Rationis Sectione* is the only extant work of Apollonius other than the *Conics*. It is preserved only in an Arabic version which appears to be an adaption rather than a literal translation. According to Pappus, the general problem in this treatise is 'to draw through a given point a straight line to cut off from two given straight lines two sections measured from given points on the two given lines, so that the two sections cut off have a given ratio.'

De Spatii Sectione deals with a general problem similar to that of De Rationis Sectione. But in this case the intercepts cut off from the two given lines must contain a given rectangle rather than being in a given ratio.

The treatise De Sectione Determinata dealt with what Boyer says 'might be called an analytic geometry of one dimension.' The general problem is: given four points on a straight line – A, B, C, D – to determine a point P such that $AP \cdot CP / BP \cdot DP$ has a given value. Here again the problem reduces to the solution of a quadratic equation.

The treatise De Tactionibus is different from the three just considered. The general problem, now known as the Problem of Apollonius, is the following: given three things, either points, straight lines or circles, describe a circle passing through the given points and touching the given straight lines or circles. The most difficult case, when the three things are circles, attracted the attention of Newton, one of whose solutions was obtained by the intersection of two hyperbolas.

The general problem in De Inclinationibus is to demonstrate how a straight line of a given length, tending towards a given point (that is, it will, if produced, pass through the point), could be inserted between two given lines that are either straight or curved.

A number of other lost works in pure mathematics by Apollonius are mentioned by later writers. There is detailed information about the contents of only one of these, a work described by Pappus in Book II of his Treasury. The beginning of Pappus' description is lost and so the title of this work is unknown. It develops a method of expressing extremely large numbers, which, as we have seen, Archimedes had already done in The Sand Reckoner. Apollonius did this by using a place-value notation with a base of 1,000, whereas Archimedes' base was $10,000^2$.

Another lost work of Apollonius is his Comparison of the dodecahedron with the icosahedron, where both of these perfect figures are inscribed in the same sphere. According to Heath, 'he proved that the perpendiculars from the centre of the circumscribing sphere to a pentagonal face of the dodecahedron and to a triangular face of the icosahedrons are equal, so that the volumes of the solids are to one another as their areas.'

There is an allusion to a General Thesis by Apollonius that must have dealt with the foundations of geometry. This treatise would seem the source of several remarks made by Apollonius on the fundamental principles of geometry, quoted by Proclus in his commentary on Book I of Euclid's *Elements*. Proclus also mentions another work of Apollonius, *On the Cochlias*, or cylindrical helix, now lost.

A lost work of Apollonius *On unordered irrationals* is referred to by Pappus in his commentary on Book X of the *Elements*. According to Pappus, this thesis contains some extensions and generalizations of Euclid's theory of irrationals in the *Elements*.

Apollonius appears to have written one or two works on mathematics applied to optics, both lost. A fragmentary palimpsest known as the 'Bobbio Mathematical Fragment' refers to a work of Apollonius entitled *On the Burning Mirror*, in which he found the focal points for parallel rays reflected from a spherical mirror. The same passage also mentions another work of Apollonius called *To the Writers on Catoptrics*, in which he states that his predecessors were wrong in saying that such rays would be focused at the centre of curvature.

Eutocius mentions a work of Apollonius entitled *Quick Delivery*, which seems to have taught methods of rapid calculation. Here Apollonius appears to have developed a closer approximation to π than the one given by Archimedes, probably the one generally used today, 3.1416.

Apollonius is also noted for his astronomical studies. But the only specific information about his work in this field is given by Ptolemy in his *Almagest*. There he describes how Apollonius developed theories of epicycles and eccentric circles to determine the 'stations,' or turning points, of a planet undergoing retrograde motion as seen by an observer on earth. The first of these theories has the planet moving on the circumference of a circle, the epicycle, whose centre moves around the periphery of a second circle called the deferent. The second theory has the planet moving in a circular orbit whose centre is a point other than the centre of the earth. Apollonius also showed that the epicycle and eccentric circle theories were equivalent to one another. These would be the basic theories for the motion of the celestial bodies for the next 17 centuries.

The first to use Apollonius' epicycle and eccentric circle theories was Hipparchus of Nicaea, the greatest astronomer of antiquity, who was born around the time that the Great Geometer died. Despite his fame, virtually nothing is known of Hipparchus other than the fact that he was born in Nicaea (Turkish Iznik), in the region in northwestern Asia Minor known as Bithynia, and that he spent much of his later life in Rhodes.

Ptolemy, writing in the mid-second century AD, records in his treatise on the *Phases of the Fixed Stars* that the observations he took from Hipparchus were made in Bithynia, presumably in Nicaea. In his *Almagest* Ptolemy records a number of observations by Hipparchus ranging in date from 147 BC to 127 BC, and he notes that those in the period 141–127 BC were made on Rhodes, where he seems to have spent the latter part of his career.

The only work of Hipparchus that has survived is his *Commentary on the Phaenomena of Aratus and Eudoxus* in three books. As noted above, early in the third century BC Aratus had written a poem, entitled *Phenomena*, based on a pioneering work by Eudoxus, now lost, naming and describing the constellations. Hipparchus, in his *Commentary*, remarks that 'Several other writers have compiled commentaries upon the *Phaenomena* of Aratus, but the most careful of them is that of Attalus, the mathematician of our own time.' Hipparchus goes on to say that his aim in writing his own commentary is to give a critique of these earlier works, 'to set out the details which seem to me to have been incorrectly given.'

In the latter part of his commentary, Hipparchus gives an account of the risings, settings and culmination of the principal constellations for a latitude where the longest day is 14½ hours, along with the corresponding degrees of the ecliptic. At the end of Book III he gives a list of bright stars that lie on or near the 24 great circles that mark the hours on the celestial sphere, beginning with the one through the point of the summer solstice, thus enabling an observer to tell the time at night.

Several authorities have credited Hipparchus with the compilation of a catalogue of some 850 stars. It has been suggested that this formed the basis for Ptolemy's star catalogue in the *Almagest*, which contains the coordinates of 1,025 stars. This led to a charge that Ptolemy had plagiarized Hipparchus, whom he refers to frequently and with due credit in the *Almagest*. Prevailing opinion now is that the charge is unfounded.

Hipparchus' main claim to fame is his discovery of the precession of the equinoxes, that is, the slow movement of the celestial pole in a circle about the perpendicular to the ecliptic, as illustrated in Figure 5. The earth's precession manifests itself by a gradual advance of the spring equinox along the ecliptic, thus causing a progressive change in the celestial longitude of the stars, with a period of somewhat less than 26,000 years. Hipparchus discovered this effect in 135 BC by comparing his star catalogue with observations made 128 years earlier by the astronomer Timocharis, finding that the celestial longitude of the star Spica in the constellation Virgo had changed by some two degrees in that interval of time. Hipparchus thus concluded that the solstices and equinoxes shift westward with respect to the stars 'not less than 1/100°' in a year, whereas the actual rate is about 1° in 72 years.

Hipparchus wrote a treatise *On the Length of the Year*, now lost, which is cited by Ptolemy in the *Almagest*. According to Ptolemy, Hipparchus had made an accurate determination of the length of the so-called tropical year by measuring the time between two summer solstices, one that he himself observed in 135 BC, the other recorded by Aristarchus in 280 BC, 145 years earlier. Hipparchus found that the time between the two observations was 12 hours less than 145 years, assuming that each year was 365¼ days. The value that he found was equivalent to 365.2467 days, about 6.6 minutes longer than the currently accepted value.

After determining the length of the tropical year, Hipparchus wrote a treatise *On Intercalary Months and Days*. Here he proposed a lunisolar intercalation cycle as a modification of the Callippic cycle. His cycle comprised 304 tropical years, 112 with 13 synodic months (the time between successive conjunctions and oppositions of the sun and moon), and 192 with 12, giving a total of 111,035 days. This implies that the mean synodic month is equal to 29.530585 days, which is less than one second in error.

Hipparchus also made detailed studies of the motions of both the sun and the moon, in which he used the epicycle and eccentric circle theories that had been developed by Apollonius of Perge. Hipparchus used the eccentric circle theory to account for the solar anomaly, the fact that the seasons have different lengths, which had been noticed by Callippus as early as 330 BC. Hipparchus observed the times of the solstices and equinoxes to give him the lengths of the seasons around 130 BC, recording the following lengths: spring = 94½ days, summer = 92½ days, autumn = 88⅛ days, winter = 90⅛ days, adding up to 365¼ days. Today the lengths of the seasons have changed, so that summer is the longest season rather than spring. If the earth were the centre of its orbit the sun would appear to move along the ecliptic with uniform speed and the seasons would all have the same duration. Hipparchus accounted for the solar anomaly by having the sun move along an eccentric circle, that is, one whose centre is displaced from the earth. Using Hipparchus' eccentric model, the sun moves at uniform velocity on its circle, but its varying distance from the earth makes it appear to travel more swiftly at perigee and more slowly at apogee. The model was highly successful and was used in turn by Greek, Arabic and European astronomers up until the sixteenth century.

Hipparchus was faced with much greater difficulties in formulating a lunar theory, for whereas the sun has only one period, its return to the same longitude, namely the year, the moon has three different periodicities besides the synodic month. These are the period of the moon's return in longitude, the period of its return to the same velocity ('anomalistic month'), and the period of its return to the same latitude ('dracontic month'). According to Ptolemy, Hipparchus determined these periods 'from Babylonian and his own observations.' Hipparchus used this data to determine the parameters of his lunar theory, in which he used a simple epicycle model together with the equivalent eccentric model. The data involved eclipses of the sun and moon, one of which was the lunar eclipse of 27 January 141 BC, which Toomer says gives 'a *terminus post quem* for the lunar theory.'

The ultimate goal of Hipparchus' study of lunar motion was to formulate a theory of eclipses. In order to predict a solar eclipse it is necessary to know the relative sizes and distances of the sun, moon and earth, while for a lunar eclipse it is sufficient to know the apparent sizes. Hipparchus was thus led to write a treatise in two books *On Sizes and Distances*, which was commented upon by both Ptolemy and Pappus, so that its essentials can be reconstructed. Toomer notes that Hipparchus' measurements had established the following data:

> 1) The moon at mean distance measures its own circle 650 times. 2) The moon at mean distance measures the earth's shadow (at the moon) 2½ times. 3) The moon at mean size is the same apparent size as the sun. He had also established by observation that the sun has no perceptible parallax. But from this he could only deduce that the sun's parallax was less than a certain amount, which he set at seven seconds of arc.

In the first book of *On Sixes and Distances* Hipparchus analyzed a solar eclipse that had occurred on 14 March 190 BC, in which the sun had been totally eclipsed near the Hellespont but only four-fifths obscured at Alexandria. Assuming that the sun had zero parallax and that the sun was in the meridian at both Alexandria and the Hellespont, whose longitudes differ by 10 degrees, he calculated the distance of the moon as being greater than 71 earth radii and less than 81, for a mean distance of 76 earth radii.

In the second book Hipparchus assumed that the sun had a parallax of seven minutes of arc, the minimum that he thought to be measurable. He then calculated that the minimum distance of the moon was 62 earth radii and the maximum 72⅔, giving a mean of 67⅔ earth radii.

Hipparchus also computed the sizes of the sun and moon. Theon of Smyrna says that Hipparchus computed that the sun was about 1,880 times the size of the earth, and that the earth was 27 times the size of the moon, where he is obviously referring to comparative volumes. This means that he had found the diameter of the sun to be 12⅓ that of the earth and the diameter of the earth to be three times that of the moon. Therefore, using the method of the second book, he would have found that the distance of the sun was some 2,500 earth radii and that of the moon some 60½ earth radii.

According to Ptolemy, Hipparchus measured the apparent diameters of the sun and moon with an instrument he called the 'four cubit diopter'. This was a four-foot rod with a sighting hole at one end, and a wedge that could be slid in a groove along a scale until it exactly obscured the disk of the moon or sun. The ratio of the breadth of the prism to its distance from the sighting hole gave the chord of the apparent diameter of the object.

There is some evidence that Hipparchus used and perhaps invented stereographic projection, as evidenced by his ability to compute the simultaneous risings and setting of various stars. This has led to the suggestion that it was he who invented the plane astrolabe, which in its subsequent development became the most widely used instrument in Arabic astronomy. The astrolabe is based on stereographic projection, in which the celestial sphere is mapped onto a plane in such a way that circles are preserved conformally, that is, angles of intersection will be mapped without change.

Hipparchus is renowned as the father of trigonometry, for he seems to have been the first to compile the equivalent of a trigonometric table. This was a table of chords of arcs subtended at the centre of a circle by angles ranging at intervals of $1/48^{th}$ of a circle, i.e., 7½°, using linear interpolation between the computed points to obtain other values. Such a tabulation of chords is exactly the same as a trigonometrical table of the sine function, for, using modern notation, the chord of an angle equals twice the sine of half the angle, i.e., chord $(A) = 2 \sin (A/2)$. In compiling his table of chords, Hipparchus seems to have introduced the Babylonian system of dividing the circle into 360 degrees of 60 minutes each, apparently the first in the Greek world to do so.

Sphaeric, or the geometry of the sphere, was already so far advanced by the time of Euclid that he quotes propositions as generally known. These propositions and others, particularly those used in astronomy, were collected in a treatise called *Sphaerica* by Theodosius of Bithynia, a younger contemporary of Hipparchus. The treatise is in three books, of which the second half of Book II and all of Book III are of astronomical interest only. According to Heath: 'The object of the propositions is to prove such results as Euclid obtained in the *Phaenomena*, e.g., that different arcs of the ecliptic having the same length take a longer or shorter time to rise according as they are nearer to or farther from the tropic circle.'

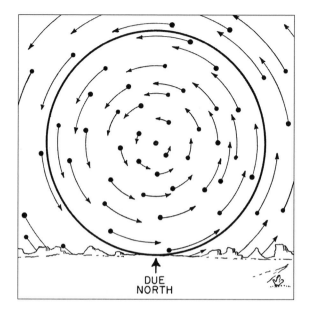

1 Apparent motion of the stars about the celestial pole

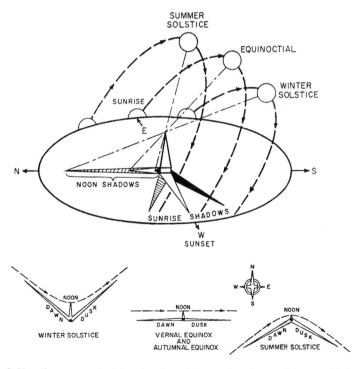

2 Use of a gnomon to determine the solstices and equinoxes (above and below)

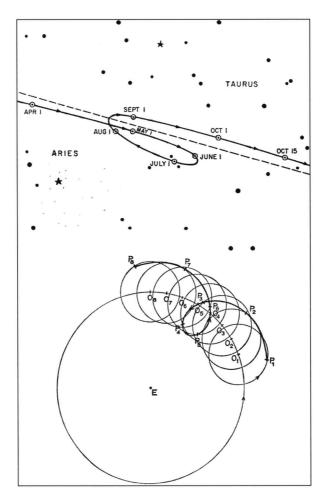

3 Apparent retrograde motion of a planet (above). Epicycle theory
of Apollonius to explain the retrograde motion of the planets (below)

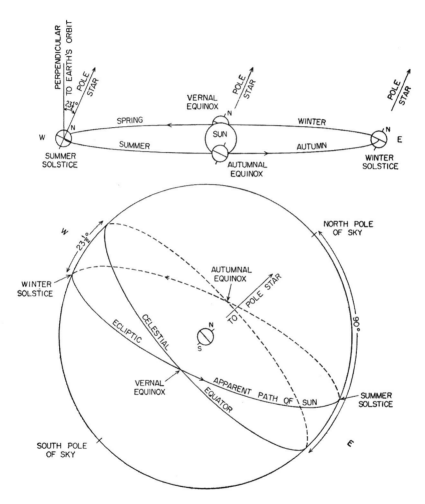

4 The tilt of the earth's axis as the cause of the seasons (above).
The equinoxes and solstices shown on the celestial sphere (below)

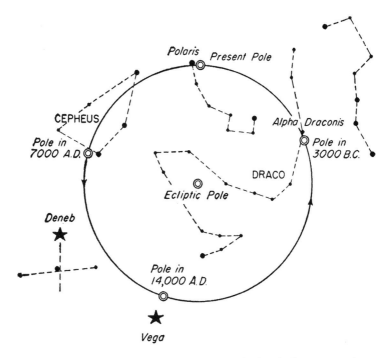

5 The rotation of the celestial pole about the ecliptic pole due to precession

6. Aristotle's cosmology

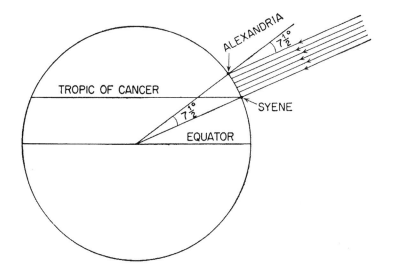

7 Measurement of the earth's circumference by Eratosthenes

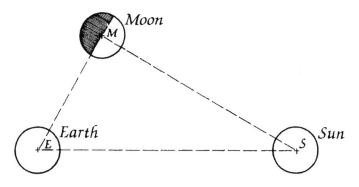

8 From Aristarchus' *On the Sizes and Distances of the Sun and Moon*; the lunar dichotomy

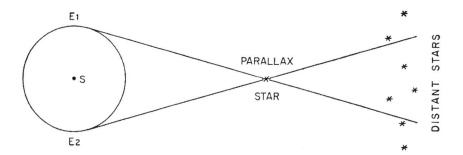

9 Stellar parallax

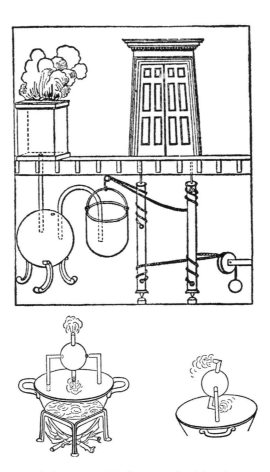

10 Hero's inventions: temple doors opened by fire on an altar (above), steam engine (below)

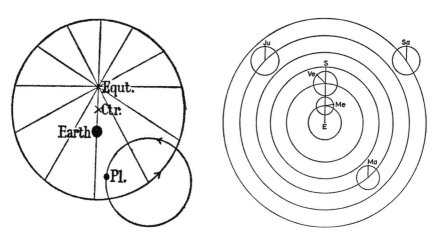

11 Ptolemy's concept of the equant (left). Simplified version of
Ptolemy's planetary model (right)

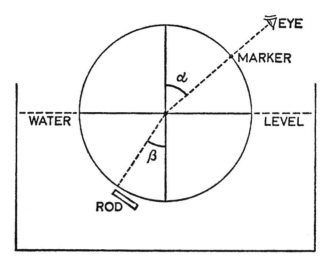

12 Ptolemy's experimental investigation of refraction

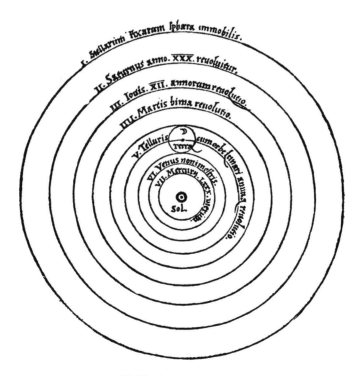

13 The Copernican system

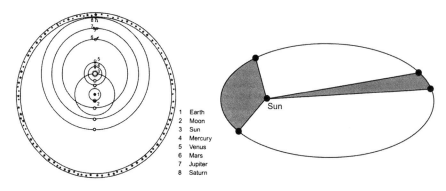

1	Earth
2	Moon
3	Sun
4	Mercury
5	Venus
6	Mars
7	Jupiter
8	Saturn

14 Tycho Brahe's system (left). Kepler's first two laws of planetary motion (right)

15 Galileo's telescopic view of the moon

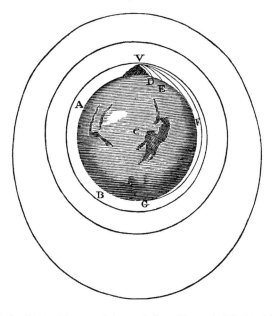

16 Projectile in orbit around the earth, from Newton's *Principia*, 1687

Another treatise entitled *Sphaerica* was written about AD 100 by Menelaus of Alexandria, who generalizes a number of theorems from the work of Theodosius. The work is in three books, of which the third contains the well-known 'theorem of Menelaus', one of the most fundamental relationships in the application of spherical trigonometry to astronomy.

Hipparchus also wrote a treatise entitled *Against the Geography of Eratosthenes,* now lost except for fragments. Here he gives a detailed criticism of the work of Eratosthenes, but he appears to have accepted his estimate that the circumference of the earth is 252,000 stades. But he did not use this measurement to compute the sizes and distances of the sun and moon in *stades.*

Hipparchus' work on geography is known principally through the Greek geographer Strabo. The lifetime of Strabo (64/63 BC–*ca.* AD 25) extended from the end of the Ptolemaic period through the first half-century of the Roman imperial era. He was born at Amaseia in the Pontus, and in his youth he studied first at Nysa in Asia Minor, then in Alexandria, and later in Rome. He lived in Alexandria in the years 25–20 BC and may have studied in the great library, where he would have read the works of Eratosthenes and other Greek geographers whom he mentions. His earlier historical work is lost, but his more important *Geographica* in 17 books has survived.

The first two books of the *Geographica* are a general introduction; Books 3 and 4 deal with Spain and Gaul; 5 and 6 with Italy and Sicily, 7 with northern Europe, 8–10 with Greek lands, 11–14 with Asia Minor and the eastern Aegean islands, 15 with India and Iran, 16 with Assyria, Babylonia, Syria, Phoenicia, Palestine and Arabia, 17 with Egypt, Ethiopia and northern Libya.

Strabo followed Eratosthenes in showing the *oikoumene,* or inhabited world, as a single ocean-girth land-mass comprising Europe, Asia, Africa and their associated islands. He represented the *oikoumene* as being entirely north of the equator on a sphere 25,200 miles in circumference, extending eastward for about 7,000 miles along a parallel drawn from Spain through Rhodes to the Ganges, and northward for some 3,000 miles along the main meridian drawn through Rhodes. He followed Hipparchus in dividing the equator into 360 degrees and establishing parallels of north latitude and meridian lines of longitude. He also followed his predecessors in adopting the notion of five zones in latitude: north frigid (uninhabitable), north temperate (inhabited), torrid (partly uninhabitable), south temperate (habitable) and south frigid (uninhabited).

Strabo went beyond Eratosthenes and his other predecessors in adding encyclopedic descriptions 'of things on land and sea, animals, plants, fruits, and everything else to be seen in various regions.' He says that near the northern limit of the inhabited world is Ireland, which he calls Ierne, whose 'inhabitants are more savage than the Britons, since they are man-eaters as well as herb-eaters, and since, further, they count it an honourable thing, when their fathers die, to devour them, and openly to have intercourse, not only with the other women, but with their mothers and sisters.'

Strabo, as is evident from the above, was given to adding fabulous tales in his description of those who lived in the more remote regions of the *oikoumene*, and he also made frequent historical and mythological digressions. His historical digressions include interesting information about the notable people who were associated with the places he describes, such as Miletus: 'Notable men were born at Miletus: Thales, one of the Seven Wise Men, the first to begin the science of natural philosophy and mathematics among the Greeks, and his pupil Anaximander and again the pupil of the latter, Anaximenes, and also Hecataeus, the author of the *History* ... .'

One of the most interesting of his mythological digressions concerns the Amazons, the fabled women warriors who, according to Strabo, once lived 'on the borders of the Gagarians, in the northern foothills of those parts of the Caucasian Mountains which are called Ceraunian.' He goes on to describe the Amazons and their way of life:

> The Amazons spend the rest of their time off to themselves, performing their several individual tasks, such as ploughing, planting, pasturing cattle, and particularly in training horses, though the bravest engage mostly in hunting on horseback and practice warlike exercise; that the right breast of all are seared when they are infants, so that they can easily use their right arm for every needed purpose, and especially that of throwing the javelin ... . They have two special months in the spring in which they go up into the neighbouring mountain which separates them and the Gagarians. The Gagarians also, in accordance with an ancient custom, go up thither to offer sacrifices with the Amazons and also to have intercourse with them for the sake of begetting children, doing these in secrecy at random with any Amazon; and after making them pregnant they send them away; and the females that are born are retained by the Amazons themselves, but the males are to the Gagarians to be brought up.

Strabo devoted much space to discussions of the ideas of earlier writers concerning the natural phenomena that had formed the *oikoumene*, particularly Aristotle's theories about earthquakes and volcanic activity, and

Strato's belief that the Mediterranean had once been a lake, before the rivers that emptied into it caused it to overflow and break through the straits of Gibraltar, a theory that has been substantiated by modern scientists.

Strabo's boundless interest makes his work utterly unlike any other surviving work of ancient geography, giving us a picture of what was known of the *oikoumene* in the late Hellenistic period, when, as he remarks, 'the spread of the empires of the Romans and the Parthians has presented to geographers of today a considerable addition to our empirical knowledge of geography, just as did the campaign of Alexander to geographers of earlier times, as Eratosthenes points out.'

CHAPTER 11

INGENIOUS DEVICES

Although Archimedes did not have a high regard for his inventions, dismissing them as being merely the 'diversions of a geometry at play', his ingenious mechanical devices represent the beginning of a tradition in the Greek world that produced a number of remarkable inventors, most notably Ctesibius of Alexandria, Philo of Byzantium and Hero of Alexandria.

Little is known about the life of Ctesibius other than that he was the son of a barber in Alexandria and flourished around 270 BC. This date comes from an epigram quoted by Athenaeus of Naucratis concerning a singing cornucopia that Ctesibius made for Arsinoë, sister and wife of Ptolemy I Soter. Despite his fame Ctesibius seems to have ended his days in abject poverty, at least according to an anecdote told by Diogenes Laertius concerning the philosopher Arcesilaus. As Diogenes tells the story, Arcesilaus, 'when he had gone to visit Ctesibius who was ill, seeing him in great distress from want, he secretly slipped his purse under his pillow; and when Ctesibus found it, "This," he said, "is the amusement of Arcesilaus".'

Ctesibius wrote a book about his inventions, now lost, some of which are described by the Latin writer Vitruvius in his *De architectura*, dedicated shortly before 27 BC Vitruvius, in his description of a water clock made by Ctesibius, mentions one of his other inventions:

> Methods of making water clocks have been investigated by the same writers, and first of all by Ctesibius the Alexandrian, who also discovered the natural pressure of air and pneumatic principles .... Preëminent for natural ability and great industry, he is said to have amused himself with ingenious devices. For example, wishing to hang a mirror in his father's shop in such a way that, on being lowered and raised again, its weight should be raised by means of a concealed cord, he employed the following mechanical contrivance.

114

Vitruvius goes on to describe how the mirror was raised and lowered by a system of pulleys, activated by a lead ball falling down a pipe: 'As the weight fell into the narrow limits of the pipe, it naturally compressed the enclosed air, and, as its fall was rapid, it forced the mass of compressed air through the outlet into the open air, thus producing a distinct sound by the concussion.'

Vitruvius then writes of how 'Ctesibius, observing that sounds and tones were produced by the contact between the free air and that which had been forced from the pipe, made use of this principle in the construction of the first water organs. He also devised methods of raising water, automatic contrivances, and amusing things of many kinds, including among them the construction of water clocks.'

Vitruvius gives a detailed description of a water clock invented by Ctesibius. This was based on the ancient clepsydra, in which time was measured through the rate at which water flowed from a container. Since the rate of flow varies with the level of water in the clepsydra, Ctesibius kept the level from changing by having water flow into it at a constant rate from a second container. This in turn was fed from a third container, with a floating valve cutting off the supply to the second container as soon as its level dropped perceptibly. This floating valve is similar to the mechanism used in the modern flush toilet. After the toilet is flushed, the bulb sinks as the water level goes down, with its metal arm opening the valve so that water flows into the cabinet. The incoming water raises the bulb up to its original level, at which point the valve closes and the flow is stopped. Vitruvius describes how this steady flow of water is used to measure time:

> A regular flow of water through the orifice raises an inverted bowl, called by mechanicians the 'cork' or 'drum.' To this are attached a rack and a revolving drum, both fitted with teeth at regular intervals. These teeth, acting upon one another, induce a measured revolution and movement.
>
> Other racks and other drums, similarly toothed and subject to the same motion, give rise by their revolution to various kinds of motions. By which figures are moved, cones revolve, pebbles or eggs fall, trumpets sound, and other incidental effects take place.

The floating drum was attached to a rod surmounted by a figure with a pointer, which indicated the time on a scale. Vitruvius describes how the hours were marked, taking into account the changing of the length of the daylight hours with the seasons, as was the custom in ancient times.

The hours are marked on these clocks on a column or pilaster, and a figure emerging from the bottom points to them with a rod throughout the whole day. Their decrease or increase in length with the different days and months must be adjusted by inserting or withdrawing wedges .... . Let the hours be marked off transversely on the column from the analemma, and let the lines of the months also be marked upon the column. Then let the column be made to revolve, in such a way that, as it turns continuously towards the figure and the rod with which the emerging figure points to the hours, it may make the hours short or long according to the respective months.

The analemma mentioned by Vitruvius is a two-dimensional projective drawing of the celestial sphere, its purpose being to determine the position of the sun at any time in the day throughout the year, which one needs to know in designing a sundial. A number of Greek mathematicians and astronomers wrote on the design of sundials, and they must have used some sort of analemma, but the only extant Greek work on the subject is by Ptolemy, who is later than Vitruvius.

Vitruvius also describes another invention of Ctesibius, a machine 'which raises water to a height.' He goes on to tell of many other ingenious devices of various kinds invented by Ctesibius. 'This, however,' he writes, referring to the water pump, 'is not the only apparatus which Ctesibius is said to have thought out, but many more of various kinds are shown by him to produce effects, borrowed from nature, by means of water pressure and compression of the air; as, for example, blackbirds singing by means of waterworks and ... figures that drink and move, and other things that are pleasing to the eye and the ear.'

The siphon has also been attributed to Ctesibius, but since none of his works have survived the invention of this device is often credited instead to either Philo of Byzantium or Hero of Alexandria. According to Philo, Ctesibius invented two types of catapults, one powered by compressed air and the other by bronze springs.

Little is known of Philo except that he was born in Byzantium, the city that was later to become Constantinople, and that he travelled to Rhodes and Alexandria, probably as a state-sponsored military engineer. While in Alexandria he was shown a catapult powered by a bronze spring that had recently been invented by Ctesibius, and from this it inferred that Philo flourished around 250 BC.

Philo is known for only one work, a great mechanical treatise called *Syntaxis tis mechanicis*, divided into nine books, of which only four have survived. As reconstructed by A. G. Drachmann the table of contents is: 1. Introduction; 2. On the lever (*Mochlica*); 3. On the building of seaports (*Limenopoeica*);

4. On catapults (*Belopoeica*); 5. On pneumatics (*Pneumatica*); 6. On automatic theatres (*Automaticapoeica*); 7. On the building of fortresses (*Paraskeuastica*); 8. On besieging and defending towns (Poliorcetica); 9. On secret letters (*Peri Epsilon*) and other strategems and weapons useful in besieging a city.

Books 4, 5, 7 and 8 are extant, the others are lost. The Greek text exists for Book 4 and for parts of Books 7 and 8. Up until the beginning of the twentieth century Book 5, the *Pneumatica*, was known only through a Latin translation of the first 16 chapters, but then Carra de Vaux discovered three manuscripts that allowed him to publish a fuller Arabic text.

Book 4, the *Belopoeica*, is devoted to the design and construction of catapults. Here Philo says that he talked about the catapults with experts in Alexandria, and also examined catapults on Rhodes. He also says he spoke with technicians who described to him the bronze-spring catapult that Ctesibius had made, although he did not actually see one himself. He gives the laws involved in designing a catapult that would fire a missile twice as heavy as that hurled by another catapult. This was equivalent to solving the famous problem of doubling the cube, since the weight of a spherical missile is proportional to the cube of its diameter.

The first eight chapters of Book 5, the *Pneumatica*, give descriptions of experiments which were, according to Drachmann, 'almost certainly taken from Ctesibius, the founder of the science of pneumatics.' Drachmann goes on to say that the rest of the book 'consists of descriptions of pneumatic toys – trick jars, inexhaustible bowls, and other apparatus for parlor magic.' Among these pneumatic toys is an automaton in which a bird and her chicks nesting in the branches of a tree are threatened by a snake, all of the action being produced through the motion of floats rising and falling in a vessel filled by either water or wine.

One of the experiments described by Philo in Book 5 involves a thermoscope, a device demonstrating the expansion of air when heated. The device consists of a hollow lead sphere, a vessel filled with water, and a bent tube which has one end in the sphere and the other in the vessel, in both cases with the end close to the bottom. Philo describes what happens when the sphere is heated in various ways:

> I say, then, that if you expose the sphere to the sun, part of the air enclosed in the tube will pass out when the sphere becomes hot. This will be evident because the air will descend from the tube into the water, agitating it and producing a series of bubbles. Now if the sphere is put back in the shade … the water will rise and pass through the tube until it descends into the sphere. If you put the sphere back in the sun the water will return to the

vessel, but it will flow back to the sphere once more if you place the sphere in the shade .... In fact, if you heat the sphere with fire, or even if you pour hot water over it, the result will be the same. And if the sphere is then cooled, water pours from the vessel to the sphere.

Another experiment described in Book 5 is one demonstrating the effects of combustion on air. Philo describes the device, which anticipates experiments done in the late eighteenth century by Lavoisier to demonstrate oxidation:

> Hence we shall prove that a place cannot be empty of air and of all other bodies as well. For example, pour water into a vessel, A. In the center of A let a sort of candle-holder, B, be set up protruding over the water, and let a lighted candle, C, be placed at the top of B. Over C invert vessel D in such a way that its mouth is near the water [i. e., barely immersed] and the candle is in the center of D. A short while after this is done you will see water rise from the lower to the upper vessel. Now this will not happen except for the reason we have indicated, namely that the air enclosed in vessel D is destroyed by the fire, because air cannot remain in proximity to fire. After the air has been destroyed by the fire, the latter will raise the water in proportion to the amount of air which is lost .... Thus the air in this vessel (D) placed over the candle is destroyed because it is, so to speak, destroyed by the fire.

Philo also describes two ingenious devices in Book 5 of the *Pneumatica*, the most interesting of which is an eight-sided inkwell that he describes as follows:

> We may make an inkstand which is octagonal, hexagonal, square, pentagonal or of any prismatic form in which glass is shaped. This inkstand may be used for writing no matter which face is uppermost. No matter how you place the ink-stand it always presents on its upper face an opening to receive the pen, without any ink upsetting. You may insert the pen, obtain ink and write. Suppose the inkstand is hexagonal, as you see it. In the interior there is a ring on a pivot AB; within this ring is another ring on another pivot CD. Within this second ring is a cup on a pivot EZ. It is this cup which is the inkwell .... Its construction resembles that of a censer which turns without losing its equilibrium. In constructing this inkstand measure accurately and make adjustments carefully so that, when you place it on any side, your pen will enter the top of the inkwell.

This device is now known as 'Cardan's suspension,' named for the Italian mathematician Geronimo Cardano (1501–1576), who described the mechanism in detail but did not claim to have invented it. The basis for the mechanism is a set of two or more gimbals, one mounted on the other with their axes mutually perpendicular, which allows an object mounted on the innermost gimbal to remain fixed when the orientation of the device is changed. Modern shipboard compasses and barometers are mounted on two-axis gimbals so that they remain upright as the vessel pitches and rolls. Inertial navigation systems for ships, aircraft and spacecraft use gyroscopes mounted on three or more orthogonal gimbals to sense rotation about all three axes in space, all based on the suspension in Philo's ingenious inkwell.

Book 7, the *Paraskeuastica*, comprises 87 chapters devoted to the techniques of fortifying a city: building walls and towers, digging moats, constructing palisades and putting catapults in place. These techniques would have been exemplified in the defence walls of Byzantium, which withstood a memorable siege by Philip of Macedon in 340–339 BC.

Book 8, the *Poliorcetica*, is concerned with the practices involved in defending a besieged city. The book is divided into two section, the first of which has 57 chapters on preparing a city to withstand a siege, including the stockpiling of food and other materials, rationing and communications, the latter including an optical telegraph employing a clepsydra to signal allies beyond enemy lines. The second section is devoted to tactics to be used in defending both the land and sea walls of a coastal city such as Byzantium.

The ninth and last book, divided into 111 short chapters, is devoted to the use of catapults and other weapons in besieging a city, as well as various strategems including secret letters, cryptography, bribery, poisoning of the city's water sources and cutting off its supplies of food to starve the enemy into submission.

Philo's other devices include the earliest-known application of a chain drive, which he used in designing an automatic repeating crossbow. He also designed the first-known escapement mechanism, which he used in constructing a washstand automaton. Philo noted of this device that 'its construction is similar to that of clocks,' indicating that such escapement mechanisms were already used in ancient water clocks, whereas they were not employed in mechanical clocks in Europe until the late thirteenth century.

The tradition of Ctesibius and Philo was continued by Hero of Alexandria, who absorbed and developed the works of his predecessors. Virtually nothing is known of Hero's life, though it would seem that he was associated with the Museum in Alexandria, where he probably taught mathematics and physics, particularly pneumatics and mechanics, and wrote textbooks on these subjects as well as other works. The dates of his lifetime have long been a matter of speculation, and various scholars have suggested times varying from the second BC to the third century AD. But a more definite dating was finally established by Otto Neugebauer in a paper published in 1938, where he computed that a lunar eclipse described by Hero in his *Dioptra* took place in AD 62.

The extant works that have been attributed to Hero are divided into two categories, technical and mathematical. The technical works are *Pneumatica, Mechanica, Dioptra, Belopiica, Automata, Catoptrica* and *Cheirobalistra.* The mathematical books are *Definitiones, Metrica, Geometrica, Stereometrica, Geodaesia, De mensuris* and *Commentary on Euclid's Elements.* According to Drachmann: 'All the technical books, except the *Cheirobalistra,* seem to have been written by Hero; of the mathematical books only the *Definitiones* and the *Metrica* are direct from his hand. The others are, according to J. L. Heiberg, "Byzantine schoolbooks with so many additions that it is impossible to know what is genuinely Heronian and what is not".'

The *Pneumatica* is by far the longest of Hero's works, comprising an introduction and two books, the first with 43 chapters and the second with 37. A slightly different text, translated into English in 1851 by Bennet Woodcroft, has 78 chapters. The introduction discusses the nature of a vacuum in air, probably derived from Strato, and phenomena involving the pressure of air and water. Each of the chapters describes a device operated by air and water pressure, illustrated with figures that were probably drawn by Hero himself. The devices include useful mechanisms including siphons, a valve for a pump, a fire-engine, a self-trimming lamp, a water clock, and an organ powered by a windmill. But, as Drachmann remarks 'all the rest are playthings, puppet shows, or apparatuses for parlor magic: trick jars that give out wine or water separately or in constant proportions, singing birds and sounding trumpets, puppets that move when a fire is lit on an altar, animals that drink when they are offered water ....' Chapter 21, for example, describes an automaton in the form of a 'Sacrificial Vessel which flows only when Money is introduced', the ancestor of the modern coin-operated vending machine.

One of these frivolous automata is described in Chapter 14, where Hero writes of a device in which the figure of a bird he calls a black-cap is perched on the branches of a tree and is heard whistling when water pours from a lionhead fountain through a funnel into a tank. He explains how the sound is produced, and then goes on to write of more elaborate automata involving several different birds in various settings:

These sounds are produced through pipes; but the quality of the sounds will vary as the pipes are more or less fine, or longer, or shorter; and as a larger or smaller portion of the pipe is immersed in the water; so that by this means the distinct notes of many birds can be produced. The figures of several different birds are arranged near a fountain, or in a cave, or in any place where there is running water: near them sits an owl, which, apparently of her own accord, turns at one time towards the birds, and then away from them; and when the owl looks away the birds sing, when she looks at them they are mute; and this may be repeated frequently.

One of the most famous of these devices is Hero's steam engine, known in Greek as an *aeolipile*, in which a hollow ball is made to rotate by two jets of steam escaping from it at either end of a diameter (see Figure 12).

The *Mechanica* was preserved only in an Arabic translation, published in 1893 with a French translation and in 1900 with a German translation. An English translation of many of the chapters was published in 1962 by Drachmann as part of a work on Greek and Roman technology. Designed as a textbook for architects and builders, the *Mechanica* is divided into three books. Book 1 covers the theory and technical knowledge required for an architect, including the notions of centre of gravity, equilibrium, and the theory of the balance, largely derived from Archimedes. Book 2 covers the theory of the five simple machines: the lever, pulley, wheel and axle, screw and wedge or inclined plane, along with numerous practical problems and applications. Book 3 describes devices for transport and miscellaneous devices and practical applications.

As Pappus remarks in his *Mathematical Collection*, which gives an abridged account of Hero's theory of simple machines: 'Now both Hero and Philo have shown that these machines, though they differ considerably from one another in their external form, are reducible to a single principle.' Hero demonstrates that the basic principle in all these machines is the law of the lever. He also makes the point, referring to the wheel and axle, that 'In this and similar machines in which great force is developed there is a retardation since we must use more time as the moving force is smaller than the weight to be moved.'

The *Dioptra* contains a description of the surveying instrument of that name, which served the same purpose as the modern theodolite. The instrument is described in the first five chapters, after which Hero goes on to deal with the measurement of heights and distances. He also gives solutions of engineering problems, such as how to dig a tunnel through a mountain working from both ends, fixing the directions so that the excavations will meet in the middle. Hero also shows how the dioptra can be used in astronomical observations, particularly the angular separation of two stars in the celestial sphere.

Chapter 34 of the *Dioptra* describes a hodometer powered by the wheel of a car to measure road distances. Chapter 38 develops a method for finding the distance between Alexandria and Rome by simultaneously observing an eclipse of the moon in the two cities. This is the lunar eclipse that Neugebauer dated to AD 62, establishing the only known date in Hero's life.

The *Belopiika* contains the description of a type of crossbow called a gastraphetes, as well as those of two catapults powered by stretched animal sinews and worked by winches.

The *Automata*, known in English as the *Automatic Theater*, deals with two automated puppet shows, one of them mobile and the other stationary. The first of these, which moved among the audience under its own power, showed Dionysus pouring out a libation while bacchantes danced around him to the sounds of trumpets and drums. The other represented a naval battle in which Athena destroyed the ships of Ajax with thunder and lightning.

The *Catoptrica* survives only in a Latin version. The book deals with reflection from both plane and curved mirrors, as well as instructions as to how to arrange mirrors for optical illusions. Hero's optical demonstrations were based on the theory that light proceeded from the eye in linear rays to the object being viewed, and on striking a mirror the incident and reflected rays make the same angle with the perpendicular to the surface. His proof of the law of reflection makes the assumption that a light ray will travel the shortest possible path, a principle that would be revived in the modern study of optics.

As he writes, referring to the drawing in Figure 11: 'If one mirror (ZH into which the observer looks) is kept unmoved, while the other (DE, behind the observer) is moved up and down, the ray will reach a point where the heel [Ki, in the figure on the left] of the observer will appear in the mirror and he will think that he is flying.'

Barulkos, 'the lifter of weights', is a description of a device which would allow a workman to lift 200 times his own weight, using an arrangement of cogwheels and winches.

Hero's mathematical treatise, the *Definitiones*, contains 133 definitions of geometrical terms, obviously intended for a course in geometry and mensuration. According to Michael S. Mahoney, the *Definitiones* 'is a valuable source of knowledge about alternative notions of geometry in antiquity and about what was taught in the classroom.'

Hero puts the lie to the notion that Greek science neglected practice in favour of theory, for his inventions and demonstrations, together with his application of mathematics to problems in physics, make him a forerunner of the experimental science that developed during the seventeenth-century Scientific Revolution.

CHAPTER 12

THE ART OF HEALING

Greek medicine reached its peak in the second century AD with the work of Galen of Pergamum, whose writings dominated medical teaching and research up to the time of the Renaissance.

The most comprehensive collection of Galen's extant works is the Greek-Latin edition by C. G. Kühn in 22 thick volumes published at Leipzig in the years 1821–33, all together coming to some 20,000 pages. As George Sarton writes in his biography of Galen, his writings covered many fields: 'anatomy and physiology, theory of the pulse, hygiene, dietetics, pathology, therapeutics, pharmacy, medical polemics, medical philosophy, logic and philosophy, philology, - in short, the universe of thought as it was refracted by the brain of an illustrious physician.'

Galen was born in Pergamum in AD 129, by which time all of the Greek world was under Roman rule, the last of the Pergamene kings having bequeathed his kingdom to Rome in 133 BC. Pergamum prospered under Roman rule and its population reached a peak of 150,000 in the mid-second century AD. The city had been a centre of Greek culture since the early Hellenistic period, with a renowned library. During the Roman imperial era it was famed for its Asclepieum, the great healing shrine of Asclepius, which attracted pilgrims and patients from all over the Graeco-Roman world. The buildings of the Asclepieum that one sees today, restored during the past half century, were erected early in the lifetime of Galen, and it was here that he began his medical studies and researches.

Most of what is known of Galen's life comes from his own writings. He says that his first teacher was his father Nikon, an architect and geometer, who taught him mathematics, grammar, logic and philosophy. When Galen was 14, Nikon had him attend lectures on the four great schools of Greek philosophy: Platonism, Aristotelianism, Stoicism and Epicureanism. Galen was most deeply influenced by Platonism, just as Hippocratic thought shaped his thought in medicine, and he connects the two in his great treatise *On the Doctrines of Hippocrates and Plato.*

When Galen was 16, Nikon was persuaded by a dream to have his son begin medical studies as well. He thereupon arranged for Galen to study at the Asclepieum with the famous anatomist Satyrus, who had come to Pergamum four years before.

Galen studied with Satyrus for four years, during which time he wrote several medical treatises, three of which he himself names. These are *On the Anatomy of the Uturus,* which he wrote at the request of a midwife, *The Diagnosis of Diseases of the Eye*, now lost, and *On Medical Experience.* The latter work reports on a two-day debate on medicine at Smyrna between the physicians Pelops and Philippus, and was written at the end of Galen's studies with Satyrus.

In *On Medical Experience* Galen refers to an earlier treatise called *On the Best Sect,* which must have been his first works. Another work on the same subject entitled *On the Best Sect, for Thrasybulos,* is sometimes attributed to Galen, but it is probably one of the many forgeries written under his name. Here the word 'sect' refers not to a religious group but to a school of medical thought, of which there were six in Galen's time, three of them from ancient Greece and the three others 'modern', in other words, from the Roman era. As Sarton writes in his biography of Galen, quoting from Galen's *de libris propis*: 'One of his Roman colleagues, an old anatomist called Martialis, asked, "To what sect does Galen belong?" and was answered: "He belongs to none and calls slaves those who accept as final the teachings of Hippocrates or Praxagoras or anybody else."'

The most ancient sect was that of Hippocrates, whom all physicians of antiquity venerated, with some claiming that all medical knowledge was to be found exclusively in the Hippocratic corpus. The Dogmatic sect emerged in the fourth century BC under the influence of Aristotle, its early leaders being Diocles of Carystus and Praxagoras of Cos, who tried to reconcile Hippocratic ideas with those that had emerged in Sicily from the time of Empedocles. The Empirical sect was founded in the first half of the second century BC by Serapion of Alexandria, whose practice, as Sarton notes, was based 'on watching and vigilance, clinical stories and if necessary on analogies. His empirical tendencies were such that he did not dare to reject popular remedies.'

The earliest and most important of the 'modern' sects was that of the Methodists, founded in Rome by Asclepiades of Bithynia early in the first century BC. Asclepiades was influenced by the atomic theory of Epicurus and believed that the body was composed of invisible particles, good health coming from their free and balanced motion through pores in the body, disease from a blockage, flood or imbalance. But, as Vivian Nutton, remarks, 'What gained Asclepiades his reputation in Rome, however, was less his theories than his therapies. His slogan "swiftly, safely, pleasantly," an adaptation of ideas in the Hippocratic corpus, and his liberal use of wine and gentle exercise were as notorious among later opponents as they were congenial to his patients.'

The two other sects, Pneumaticism and Eclecticism, emerged in the latter half of the first century BC. The founder of the first of these sects was Athenaeus of Attaleia, whose ideas are described by Nutton as 'a mixture of Stoicism and Hellenistic dogmatic, or Hippocratic, medicine.'

The Eclectic sect was founded by two followers of Athenaeus, Agatheinus of Sparta and Archigenes of Apamea. Agatheinus combined ideas and practices he had learned from Athenaeus with material from Methodist and Empiricist sources. Following Athenaeus, he devoted much attention to the therapeutic effects of bathing, recommending cold baths rather than hot.

Nikon died when Galen was 20, and he decided to leave Pergamum for Smyrna. There he began studying with Pelops, whom he calls his second medical teacher, and at the same time he attended the lectures of the Platonist Albinus. While at Smyrna he wrote a treatise in three books on the movements of the lungs and thorax.

Galen then moved to Corinth, where he stayed only briefly before going on to Alexandria, where he remained for about five years. While in Alexandria he studied anatomy and medicine under a number of teachers, most notably the anatomist Heracleinos. Here for the first time he had the opportunity to examine human skeletons, though not cadavers, because of the Greek taboo on desecrating the human body.

Galen returned to Pergamum in the autumn of 157, when he would have been about 28. Soon after his return he was appointed as surgeon of the gladiatorial troupe owned by the high priest of Asclepius, who was also president of the athletic games celebrated in the Asclepieum. He proved to be exceptionally competent, as Nutton notes in describing this phase of Galen's career:

Galen's duty was to keep his gladiators alive, and not only in the immediate aftermath of their appearance in the arena. He attended to their diet, cleaned and stitched up their wounds, principally to their thighs, arms and buttocks (which would produce much blood, but not necessarily lasting damage), and oversaw their general health. He claims that under his supervision only two gladiators died in his first period in office, compared with

126

the sixteen lost by his predecessor, and he was thus re-engaged by the next high-priest, seven and a half months later, and by his three successors.

Galen left Pergamum in the summer of 161 because of civil strife and moved to Rome, at the beginning of the joint reigns of Marcus Aurelius (r. 161–80) and Lucius Verus (r. 161–69). He successfully treated several prominent patients, including the Aristotelian philosopher Eudemus, who introduced him to the consul Flavius Boethus and other prominent Roman officials. Flavius Boethus commissioned Galen to write his first major works on anatomy and physiology, beginning with the original version of his *Anatomical Procedures.* He also began to give public lectures and demonstrations on anatomy, which attracted high Roman officials as well as famous Greek sophists and rhetoricians who had taken up residence in Rome.

Galen left Rome in the summer of 166 and returned to Pergamum, where he remained for more than two years. Late in 168 he was summoned to attend the emperors Marcus Aurelius and Lucius Verus in Aquileia, near the head of the Adriatic, where they were preparing for a campaign against the German tribes. Shortly after he joined them the emperors left Aquileia to avoid the plague, but Verus had already been infected and died a few days later, early in 169, after which Marcus Aurelius conducted his remains back to Rome for the state funeral. Marcus Aurelius set out on campaign later that year, leaving Galen to look after the health of his son Commodus, the heir apparent. When Commodus succeeded as emperor in 180 Galen remained on friendly terms with him, and when Septimius Severus became emperor in 193 he enjoyed his friendship too.

Aside from a visit to Pergamum in the 190s, Galen remained in Rome or nearby for the rest of his days, serving as one of the court physicians into at least the first decade of the third century. In 192 he suffered the great misfortune of losing many of his treatises in the fire that destroyed the Temple of Peace, where they had been deposited. The latest datable incident in his extant writings refers to an accident that took place during the secular Games of 204. According to Nutton, Galen's treatise *On Theriac, for Piso* 'cannot have been written before 204 and perhaps not before 207.' Nutton also writes of Galen that 'a strong tradition in Arabic authors, perhaps also reflected in Byzantine chronographers, has him dying aged 87 – that is in 216–17. '

Although Galen is renowned for his medical writings he was noted in his own time as a philosopher and philologist. His philosophical writings span the whole of his adult life: *On Medical Experience* was a product of his student days at Smyrna, while his last work, *On My Own Opinions*, was written almost

60 years later. His treatise *That the best doctor is also a philosopher* gives his view that training in philosophy is an essential part of the training of a physician. He gives three reasons for this view, one corresponding to each of the three main branches of philosophy, namely logic, physics and ethics. Logic is necessary, he says, because a physician must be trained in scientific method so as to distinguish between valid and invalid arguments. A knowledge of physics is essential in studying the nature and function of the body and its constituent organs. And a doctor must have a deep understanding of the ethical basis of his profession, which will lead him to despise money and treat his patients without charge, as Galen himself claims to have done.

Only three of his many logical treatises have survived: *On Demonstration, Introduction to Logic* and *Ambiguities of Speech.* The lengthiest of Galen's extant philosophical works is his thesis *On the Doctrines of Hippocrates and Plato*, in which he defends Plato's ideas on physiology and psychology against the Stoics.

Leonard G. Wilson describe Galen's system, which was the basis for the explanation of the physiology of the body up to the time of the English physician and anatomist William Harvey (1578–1657):

> His physiological theories are of particular interest because they included concepts of digestion, assimilation, blood formation, the maintenance of the tissues, nerve function, respiration, the heart beat, the arterial pulse, and the maintenance of vital warmth throughout the body – concepts which together formed a comprehensive and connected account of the functioning of the living animal body.

Galen held that this tripartite physiological system linked body and soul together, explaining why physical and mental states influenced one another. Based on the ancient theory of the four humours – blood, phlegm, bile and black bile – Galen posited nine possible mixtures or temperaments, one of them an exact balance of the four Aristotelian primary qualities – hot, cold, wet and dry – the others with one or two qualities dominating. Each mixture predisposed an individual to certain types of illness; a good physician should determine the particular temperament of his patient and restore it with the proper treatment.

Nutton remarks that 'Later Galenists developed this notion still further so that today terms such as "phlegmatic" and "sanguine" are applied to behavior and attitude rather than to physical condition.'

Galen, in his short treatise on *Whether Blood is Contained in the Arteries in Nature*, refuted the common Greek view that the arteries contain nothing but *pneuma*, and showed that in fact they are always full of blood. Wilson explains how Galen demonstrated that both the left ventricle of the heart and the arteries always contain blood:

> Galen also observed the presence of blood in the arteries of the transparent mesentery, and then he showed experimentally that when he isolated a portion of an artery in a living animal – he tied it off with ligatures so that no blood could flow into it from elsewhere and then opened it – he always found it full of blood. By opening the chest of a living animal he demonstrated that blood was present in the left ventricle of the heart.

Galen's anatomical works include *On Bones, On Veins, On Veins and Arteries, On the Anatomy of Muscles, On the Use of Parts* and *On Anatomical Procedures*. The latter, a huge work in 15 books, is a detailed guide to dissection, which he says he first learned from demonstrations in Alexandria.

> Make it your serious endeavor not only to learn precisely from books the form of each bone but also to examine assiduously with your own eyes the human bones themselves. This is quite easy at Alexandria because the physicians there employ ocular demonstrations (*autopsia*) in teaching their students. For this reason, if for no other, try to visit Alexandria. But if you cannot, it is still not impossible to see something of human bones. I, at least, have done so very often on the breaking open of a grave or tomb .... If you have not the luck to see something of this sort, choose an ape, and having removed the flesh, observe each bone precisely.

Galen's treatise *On Anatomical Procedures* also deals with vivisection. In Book VII, chapter 15 he describes his examination of the beating heart of a living animal, after first giving detailed instructions on the surgical procedures in exposing the organ:

> All this will be clear to you at once when the heart is exposed. As time passes, the movements of each ventricle become brief, long pauses intervening, and also there becomes apparent the expansion [*diastole*] of the right ventricle, accomplishing its function according to its own nature, as you will see particularly when those parts approach immobility. For in each ventricle the apex stops moving first and then the part next to it, and so on until only the bases are still left moving. When even these have stopped an ill-defined movement at short intervals is still seen in the 'auricles.' The cause of this phenomenon we must seek at leisure, for it's not reasonable that its outgrowth should move longer than the heart itself. But here we do not aim to seek causes in this matter, but observed anatomical phenomena only.

Galen made a number of errors, the most notorious, as G. E. R. Lloyd points out, being 'the belief that blood is carried over directly from the right into the left side of the heart through the interventicular septum, the solid musculo-membraneous partition that divides the two sides of the heart.'

Galen's methods in proceeding to a diagnosis, course of treatment and prognosis are described in detail by Nutton, who notes that Galen always takes full credit for his successes but lays the blame for any failures elsewhere:

> Having made his observations and gathered as much information as he could, Galen then proceeded to a diagnosis and forecast. His usual method was to employ logic to establish a differential diagnosis, classifying the patient's condition with ever-increasing prediction until he could identify what was wrong and assign a cause .... Once a diagnosis had been established and the chain of causation identified, one could select an appropriate treatment to restore the functional or humoral imbalance. At the same time, one could predict the future outcome of the illness with confidence .... By following the method of prognosis carefully one could never fail – or if one did, the fault did not lie with the physician .... Credit for success thus rested with Galen, and with those who followed him, responsibility for failure with others.

Dietetics was an important part of Galen's treatment of illness, and for him, as Nutton remarks, this 'encompassed one's whole lifestyle, including exercise, sleep and environment.' Nutton goes on to say that 'Most of Galen's recommendations would meet with the approval of a modern dietician, with one major exception. He placed an almost total ban on fresh fruit, which he considered a frequent cause of illness. His father had warned him of the dangers of eating such fruit, but he had once been led astray by friends into eating a lot of fresh fruit in autumn. The result was an acute illness.'

Nutton remarks that 'If dietetics failed, Galen turned next to drugs, seeking to regulate the body's original balance.' His major works in this field are *On the Properties of Simples* and his two huge treatise *On the Compositions of Drugs*, which Nutton says 'all formed part of a single overall conception of therapeutics and of a project that occupied him for more than half a century.'

Nutton goes on from this to give a general appraisal of the man who was to be known in Renaissance Europe as 'The Prince of Physicians':

> Galen's pharmacological writings thus display his typical combination of intelligent reasoning, detailed observation, and empirical testing alongside

a passionate urge to correct the mistakes of others and to demonstrate his own superiority. He saw his therapeutics, the healing of the sick, as the culmination of a range of other skills, in logic, argument, understanding and experiment. The ideal doctor, as represented by Hippocrates and by the statue of Pergamene Asclepius, combines reason and experience, book learning and personal skills, anatomical knowledge and speculation about the natural world in general ... enough remains in his writings to show how he came to acquire so quickly the reputation of being a great and effective doctor.

Much of Galen's pharmacological information comes from earlier sources, most notably Dioscorides of Anazarbus (fl. AD 50–70). Dioscorides' only extant work is a treatise of five books in Greek, known in its Latin translation as *De materia medica*. John M. Riddle notes that in *De material medica* Dioscorides 'discusses over 600 plants, thirty-five animal products and ninety minerals in simple, concise Greek .... Of the approximately 827 entries, only about 130 substances are described in the Hippocratic corpus .... Galen, always a severe critic, acknowledged Dioscorides' work to be the best of its kind and showed his respect by numerous citations.'

According to Galen, Dioscorides was born in Anazarbus, a Greek city north-east of Tarsus in Asia Minor. Otherwise, virtually all that is known about the life of Dioscorides comes from a dedicatory letter attached to *De material medica*. The letter is addressed to his friend and mentor Laecanius Areius of Tarsus, under whom he seems to have studied pharmacology. Dioscorides mentions in the letter that he had 'led a soldier's life', which has led to the supposition that he served as a physician in the Roman army, perhaps in the Armenian wars of 55–63.

According to Riddle, *De Materia medica* is organized by subject matter, where the number of items in the various books is approximate 'since modern subspecies do not always correspond to Dioscorides' varieties.' He writes that 'book I (129 items), deals with aromatics, oils, salves, trees, and shrubs (liquids, gums, and fruits); book II (186), with animals, animal parts, animal products, cereals, pot herbs, and sharp herbs; book III (158), with roots, juices, herbs and seeds; book IV (192), with roots and herbs not previously mentioned; and book V (162), with wines and minerals.'

Dioscorides claims that his knowledge of medicinal herbs was gained both from historical research and direct experience in his travels, which seem to have taken him all over the Greek world, with references farther afield probably deriving from the reports of travellers. He describes the scope of his work on pharmacology, which he believed to be an essential element in what he called the Art of Healing:

> Now it is obvious that a Treatise on Medicines is necessary, for it is conjoined to the whole Art of Healing, and by itself yields a mighty assistance to every part. And because its scope may be enlarged both in the direction of methods of preparation, and of mixture, and of experiments on diseases and because a knowledge of each separate medicine contributes much hereunto, we will include matter that is familiar and closely allied, that the book may be complete.

Dioscorides writes at length about the great care that must be taken 'both in the storing up and in the gathering of herbs each at its due season, for it is according to this that medicines either do their work, or become quite ineffectual ... . Therefore the man who will observe his herbs oftentimes and in divers places will acquire the greatest knowledge of them.'

> We ought to gather herbs when the weather is clear, for there is a great difference whether it be dry or rainy when the gathering is made. The place also makes a difference: whether the localities be mountainous and high, whether they lie open to the wind, whether they be cold and dry; upon this the strongness of drugs depend ... . It must also not be forgotten that herbs frequently ripen earlier or later according to the characteristics of the country and the temperature of the year, and that some of them by an innate property bear flowers and leaves in winter, others flower twice in a year. Now it behooves anyone who would be a skilful herbalist, to be present when the plants first shoot out of the earth, when they are fully grown, and when they begin to fade.

One of the medicinal plants described by Dioscorides is cannabis, which he writes of in Book III of *De material medica*, distinguishing between the cultivated and wild varieties, the latter known in Greek as *Althaea cannabina*:

> Cannabis: a plant useful for the plaiting of the most resilient ropes. It bears leaves like the ash but bad-smelling, has long hollow stems, and a round edible fruit which if eaten in quantity quenches sexual desire; pureed when green it's good for analgesic ear-drops. Wild cannabis bears shoots like those of the elm but darker and smaller; it's a cubit tall; the leaves are like the tame sort, rougher and darker, the flowers reddish like rose campion, and the seeds and roots like mallow.

Each of the items was illustrated by a miniature painting of the entire plant, including the roots, flower and fruit. The Roman senator Cassiodorus, writing in the sixth century, advises the monks of his monastery at Vivarium to read *De materia medica*: 'If you have not sufficient facility in reading Greek then you can turn to the herbal of Dioscorides, which describes and draws the herbs of the field with wonderful faithfulness.'

De material medica survived in Byzantium as well as in Arabic and Latin translations. There is also at least one Old English version of Dioscorides. The printing of Greek medical texts began in 1499 with the publication of *De materia medica* by Aldus Mantius in Venice. This programme continued the following year with the first volume of a projected edition of Galen by Kallierges and Blastos, but the project was never completed. Nevertheless this marked a turning point in the survival of Greek medical works, since, as Nutton remarks, 'What remains for consultation today is largely what was published between 1499 and 1540,' most notably the 1538 Basle edition of the complete works of Galen.

And in this way the ancient Greek art of healing eventually made its way to Western Europe, where the works of Dioscorides and Galen and others would stimulate the emergence of modern medicine.

CHAPTER 13

SPHERES WITHIN SPHERES

Ancient Greek astronomy culminated with the work of Claudius Ptolemaeus (*ca.* 100–*ca.* 170), known more simply as Ptolemy. The most influential of his writings is his *Mathematiki syntaxis* (*Mathematical synthesis*), better known by its Arabic name, the *Almagest,* the most comprehensive work on astronomy that has survived from antiquity. Ptolemy also wrote treatises on astrology, geography, optics and musical theory, as well as making important advances in mathematics in his astronomical and other works.

Most of what is known of Ptolemy's life is based on references from his extant works, along with uncertain information from later sources. The only definite evidence concerning his life comes from a series of observations recorded in the *Almagest,* all made during the successive reigns of the emperors Hadrian (r. 117–38) and Antoninus Pius (r. 138–61), the earliest 26 March 127 and the latest 2 February 141. This agrees with the statement of a later source who says that Ptolemy flourished under Hadrian and lived until the reign of Marcus Aurelius (r. 161–80). As G. J. Toomer writes, 'the only place mentioned in any of Ptolemy's observations is Alexandria, and there is no reason to suppose that he ever lived anywhere else . . . . His name "Ptolemaeus" indicates that he was an inhabitant of Egypt, descended from Greek or Hellenized forebears, while "Claudius" shows that he possessed Roman citizenship, probably as a result of a grant to an ancestor by the emperor Claudius or Nero.'

The *Almagest* is Ptolemy's earliest extant work, and was evidently published before the year 150. As Toomer writes in the introduction to his translation of the *Almagest*: 'As is implied by its Greek name, *Mathematiki syntaxis* ... the *Almagest* is a complete exposition of mathematical astronomy as the Greeks understood the term.' He notes that 'by the early fourth century (and probably much earlier), when Pappus wrote his commentary on it, the *Almagest* had become the standard textbook in astronomy which it was to remain for more than a thousand years ... . It was dominant to an extent and for a time which is unsurpassed by any other scientific work except for Euclid's *Elements*.'

Owen Gingerich, in his foreword to Toomer's translation, remarks that 'What Ptolemy has done is to show – as far as we know for the first time in history – how to convert specific observational data into the numerical parameters for his planetary models, and with the models to construct tables [ephemerides] whereby the solar, lunar and planetary positions and eclipses can be calculated for any given time, past or future.'

The topics in the *Almagest* are treated in logical order through the 13 books. Book I begins with a general discussion of astronomy, including the justification of the Aristotelian view that the earth is stationary 'in the middle of the heavens.' The rest of Book I and all of Book II are devoted principally to the development of the spherical trigonometry necessary for the whole work. Book III deals with the motion of the sun and Book IV with lunar motion, which is continued at a more advanced level in Book V along with solar and lunar parallax. Book VI is on eclipses; Books VII and VIII are on the fixed stars, including a star catalogue; and Books IX through XIII are on the planets.

Toomer notes in his introduction that Ptolemy generally uses the Babylonian sexagesimal system, although for convenience he sometimes employs the traditional Greek fractional system when precision is not required.

Toomer also adds a note in his introduction concerning Ptolemy's chronology and calendars: 'Ptolemy's own chronological system is very simple. He uses the *Egyptian year* and the *era Nabonassar*. The Egyptian year is of unvarying length of 365 days consisting of twelve 30-day months and 5 extra ('epagomenal') days at the end.' Ptolemy himself gives his reason for choosing as his reference point the date when the Babylonian ruler Nabonassar began his reign, on 26 February 746 BC: 'For that is the era from which the ancient observations are, on the whole, preserved down to our own time.'

The trigonometry developed in Books I and II is applied by Ptolemy to various phenomena associated with the annual variation in solar declination, the angular distance of the sun from the ecliptic. The only numerical parameter he uses is the inclination of the ecliptic, which is also the maximum solar declination. He describes two simple instruments that he used to make this measurement, one of which, known as a plinth, is essentially a sundial. The other, a meridional armillary, consists of two concentric brass rings in which the inner ring can rotate freely with a north-south motion. In Book I chapter 12, Ptolemy explains how the instrument is set up so that the lateral plane of the rings is perpendicular to the plane of the horizon and parallel to the plane of the meridian, after which the measurement of the sun's altitude at noon can be measured as follows: 'Having set the instrument up in that way, we observed the sun's movement towards the north and south by turning the inner ring at noon until the lower plate was completely enshadowed by the upper one. When this was the case, the tips of the pointers indicated to us the distance of the sun from the zenith in degrees, measured along the zenith.'

Ptolemy measured the noon altitude of the sun at the summer and winter solstices. The difference between the two is the angle between the tropics, which he found to be greater than $47\frac{2}{3}°$ and less than $47\frac{3}{4}°$. The value found by Eratosthenes and Hipparchus, $11/83$ of a circle, falls within these limits, and so Ptolemy adopted their value. When that value is divided by two it gives the obliquity of the ecliptic, which he thus found to be $23°51'20''$. The present value for the obliquity is $23°26'$, which is nearly half a degree less than Ptolemy's value.

There are two reasons for this difference, one being that his and all other ancient measurements of the obliquity of the ecliptic were a little too high, a systematic error due to the crudity of the instruments used. Secondly, the obliquity of the ecliptic really has decreased slightly since Ptolemy's time, by about $\frac{1}{4}°$. The tilt of the earth's axis varies from 22.1 to 24.5 degrees over a 41,000 year period; the current value is 23.44 degrees and is decreasing. This is one of the so-called Milankovich cycles, named for Milutin Milankovitch (1879–1958), a Serbian civil engineer and geophysicist, who studied the effect of variations in the earth's orbit upon climate changes.

Ptolemy's determination of the obliquity of the ecliptic allowed him to construct a table of the declination of the sun as a function of its longitude, which is necessary for solving problems involving celestial rising times. Most of Book II of the *Almagest* is devoted to calculating tables of rising times for various latitudes, which were used to determine the length of daylight for a given date and latitude.

Ptolemy begins his study of solar motion in Book III with a discussion of the length of the year. Comparing an autumnal equinox that he observed in AD 139 BC with one seen by Hipparchus in 147 BC, he found that the length of the tropical year is less than 365¼ days by one day in 300 years, just as Hipparchus had determined. Ptolemy found the same value when he compared a spring equinox he observed in AD 140 with one witnessed by Hipparchus in 146 BC, and again when he compared his observation of the spring equinox in AD 140 with one made by Meton and Euctemon in 432 BC. All three of Ptolemy's observations contain significant errors, but when compared with the earlier observations they give a tropical year that agrees exactly with the value found by Hipparchus. As Toomer remarks, 'it is likely that in this case Ptolemy was influenced by his knowledge of Hipparchus' value to select such of his own observations as best agreed with it. For Hipparchus' solar and lunar theory represented the known facts (that is, eclipse records) very well, and Ptolemy would be reluctant to tamper with those elements if that would seriously affect the circumstances of eclipses.' In any event, the result obtained is a little high compared to the value of the tropical year used in the modern Gregorian calendar, which is less than 365¼ days by 3 days in 400 years.

Using the length of the tropical year that he had determined, Ptolemy created a table of the mean solar motion that set the pattern for all other mean motion tables in the *Almagest*. The data is written to six places in the sexagesimal system, tabulated for hours, days, months, years and 18-year periods.

Chapter 4 of Book III is 'On the apparent anomaly of the Sun,' the variation of the velocity of the sun along the ecliptic evidenced by the fact that the seasons are of unequal length. Ptolemy presents a model for representing anomalistic motion in general, for the sun, moon and planets, using eccentric circles as well as epicycles, showing, as had Apollonius, that the two models are equivalent.

Using his observations of solstices and equinoxes Ptolemy found the same lengths for the seasons as Hipparchus. He concluded that the longitude of the sun's apogee, or greatest distance from the sun, is constant, and thus he represented the solar motion by a simple eccentric circle. With this model the sun moves fastest at its perigee, its closest approach, and slowest at its apogee. Since Ptolemy used the same data and method as Hipparchus he found the same values for the eccentricity and apogee longitude. The eccentricity is the ratio of the distance between the centre of earth and that of the eccentric circle to the radius of the circle, while the longitude is the angle between the spring equinox and the apogee. These quantities are not constant and had changed since the time of Hipparchus, but the instruments that Ptolemy used for his equinox and solstice observations were not sufficiently sensitive to detect the changes.

According to Toomer, the final stage in Ptolemy's solar theory was to develop the so-called equation of time:

> Since the sun travels in a path inclined to the equator and with varying velocity, the interval between two successive meridian transits of the sun (the true solar day) will not be uniform but will vary slightly through the year. Since astronomical calculations employ uniform units (that is, mean solar days), whereas local time, in an age when the sundial is the main chronometer, is reckoned according to the true solar day, one must be able to convert from one to the other, the calculation of which is done by the equation of time, the calculation of which Ptolemy explains.

The lunar theory is developed in Book IV and V. There, four periodicities must be distinguished: the time for the moon to return to the same longitude, the time for it to return to the same velocity (period of anomaly), the time to return to the same latitude, and the synodic month, the time between successive conjunctions (when the moon is between the sun and earth) and oppositions (when the earth is between the sun and moon). Ptolemy mentions a number of earlier attempts to find a period containing an integer number of each of these periodicities, which would thus be an eclipse cycle. One of these attempts that he quotes is by Hipparchus, whom he said establishes these relations 'from Babylonian and his own observations,' where the length of the synodic month is given in the sexagesimal system: '(1) In 126,007 days, 1 hour, there occur 4,267 synodic months, 4,563 returns in anomaly, and 4,612 sidereal revolutions less 7½° (hence the length of a mean synodic month is 29; 31, 50,2, 20 days) [approximately 29.6 days]. (2) In 5,458 synodic months there occur 5,923 returns in latitude.'

Thus, as Toomer explains, Ptolemy 'is able to construct tables of the mean lunar motion in longitude, anomaly, argument of latitude (motion with respect to the nodes in which the orbit of the moon intersect the ecliptic) and elongation (motion with respect to the mean sun).'

In Book IV, Ptolemy develops a simple lunar theory, using an epicycle model, which is essentially the same as that of Hipparchus. When Ptolemy compared his observations of the moon with those predicted from this theory, he found good agreement at conjunction and opposition, but there were large discrepancies at intermediate positions, reaching a maximum at quadrature, when the elongation is 90°. Ptolemy deals with this problem in

Book V, where he develops his own lunar theory, introducing what Toomer calls 'a "crank" mechanism that "pulls in" the epicycle as it approaches quadrature, thus making it appear larger.'

Ptolemy then goes on to deal with the problem of lunar parallax, the angular difference between the true and apparent positions of the moon because it is observed from the earth's surface rather than its centre. He measured the lunar parallax by comparing the moon's position as observed at Alexandria with a theoretical value obtained from his lunar theory. This allowed him to compute the mean distance of the moon, which he found to be 59 earth radii. Then, using the same methods as Eratosthenes, he went on to calculate the mean distance of the sun as 1,210 earth radii, the diameter of the moon as 0.292 earth diameters, and the diameter of the sun as 5.5 earth diameters.

Book VI is devoted to eclipse theory, which as Toomer writes, 'is easily derived from what precedes .... Ptolemy explains in minute detail how to compute the size, duration, and other circumstances of both lunar and solar eclipses for any given place. But his method does not allow one to compute the path of a solar eclipse (a development of the late seventeenth century).'

Books VII and VIII deal with the fixed stars, which serve as the background against which the other celestial bodies move. It was particularly necessary to establish the coordinates of stars in a band along the ecliptic to describe the motion of the planets. Ptolemy compared his own observations with those of Hipparchus and other Greek astronomers to show that the relative positions of the stars had not changed. He followed Hipparchus in stating that the celestial sphere was rotating about the pole of the ecliptic from east to west by approximately 1° in 100 years. A large part of the two books (61 of 97 pages in Toomer's translation) is taken up by a catalogue of stars. The catalogue contains 1,022 stars, grouped in 48 constellations, each listed with its celestial latitude and longitude as well as magnitude, the latter on a scale of 1 to 6, in which the brightest were magnitude 1 and the faintest 6. The last chapter of Book VIII is entitled 'On the first and last visibilities of the fixed stars' in other words, on the heliacal risings and settings of stars, a problem of traditional interest in Greek astronomy.

The last five books are devoted to planetary theory. Book IX begins with a chapter 'On the order of the spheres of the sun, moon and five planets'. This is of primary importance, for the order of the two inner planets, Mercury and Venus, is not fixed in the geocentric system, since either or both of them can be closer to the earth than the sun depending on their phases. Ptolemy discusses this question, giving the opinions of earlier Greek astronomers, where when he writes 'below the sun' he means 'closer to the earth than the sun', whereas 'above the sun' means the opposite. Ptolemy took the view of those earlier astronomers who put Venus and Mercury 'below the sun', adopting the order moon, Mercury, Venus, sun, Mars, Jupiter, Saturn as being more plausible.

Ptolemy then begins a discussion of planetary theory, saying that 'Now it is our purpose to demonstrate for the five planets, just as we did for the sun and moon, that all their apparent anomalies can be represented by uniform circular motions, since they are proper to the nature of divine beings, while disorder and non-uniformity are alien [to such beings].'

The most striking feature of planetary motion as seen from the earth is the looping retrograde path they take whenever they pass the earth or are passed by it. This had been first explained by Apollonius with his epicycle theory, but Ptolemy showed that this was not sufficient to account for all the anomalies of planetary motion. The principal modification made by Ptolemy to explain these anomalies is to allow the centre of the epicycle to move uniformly with respect to a point called the equant (see Figure 13), which is displaced from the centre of the deferent circle, a device that was to be the subject of controversy in later times.

Books IX–XI develops the theory of the longitudinal motion of the planets. Book XII is devoted to establishing two sets of planetary tables. The first are tables of planetary stations, that is, the points where a planet changes the direction of its motion on the celestial sphere in its retrograde loops. The second, for Mercury and Venus, are tables of greatest elongation, their maximum angular distance from the sun along the ecliptic.

Book XIII deals with planetary latitudes, for all five visible planets have orbits that are slightly inclined to the ecliptic. Toomer gives a summary of how Ptolemy solved the problem of planetary latitudes:

Ptolemy eventually reaches that solution in the *Planetary Hypotheses* (except that the deferents of Venus and Mercury are inclined to the ecliptic at a very small angle); but in the *Almagest*, misled by faulty observations and the eccentricity of the orbit of the earth, he devises a much more complicated theory in which the epicycles of outer planets undergo varying inclinations as the epicycle moves round the deferent. The resultant tables do, however, represent the actual changes in latitude fairly well and are no mean achievement. The work ends with a discussion of the traditional problem of the heliacal risings and settings of the planets.

The *Almagest* was by far the most influential of Ptolemy's works, dominating the field of theoretical astronomy until the end of the sixteenth century. It almost immediately became the standard textbook in astronomy, while Pappus and Theon of Alexandria wrote the commentaries to it. The extant writings of Ptolemy also include other treatises on astronomy: the *Handy Tables, Planetary Hypotheses, Phases of the Fixed Stars, Analemma* and *Planisphaerium*; a work on astrology called the *Tetrabiblos*, and treatises entitled *Geography, Optics* and *Harmonica*.

The *Handy Tables* contains all the astronomical tables that are scattered throughout the *Almagest*. There are additions to what appeared in the *Almagest*, including a table of the longitudes and latitudes of major cities allowing one to make conversions from the coordinates of Alexandria. Also, as Toomer notes, 'The epoch is changed from era Nabonassar to era Philip (Thoth I = 12 November 324 BC). The tables became the standard manual in the ancient and Byzantine worlds, and their form persisted beyond the Middle Ages.'

The *Planetary Hypotheses*, in two books, is a popular digest of the *Almagest*. But it goes beyond the *Almagest* in several respects, such as changing some parameters and even theories, as well as presenting physical rather than mathematical models so as to represent the celestial motions mechanically. Ptolemy also proposed a system for determining the absolute distances of the planets, assuming that they and the sun and moon were arrayed in the ascending order that he had chosen in the *Almagest*: moon, Mercury, Venus, sun, Mars, Jupiter, Saturn. His system was based on the assumption that the maximum distance from the earth of each of these bodies is exactly equal to the minimum distance of the next body in outward order. Assuming the circumference of the earth to be 180,000 stades, he computed the distances of all the celestial bodies right out to the sphere of the fixed stars in earth radii and stades, where he put the latter sphere just beyond the maximum distance of Saturn. The value that he thus obtained for the radius of the sphere of the fixed stars was the equivalent of about ten million modern miles. Toomer notes that 'This method of determining the exact dimensions of the universe became one of the most popular features of the Ptolemaic system in later times.'

Phases of the Fixed Stars is a thesis in two books dealing with the heliacal risings and settings of bright stars. Only Book II survives, most of it comprising a sort of calendar, with daily listings of helical risings and settings along with the weather forecasts associated with them by various authorities.

141

The *Analemma* survives in only a few fragments in palimpsest. As Toomer describes it: 'It is an explanation of a method of finding angles used in the construction of sundials, involving projection onto the plane of the meridian and swinging other planes into that plane. The actual determination of the angles is determined not by trigonometry (although Ptolemy shows how it is theoretically possible) but by an ingenious graphical technique which in modern terms would be classified as nomographic.'

The *Planisphaerium* treats the problem of mapping circles on the celestial sphere onto a plane, the mathematical basis of the plane astrolabe, which became the most popular of medieval astronomical instruments. As Toomer remarks: 'Since the work explains how to use the mapping to calculate rising times, one of the main features of the astrolabe, it is highly likely that the instrument itself goes back to Ptolemy (independent evidence suggests that it goes back to Hipparchus).'

Ptolemy's *Tetrabiblos* is the classic Greek work on astrology, the pseudo-science of astronomical divination based on the notion that celestial bodies influence human affairs. Ptolemy was himself sceptical about some of the credulous beliefs involved in astrology, as when he states in Book III of the *Tetrabiblos* that 'we shall dismiss the superfluous nonsense of the many, that lacks any plausibility, in favor of the primary natural causes.' Like the *Almagest*, the *Tetrabiblos* was translated into both Arabic and Latin and was very popular in the medieval world.

Ptolemy's *Geography*, divided into eight books, is an attempt to map and describe the *oikoumene*. Most of it consists of lists of places, with their longitude and latitude, along with very brief descriptions of the principal topographical features of the larger land masses. Ptolemy's *oikoumene* extends eastward 180° in longitude from his zero meridian in the outermost of the Fortunate Isles, now known as the Canaries, and in latitude from 16°25' south to 63° north. He used two systems of projection for his maps, one of which is shown in Figure 14.

One major defect of Ptolemy's *Geography* is that his value for the circumference of the earth is too small by a factor of one-third. The most conspicuous error in his map of the *oikoumene* is the extension of the Eurasian land mass over 180 degrees of longitude instead of 120 degrees. Nevertheless, Ptolemy's treatise was by far the best geographical work produced in antiquity, and it remained unsurpassed for nearly 1,400 years.

The *Geography* was first translated into Arabic around 820, and it dominated Islamic geographical studies for at least the next seven centuries. It first reached Western Europe through a Latin translation from the Greek by Jacobus Angelus around 1406 and became very popular. Ptolemy's two systems of projection influenced the subsequent development of European cartography, as evidenced by the map drawn by Bernardus Sylvanus in his 1511 edition of the Geography and Mercator's map of Europe in 1544.

Ptolemy's researches on light are presented in his *Optics*, a treatise in five books. The work is lost in Greek and survived only through an Arabic translation lacking Book I and the end of Book V. This translation, which has since been lost, was the source of the extant Latin translation done in the twelfth century by Eugenius of Sicily.

The lost Book I of the *Optics* dealt with the theory of vision, where Ptolemy, like most ancient writers, believed that vision occurs through a cone-shaped bundle of light rays emanating from the eye. He also demonstrated that light rays are propagated in straight lines. Book II deals with the role of light and colour in vision; with the perception of the position, form and motion of objects, and with optical illusions. Book III and IV are devoted to catoptrics, the theory of reflection, while Book V deals with refraction.

At the beginning of Book III Ptolemy states three elementary principles of optics concerning the formation of images by reflection in mirrors: 1) The image appears at some point along the infinite line proceeding from the eye to the surface of the mirror. 2) The image appears on the perpendicular drawn from the object to the mirror and produced. 3) The incident and reflected rays make the same angle with the surface normal, that is, the perpendicular to the mirror at the point of incidence. The latter is now known as the law of reflection, which Ptolemy was the first to explain clearly.

Ptolemy demonstrated the law of reflection experimentally, showing that the angle of incidence is equal to the angle of reflection for plane, convex and concave mirrors. The other topics dealt with by Ptolemy in Books III and IV are summarized by Toomer:

> There follows a remarkable discussion on the propriety of assimilating binocular to monocular vision in geometric proofs. Ptolemy incidentally determines the relationships between the images seen by the left and right eyes and the composite image seen by both, using an ingenious apparatus with lines of different colors. He then develops from the three laws a series of theorems on the location, size, and appearance of images, first for plane mirrors, then for spherical convex mirrors, then (in Book IV) for spherical concave mirrors and various types of 'composite' (such as cylindrical) mirrors.

Book V is entirely devoted to refraction, the bending of light when it passes from one medium to another. The apparatus Ptolemy used is described by G. E. R. Lloyd in his *Greek Science After Aristotle*, referring to the drawing reproduced here in Figure 12:

> To measure the angle he uses a circular disk, each quadrant of which is divided into ninety parts, like a protractor. This disk is set up in a bowl of clean water so that the water just covers the bottom half of the circle. A coloured marker is placed at a given point (e.g. 10°) along the circumference of the semicircle which is above the water, and the marker, the centre of the disk and the eye are aligned. A small, thin rod is then moved along the circumference of the opposite quadrant (under the water) until the extremity of the rod appears in line with the coloured marker and the centre of the disk. This enables both the angle of incidence [α] and the angle of refraction [β] to be determined, and Ptolemy remarks that the former is always greater than the latter, and that as the former increases the amount of refraction also increases.

Ptolemy then describes a series of experiments that he performed to measure the angle of refraction for various angles of incidence. He remarks that 'we have found no perceptible difference between waters of different densities and rareties.' He went on to repeat the experiment, first for light passing from air to glass and then from water to glass. The results found by Ptolemy are remarkably close to those that can be found from the modern law of refraction, derived by the Dutch mathematician Willibrod Snell (1580–1626).

The *Harmonica* is a thesis on musical theory in three books. According to Toomer, 'it deals with the mathematical intervals (on a stretched string) between notes and their classification according to various traditional Greek systems. It seeks a middle ground between the two schools of the Pythagoreans and the followers of Aristoxenus, of whom the former, according to Ptolemy (I, 2), stressed mathematical theory at the expense of the ear's evidence, while the latter did the reverse.'

The last three chapters of the *Harmonica* are lost; apparently they dealt with the rotation of the planetary spheres and the musical intervals, a revival of the ancient Pythagorean notion of the harmony of the celestial spheres. According to Toomer, 'Kepler intended to publish a translation of Book III of Ptolemy's *Harmonica*, with a "restoration" of the last chapters and a comparison with his own kindred speculations, as an appendix to the *Harmonices mundi*. The appendix never appeared, but the whole work is a tribute to his predecessor.'

CHAPTER 14

CLASSICAL TWILIGHT

Athens and Alexandria continued as centres of Hellenic culture even as Rome extended its rule eastward over the Greek world. At the same time Rome had been absorbing Greek culture, as evidenced by the development of Roman literature based on Hellenic models.

This cultural exchange accelerated after 155 BC when an Athenian embassy arrived in Rome to appeal an unfavourable decision made by Greek arbitrators in a dispute with Oropus. The ambassadors were the directors of three of the four renowned philosophical schools of Athens: Carneades of Cyrene, head of the Academy; Critolaos of Phaselis, director of the Lyceum; and Diogenes of Babylon, leader of the Stoic school. The Epicurean school was not represented in the embassy, probably because in their pursuit of happiness its members chose to avoid involvement in public life.

A decade later the Stoic philosopher Panaetius of Rhodes (*ca.* 185–109 BC) came from Athens to Rome, where he remained for the most part until he returned to Athens in 129 BC to head the Stoa. Cicero, who was deeply influenced by Panaetius, writes of him that 'he fled from the gloom and harshness [of the rigorous Stoics] and did not approve of their thorny arguments. In one branch of philosophy [i. e., ethics] he was more gentle, in the other [i.e., physics and logic] clearer. He was always quoting Plato, Aristotle, Xenocrates, Theophrastus, Diocaearchus, as his writings clearly show.'

Posidonius (*ca.* 135–*ca.* 51 BC), one of last original thinkers of the Stoic school, studied at Athens under Panaetius before moving to Rhodes. There he attracted students from Rome, including Cicero, and was visited by leading Romans during their eastern journeys, most notably Pompey. He represented the Rhodians on an embassy to Rome in 87 BC, and his extensive travels took him as far as Gadeira (Cadiz) in Spain, where he observed the tides of the Atlantic. He described the tides in his treatise *On Ocean*, where he ascribes the phenomenon to the combined actions of sun and moon. None of his wide-ranging works survive other than in fragments, though he was extremely influential in the subsequent intellectual history of the Roman world and of medieval Europe.

The Roman poet Lucretius (*ca.* 94–*ca.* 50 BC) is said to have followed the Epicurean maxim 'Live unnoticed' so carefully that virtually nothing is known about his life. St Jerome reports that Lucretius was born in 94 BC, that an overdose of an aphrodisiac drove him mad, and that in his intervals of sanity he wrote several books, which were later edited by Cicero, and that he committed suicide at the age of 44.

Lucretius is renowned for a superb didactic poem in six books entitled *De Rerum Natura (On the Nature of Things)*, based on the atomic theory and the teaching of Epicurus In the first book of the poem Lucretius reveals his intention of using the atomic theory to overthrow 'this very superstition which is the mother of sinful and impious deeds.' He denies creation on the grounds of the permanence of atomic matter, stating that 'Nothing is ever produced by divine power out of nothing.' The void is a frame of reference for atoms in motion and 'time by itself does not exist; but from things themselves there results a sense of what has already taken place, what is now going on and what is to ensue.' We must rely on our senses in studying nature, for 'What can be a surer guide as to the distinction of true from false than our senses.'

The second book of *De Rerum Natura* deals with the kinetics of the atomic theory, with the random movements and collisions of the atoms bringing about the groupings and separations that form the various bodies found in nature. Lucretius followed Epicurus in saying that the reason the atoms collide is that 'at quite indeterminate times and places they swerve ever so little from their course, just so much that you can call this a change in direction.' This was later interpreted to mean that the atomic theory was not deterministic, since the 'swerve' made atomic motion unpredictable. The atomic theory was in this way made more acceptable for Christians, since it allowed for free will in human actions. Thus *De Rerum Natura* became popular in medieval Europe, which eventually led to the revival of the atomic theory in the seventeenth century.

The Roman architect and engineer Vitruvius Pollio flourished in the first century BC. Virtually nothing is known of his life other than the internal evidence in his only known work, *De Architectura*, a treatise on architecture and engineering based partly on his own studies and partly on those of earlier architects, mostly Greeks. The treatise is encyclopedic in scope, dealing not only with the history and principles of architecture, but also with military and civil engineering as well as physics and astronomy, including the construction of sundials. The work of Vitruvius was revived in the European renaissance and has been influential in architectural studies from then until the present day.

Pliny the Elder (*ca.* AD 23–79) was born at Comum (Como), and was probably educated in Rome. He was in command of the Roman fleet sent to evacuate refugees during the eruption of Mount Vesuvius in AD 79, when he was asphyxiated by the volcanic fumes. His only surviving work is his *Natural History.* He notes in the preface 'that by perusing about 2,000 volumes we have collected in 36 volumes about 20,000 noteworthy facts from one hundred authors we have explored.' Pliny the Younger, his nephew and adopted son, describes the *Natural History* as 'a diffuse and learned work, no less rich in variety than nature itself.' The *Natural History* was widely known in medieval Europe, where, despite its uneven quality and generally low level, it represented a large fraction of the scientific knowledge available at that time.

The Roman writer Seneca, a Stoic who flourished in the first century AD, is best known for his dialogues, letters and tragedies, but he is also of interest in the history of science for his *Natural Questions.* This work deals principally with topics in physics, meteorology and astronomy, where his sources are principally Aristotle and Theophrastus. He writes of the low state to which general knowledge of astronomy had fallen since the days when the ancient Greeks 'counted the stars and named every one,' noting that 'there are many nations at the present hour who merely know the face of the sky and do not understand why the moon is obscured in an eclipse.' But he is hopeful that 'the day will come when the progress of research through the long ages will reveal to sight the mysteries of nature that are now concealed.'

During the early medieval period the attitude of Christian scholars was that the study of science is not necessary, for in order to save one's soul it is enough to believe in God, as St Augustine of Hippo (354–430) wrote in his *Enchiridion:* 'It is enough for Christians to believe that the only cause of created things, whether heavenly or earthly, whether visible or invisible, is the goodness of the Creator, the one true God, and that nothing exists but Himself that does not derive its existence from Him.'

The Greek philosopher Plotinus (205–270) is believed to have been born in Egypt, where he studied at Alexandria before moving to Rome at the age of 40. His works cover the whole range of philosophy, including cosmology and physics. They embody a synthesis of Platonic, Pythagorean,

Aristotelian and Stoic thought that came to be known as Neo-Platonism, the dominant philosophy in the Graeco-Roman world through the rest of antiquity and on into the medieval era.

Iamblichus (250–*ca.* 325), a Greek-speaker of Syrian origin, studied in Rome under the Neoplatonist philosopher Porphyry and later established his own school in Syria. His extant work consists of nine books on the Pythagoreans, including their number mysticism, as well as books on the use of arithmetic in physics, ethics and theology. Iamblichus goes far beyond Plato in advocating the complete mathematization of nature, for he felt that mathematics was the key to understanding not only the movement of the celestial bodies, but of terrestrial phenomena as well.

The Roman writer Chalcidius, who flourished in the fourth century, is noted for his Latin translation of Plato's *Timaeus,* as well as for his own commentary on that work. These were the only sources of knowledge about Plato's cosmology available in Europe during the early medieval era. Chalcidius was also influenced by the ideas of Aristotle and transmitted them to medieval Europe as well, though in somewhat modified form. Two of the most important ideas of Aristotelian science which were thus perpetuated were the concept of the four elements and the astronomical theory of the homocentric spheres, along with the notion of the dichotomy between the terrestrial and celestial regions. Chalcidius refers to the astronomical theories of Heraclides Ponticus, who is also mentioned by the Roman Neoplatonists Macrobius and Martianus Capella.

Macrobius, who may have been from North Africa, flourished in the early fifth century. Besides his mention of the theories of Heraclides, Macrobius also writes of the number mysticism of the Pythagoreans, and says that several Platonists believed that the interplanetary distances were such as to produce harmonious relations, the famous 'harmony of the spheres'.

Martianus Capella was of North African origin and flourished in the years 410–439. He is the author of an allegorical work on the seven liberal arts entitled *The Nuptials of Mercury and Philology.* Book VIII of this work is an introduction to astronomy, in which he states that Mercury and Venus orbit the sun, a theory that he attributes to Heraclides Ponticus, though probably mistakenly. His work was very popular in the early medieval era in Europe, when a number of commentaries were written on it.

The Roman philosopher Boethius (*ca.* 480–524) held high office under the Ostrogoth king Theodoric, who had him imprisoned and executed. His best known work is his *Consolation of Philosophy,* written while he was in prison before his execution. The other works of Boethius fall into two categories: his translations from Greek into Latin of Aristotle's logical works and his own writings on logic, theology, music, geometry and arithmetic. His writings were influential in the transmission to medieval Europe of the basic parts of Aristotle's logic and of elementary arithmetic.

Cassiodorus was another Roman who held high office under the Ostrogoths. In his *Introduction to Divine and Human Readings* he urges the monks of the monastery at Monte Cassino in Italy, founded by St Benedict in 529, to copy faithfully the classics of ancient scholarship preserved in their libraries as a cultural heritage. He listed some of the important works of science that he thought should be preserved, and in doing so he described and thus transmitted the basic Aristotelian classification of the sciences. This classification divides philosophy into theoretical and practical areas. The theoretical areas are metaphysics, physics and mathematics, where the latter is further subdivided into arithmetic, music, geometry and astronomy, while the practical areas are ethics, economics and politics. The mathematical sections of the book are briefer and more elementary, mostly dealing with definitions. There is also a section on medicine, in which Cassiodorus gives advice on the use of medicinal herbs, urging the monks to read the works of Hippocrates, Dioscorides and Galen.

Meanwhile mathematics and philosophy continued at a high level in the eastern Greek world. Nicomachus of Gerasa in Palestine, a Greek who flourished *ca.* AD 100, is noted for his *Introductio arithmeticae*, which remained influential up until the sixteenth century. This is a treatise in two books, described by Boyer as 'a handbook on those elements of mathematics that were essential to an understanding of Pythagorean and Platonic philosophy.'

The only other work of Nicomachus that has survived is his *Manual of Harmonics*, a treatise on musical theory. Leonardo Taran describes this work as characteristic of both the Aristoxenian and Pythagorean traditions, the former referring to Aristoxenus of Tarentum, who in the fourth century BC formulated an important system of musical theory quite different than that of his predecessor.

Diophantus of Alexandria (fl. *ca.* AD 250), one of the last great mathematicians of antiquity, did for algebra and number theory what Euclid had done for geometry. Little is known of his life beyond the bare facts given in an algebraic riddle about Diophantus in the *Greek Anthology*, dating from the fifth or sixth century: 'God granted him to be a boy for the sixth part of his life, and adding a twelfth part to this He clothed his cheeks with down; He lit him the light of wedlock after a seventh part, and five years after his marriage He granted him a son. Alas! Late-born wretched child; after attaining the measure of half his father's life, chill Fate took him. After consoling his grief by this science of numbers for four years he ended his life.'

Assuming that the biographical facts in this riddle are correct, Diophantus lived to be 84 years old. His most important treatise is the *Arithmetica,* of which 6 of the original 13 books are extant in Greek, while another 4 books, recently discovered, survived in an Arabic translation. As Kurt Vogel describes this unique work:

> Although Diophantus knew elementary number theory and contributed new theorems to it, his *Arithmetica* is a collection of problems. Diophantus, by a sagacious choice of suitable auxiliary unknowns and frequently brilliant artifices, succeeded in reducing the degree of the equation (the unknowns reaching as high as the sixth power) and the number of unknowns (as many as ten) and thus arriving at a solution .... In his solutions Diophantus showed himself a master in the field of indeterminate analysis, and apart from Pappus he was the only great mathematician during the decline of Hellenism.

The six books of the *Arithmetica* that survived in Greek were translated into Latin in 1621, and six years later this work inspired the French mathematician Pierre Fermat to create the modern theory of numbers. After reading Diophantus' solution of the problem of dividing a square into the sum of two squares, which is the Pythagorean theorem, Fermat made a notation in the margin of his copy of the *Arithmetica,* stating that 'It is impossible to divide a cube into two other cubes, or a fourth power or, in general, any number which is a power greater than the second into two powers of the same denomination.' He then noted that he had discovered a remarkable proof 'which this margin is too narrow to contain.' He never supplied the proof of what came to be called 'Fermat's last theorem,' which was finally solved in 1994 by Andrew Wiles, a British mathematician working at Princeton University, the last link in a long chain of mathematical development that began in ancient Alexandria. The work of Diophantus is still a part of modern mathematics, studied under the heading of Diophantine Analysis.

The philosopher Alexander of Aphrodisias in Asia Minor flourished in the second or third century AD. He is best known for his commentaries on Aristotle, which in Latin translation were very influential in late medieval

Europe. Aside from his commentaries, four of his philosophical works have survived in Greek manuscripts: *On the Soul, On Fate, On Mixture,* and *Natural Questions,* the fourth book of which deals mainly with problems in ethics.

Pappus of Alexandria, who flourished in the first half of the fourth century AD, is renowned for his work in mathematics, astronomy, music and geography. His most important work is his *Synagogue,* or *Collection,* which is thus described by Heath in his history of Greek mathematics:

> While it covers the whole range of Greek geometry, the *Collection* is a handbook or guide rather than an encyclopedia; it was intended to be read with the original works (where extant) rather than independently. Without pretending to great originality, the whole work shows, on the part of the author, a complete grasp over the subjects treated, independence of judgement, and mastery of technique; the style is concise and clear; in short, Pappus stands out as an accomplished and worthy representative of the classical Greek geometry.

Book V deals mostly with the interesting topic known as isoperimetry, defined by Heath as 'the comparison of the content of figures which have different shapes but the same contour, or (in the case of solids) equal surfaces.' The book begins with a passage on what Heath calls 'the sagacity of bees shown in their choice of the shape of the cells in which they store their honey.'

> Presumably because they know themselves to be entrusted with the task of bringing from heaven to the cultured portion of mankind a share of ambrosia in the form of honey, they do not think it proper to pour it carelessly on ground or wood or any other ugly and irregular material; but first collecting the sweets of the fairest flowers which grow on the earth, they make from them, for the reception of the honey, the vessels which we call honey-combs, with cells all equal, similar, and contiguous to one another, and hexagonal in form. They would necessarily think that the figures must be such as to be contiguous to one another, that is to say, to have their sides common, in order that no foreign matter could enter the interstices between them and so spoil the purity of their produce ... the bees by reason of their instinctive wisdom chose for their construction the figure which has the most angles, because they conceived that it would hold more honey ....

Boyer writes that 'Books VI and VIII of the *Collection* are chiefly on applications of mathematics to astronomy, optics and mechanics (including an unsuccessful attempt at finding the law of the inclined plane). Of far more significance in the history of mathematics is Book VII, in which, through his penchant for generalization, Pappus comes close to the fundamental principle of analytic geometry.'

The *Collection* is the principal, and sometimes the only, source of knowledge of the accomplishments of many of Pappus' predecessors in the Hellenistic era, most notably Euclid, Archimedes, Apollonius and Ptolemy. The extant works of Pappus also include a commentary on Ptolemy's *Almagest*, apparently part of a larger original, and also a commentary on the Ptolemaic *Planisphaerium*. He is also known to have written a commentary on Euclid's *Elements*. This is now lost except for a two-part commentary on the tenth book of the *Elements* in Arabic translation that has been attributed to Pappus, though some doubt has been cast on the attribution. The Byzantine source known as the *Suda Lexicon* mentions a work by Pappus entitled *Description of the World*, which has not survived in Greek but may be the *Geography* bearing the name of the Armenian Moses of Khoren, translated from the treatise by Pappus. It is also possible that the commentary on Ptolemy's *Harmonica*, previously attributed to Porphyry, may actually be a work of Pappus.

The work of Pappus in mathematics is known to have influenced both Descartes and Newton, among others, and one of his discoveries, known today as the Theorem of Pappus, is still taught in elementary calculus courses. Boyer, in his history of mathematics, writes of Pappus as the last great Greek mathematician: 'The *Collection* of Pappus is the last truly significant ancient mathematical treatise, for the attempt by the author to revive geometry was not successful. Mathematical works continued to be written in Greek for about another thousand years, continuing an influence that had begun almost a millennium before, but authors following Pappus never again rose to his level.'

An oath signed by 'Pappus, philosopher' in a collection of works on alchemy has been attributed to Pappus of Alexandria. If so, it may shed light on his religious views, which would seem to be a mixture of Christian, Pythagorean, alchemical and astrological beliefs. It reads: 'I therefore swear to thee, whoever thou art, the great oath, I declare God to be one in form, but not in number, the maker of heaven and earth, as well as the tetrad of the elements and things formed from them, who has furthermore harmonized our rational and intellectual souls with our bodies, who is borne upon the chariots of the cherubim and hymned by angelic throngs.'

Much of the lore of alchemy, astrology and magic is found in the so-called *Corpus Hermeticum*, a collection of writings that takes its name from the legendary Hermes Trismegestus (Thrice-Greatest), a syncretization of the

Greek god Hermes with the Egyptian divinity Thoth. Most of these writings, once thought to be of ancient Egyptian origin, are now dated to about the second century AD. The earliest full description of the *Corpus Hermeticum* is in the *Stromata* of Clement of Alexandria (*ca.* 150–*ca.* 220), who says that of the 42 books four are astrological and the remainder religious, philosophical and medical, all of them with a touch of the occult, as in one fragment which states that 'philosophy and magic nourish the soul.'

The centre of the Roman Empire moved eastward in 330, when Constantine the Great transferred his capital from Italy to the Greek city of Byzantium on the Bosphorus, which he rebuilt and expanded to make it the 'New Rome,' thenceforth known as Constantinople. Constantine was baptized just before he died seven years later, the first step in establishing Christianity as the state religion of the empire, a process that was virtually completed by the latter half of the following century.

During that period imperial sovereignty was sometimes divided between Emperor of the West and the Emperor of the East, the latter ruling in Constantinople. The third quarter of the fifth century was a chaotic period in the history of the western part of the empire. Ten men followed one another in turn as Emperor of the West, the last being Romulus Augustus, who was overthrown in 476. By that time most of Western Europe had been lost to the empire, and thenceforth the emperor in Constantinople was sole ruler of what remained.

The library in the Serapeum survived almost to the end of the fourth century, by which time the Museum seems to have vanished. The emperor Theodosius I issued a decree in 391 calling for the destruction of all pagan temples throughout the empire. The edict was only partially effective, as evidenced by the fact that later emperors found it necessary to renew the ban. Nevertheless, Theophilus, bishop of Alexandria, took this opportunity to lead his fanatical followers in demolishing the Serapeum, including its library.

The last contemporary description of the library is by Aelius Festus Aphthonius, who some time after 391 paid tribute to its role in making Alexandria the centre of Greek culture: 'On the inner side of the colonnade were built rooms, some of which served as book stores and were open to those who devoted their life to the cause of learning. It was these study rooms that exalted the city to be the first in philosophy. Some other rooms were set up for the worship of the old gods.'

The last scholar known to have worked in the Museum and Library was Theon of Alexandria, who in the second half of the fourth century wrote commentaries on Euclid's *Elements, Data* and *Optica,* as well as on Ptolemy's

Almagest and *Handy Tables*. His commentaries were really new editions of these works in a form that would make them more accessible to Theon's students. Toomer remarks that 'The most notable of Theon's editions is that of Euclid's *Elements*, which was so influential that it consigned the original text to near oblivion.'

A passage in Theon's commentary on the *Handy Tables* led to an interesting development in Arabic astronomy. This is where Theon states that 'certain ancient astrologers' believed that the points of the spring and fall equinox oscillate back and forth along the ecliptic, moving through an angle of eight degrees over a period of 640 years. This erroneous notion was revived in the so-called 'trepidation theory' of Arab astronomers, and it survived in various forms up into the sixteenth century, when it was discussed by Copernicus.

Among lost works attributed to Theon were two treatises on the astrolabe. One of these may have been the principal source of transmission of the theory of the astrolabe to the Arabs.

Theon was the father of Hypatia (*ca.* 370–415), the first woman to appear in the history of science. Hypatia was professor of philosophy and mathematics, and *ca.* 400 she became head of the Platonic school in Alexandria. She revised the third book of Theon's commentary on Ptolemy's *Almagest*, and she also wrote commentaries on the works of Apollonius and Diophantus, now lost. Like her father, Hypatia was a pagan. Her lectures on Neo-Platonic philosophy aroused the anger of St Cyril, bishop of Alexandria, who in 415 instigated a riot by fanatical Christians in which Hypatia was killed.

Proclus (*ca.* 410–485), the last great Neoplatonist philosopher, was born in Constantinople, but moved to Athens in his youth to study at the Academy. He remained in Athens for the rest of his days, except for a brief exile due to his paganism, and was head of the Academy during his latter years. He was the last great synthesizer of Greek philosophy and as such was extremely influential in medieval and Renaissance thought. His works include a commentary on Book I of Euclid's *Elements*, which contains a rich history of Greek geometry, and a treatise entitled *Outline of Astronomical Hypotheses*, a summary of the theories of Hipparchus and Ptolemy. According to Glenn R. Morrow: 'With the revival of learning in the fifteenth century and the desire of Renaissance thinkers to throw off the yoke of medieval Aristotelianism, Proclus' Platonism had a great vogue in the Florentine Academy and strongly influenced Nicholas of Cusa and Johannes Kepler.'

Proclus, remained a pagan throughout his life, though it led to his dismissal from the Academy and temporary exile from Athens. He lived in a house on the south slope of the Acropolis, under the Parthenon, the temple of Athena Parthenos, the Virgin Goddess. The Parthenon ceased to be a sanctuary of Athens in AD 435, when an edict by Theodosius II closed all pagan temples in the empire, though it took some years before the law was fully implemented. The chronicler Marianus says that after the Parthenon was finally closed, Proclus had a troubling dream that he related to his friends. It seems that a beautiful young woman appeared to him dressed in the costume of Athena Parthenos, imploring him to give her shelter for she had been evicted from her ancient sanctuary, but before he could respond to her she disappeared.

Ammonius, son of Hermias, so called to distinguish him from namesakes, directed the Platonic school in Alexandria from 485 until his death *ca.* 517–26. He was a distinguished philosopher, astronomer and mathematician, noted for his commentaries on Aristotle. He managed to remain on good terms with the Christian authorities in Alexandria, though he and several of his faculty were pagans. (He may have become a Christian, but if so it would have been only nominally.)

Ammonius was the last pagan philosopher of Alexandria, for by his time Christianity had triumphed over the old gods who had been worshipped in the Serapeum and the Greek philosophers whose works had been studied in the Museum and Library of Alexandria. As Tertullian had written two centuries earlier in attacking pagan philosophy, rejecting research in favor of revelation:

What then has Athens to do with Jerusalem, the Academy with the Church, the heretic with the Christian? Our instruction comes from the Porch of Solomon who himself taught us that the Lord is to be sought in the simplicity of one's heart .... We have no need of curiosity after Jesus Christ, nor of research after the gospel. When we believe, we desire to believe no more. For we believe this first, that there is nothing else that we believe.

CHAPTER 15

FROM BYZANTIUM AND ISLAM TO WESTERN EUROPE

Soon after Constantine the Great established his new capital at Constantinople he founded a university there. Nothing is known about the original University of Constantinople, which may not actually have functioned until until Theodosius II reorganized it in 425. The new university originally had 20 chairs of grammar, equally divided between Greek and Latin, and 8 in rhetoric, 5 of which were in Greek and 3 in Latin, as well as 2 professorships in law, 1 each in Greek and Latin, and 1 in philosophy, taught in Greek. By the following century Latin had fallen out of use in Constantinople and all of the professorships at the university were in Greek. This was part of the great cultural divide that developed in the early medieval era between Latin West and Greek East, a dichotomy that separated the newly emerging civilization of Western Europe from the Byzantine world of the Balkans and Asia Minor.

Constantine had organized the first ecumenical council of the church, which was held in 325 at Nicaea. The second ecumenical council was held at Constantinople in 381, the third at Ephesus in 431 and the fourth in 451 at Chalcedon, in the Asian suburbs of the capital, the principal business at all of these synods being doctrinal matters, particularly concerning the nature of Christ. The bishops at Chalcedon formulated what became the orthodox Christological doctrine: that Christ was both human and divine, his two natures being perfect and indivisible though separate. At the same time they condemned as heretics those who thought differently, the Monophysites and the Nestorians, whose believers, principally in southeastern Asia Minor, Syria, Mesopotamia, Persia and Egypt, then formed their own schismatic churches.

The Nestorians had already founded important schools in northern Mesopotamia at Edessa (Turkish Urfa) and Nisibis, where the language of instruction was Syriac, a Semitic language deriving from Aramaic. Among the books used at these schools were Greek treatises translated into Syriac, most notably the logical works of Aristotle. Emperor Zeno closed the school at Edessa in 489, whereupon the Nestorian scholars moved eastward to Nisibis, which was then in Persian territory.

The eastward migration of Nestorians eventually brought them to the Sassanid capital at Jundishapur in western Persia, where in the late fifth century they joined the faculty of a medical school that had been founded by King Shapur I (r. 241–72). There the Nestorian faculty taught Greek philosophy, medicine and science in Syriac translations. The school became a centre for the translation of works in medicine, cosmology, astronomy and Aristotelian philosophy, the languages involved at various times including Greek, Syriac, Sanskrit, Pahlavi and, subsequently, Arabic.

The best of the early Syriac translators was Sergius of Reshaina (d. 536), a Monophysite priest and physician who had been educated in the Platonic school of Ammonius in Alexandria. His translations from Greek into Syriac included some of Aristotle's logical works, which were at about the same time being rendered from Greek into Latin by Boethius.

He also wrote two works of his own on astronomy, *On the Influence of the Moon* and *The Movement of the Sun*, both undoubtedly based on Greek sources. Sergius was characterized by a later Syriac writer as 'a man eloquent and greatly skilled in the books of the Greeks and Syrians and a most learned physician of men's bodies. He was orthodox in his opinions ... but his morals [were] corrupt, depraved and stained with lust and avarice.'

The most distinguished Syriac scholar of the early medieval period was Severus Sebokht (d. 667), a Nestorian bishop who wrote on both scientific and theological subjects. His scientific writings included works on logic and astronomy as well as the earliest known treatise on the astrolabe. He was also the first to use the so-called Hindu-Arabic number system. Writing in 662, he praises the Hindus and 'their valuable methods of calculation, and their computation that surpasses description.' He goes on to state that 'I only wish to say that this computation is done by means of nine signs,' indicating that the symbol for zero had not yet made its appearance.

By the sixth century the character of the Roman Empire had changed profoundly from what it had been in the time of Augustus, Greek having replaced Latin as the dominant language in the capital and Christianity triumphant over the old Graeco-Roman gods. Modern historians consider the sixth century to be a watershed in the history of the empire, which from that time on they tend to call Byzantine rather than Roman. As the great churchman Gennadius was to say in the mid fifteenth century, in the last days of the Byzantine Empire: 'Though I am a Hellene by speech yet I would never say that I was a Hellene, for I do not believe as Hellenes believed. I should like to take my name from my faith, and if anyone asks me what I am I answer, "A Christian." Though my father dwelt in Thessaly I do not call myself a Thessalian, but a Byzantine, for I am of Byzantium.'

Meanwhile Alexandria and Athens continued to be cultural centres on into the sixth century, as scholars continued to study at their Platonic schools, although imperial edicts banning paganism were making it more difficult to teach classical Greek philosophy. Ammonius had two renowned students at the Platonic school in Alexandria, Simplicius and John Philoponus, who are generally considered to be the last distinguished philosophers of the ancient Greek world. Simplicius seems to have remained a pagan, while Philoponus, who succeeded Ammonius as head of the Platonic school in Alexandria, was a Monophysite Christian, probably from birth.

Simplicius went on from Alexandria to study at the Platonic Academy in Athens, where he became one of the most famous Neoplatonists of his day. He is renowned for his commentaries on Aristotle, whose thoughts he tried to harmonize with that of Plato. His commentaries contain much valuable material otherwise unavailable, including fragments of the pre-Socratic philosophers.

The Aristotelian views of Simplicius were criticized by Philoponus. Aristotle's cosmology had the celestial bodies composed of *aither*, the inde-structible fifth element, which he said 'is eternal and not subject to increase or diminution, but unaging and unalterable and unmodified.' He said that 'the stars are neither fiery nor move in fire,' and also that 'Besides, the sun, which most of all the stars is considered to be hot, is really white and not fiery.'

Philoponus rejected Aristotle's statement that the sun appears to be white, pointing out that the colour of a fire depends on the fuel: 'The sun is not white, of the kind of color which many stars possess; it obviously appears yellow, like the color of a flame produced by dry and finely chopped wood. However, even if the color of the sun were white, this would not prove that it is not of fire, for the color of fire changes with the nature of the fuel.'

Philoponus says that stars differ in their brightness, just as do terres-trial fires, depending on their fuel, indicating that celestial bodies are composite structures too. He goes on to say that even those who believe that stars are aetherial must admit that they are composed of aither and their individual form, different for each star: 'However, if one abstracts the form of all things, there obviously remains the three-dimension extension only, in which respect there is no difference between any of the celestial and terrestrial bodies.' Thus Philoponus anticipated Descartes in concluding that all bodies in the cosmos, terrestrial or celestial, are substances whose common attribute is extension.

Simplicius defended the Aristotelian notion that celestial bodies are immutable, but Philoponus pointed out the rate of change depends on the mass of a body as well as other physical properties, and so changes in the stars might not be apparent because of their great size.

Simplicius also defended the Aristotelian doctrine of the eternity of the cosmos, while Philoponus held that world began through a single act of divine creation. Sambursky writes of the shocked reaction of Simplicius to Philoponus' revolutionary view of creation and its implication concerning god and nature.

> The monotheistic dogma of the creation of the universe *ex nihilo* by the single act of a God who transcends nature implied, for Philoponus, the creation of matter imbued with all the physical faculties for its independent development according to the laws of nature, a development that he conceived of as extending from the primary chaotic state to the present organized structure of the universe. This deistic conception of a world, that, once created, continued to exist automatically by natural law, was completely foreign to the classical Greek view, which never considered the gods to be 'above nature' but associated them with nature, reigning not above it but within it. The shock created by this conception of Philoponus is reflected in the words of Simplicius, who is bewildered at the idea of a god who acts only at the single moment of creation and then hands over his creation to nature.

Philoponus also criticized Aristotelian dogmas in dynamics. He refuted Aristotle's theory that the velocities of falling bodies in a given medium are proportional to their weight, making the observation that 'if one lets fall simultaneously from the same height two bodies differing greatly in weight, one will find that the ratio of the times of their motion does not correspond to the ratios of their weights, but that the difference in time is a very small one.'

He also criticized Aristotle's doctrine of natural place and natural motion, in which, for example, air always moves upwards. He points out that air might move downward if the earth or water beneath it was removed, rushing in to fill the void. A similar cause might be responsible for the normal upward motion of air, he suggested, such as a void in the upper region.

Another criticism focused on why a projectile, such as an arrow, continues moving after it receives its initial impetus. Philoponus rejected the Aristotelian theory presented by Simplicius, which was that the air displaced by the object flows back to push it from behind, an effect called *antiperistasis*. Instead Philoponus concluded that 'some incorporeal kinetic power is imparted by the thrower to the object thrown' and that 'if an arrow or a stone is projected by force in a void, the same will happen much more easily, nothing being necessary except the thrower.' This is the famous 'impetus theory', which was revived in medieval Islam and again in fourteenth-century Europe, giving rise to the beginning of modern dynamics.

Philoponus used the impetus theory in his study of light, where he showed that light rays are not projected from the eye to the luminous object, as earlier theories supposed, but in the opposite direction. He said that light is 'an incorporeal kinetic' force emitted from the luminous object, similar to the impetus given by the thrower to the body thrown.

Philoponus also had interesting ideas in acoustics, particularly concerning the phenomenon now known as resonance. Observing the ripples produced in a cup of water when he rubbed his wet finger along the rim, he suggested that the vibrations are not transferred directly to the water but through the air enclosed by the cup: 'If we pass a wet finger round the rim, a sound is created by the air squeezed out by the finger, which air is ejected into the cavity of the cup, producing the sound by striking against the walls. Experimental evidence for it can be brought in the following way: If one fills a cup with water, one can see how ripples are produced in the water when the finger moves round the rim.' He goes on to say that no sound is produced if the cup itself is held in the hand, since 'the body struck must vibrate softly, so that the air ... is emitted continuously into the upper part, striking the walls of the cup and being reflected toward all of its parts.'

Philoponus also wrote a treatise on the astrolabe which survives in a Greek manuscript. This is the oldest extant work on the astrolabe, yet another example of the many-sided genius of Philoponus, whose work would influence later generations of scientists and philosophers in both Islam and Western Europe, including Galileo.

Eutocius (born *ca.* 480) of Ascalon in Palestine was also a student of Ammonius, to whom he dedicated his commentary on the first book of

Archimedes' *On the Sphere and Cylinder*. Eutocius later wrote commentaries on two more works of Archimedes – the *Measurement of a Circle* and *On Plane Equilibria* – as well as on the first four books of the *Conics* of Apollonius, which were dedicated to the mathematician and engineer Anthemius of Tralles. Eutocius' commentaries proved to be crucial in the survival of these works. His commentaries on Archimedes, along with the Archimedean works themselves, were translated from Greek into Latin by William of Moerbeke in 1275. The commentaries were usually printed together with the works of Archimedes and Apollonius and have never been published separately.

The peak of the Byzantine Empire came under Justinian I (r. 527–65), who reconquered many of the lost dominions of the empire, so that the Mediterranean once again became a Roman sea. Justinian also broke the last direct link with the classical past when in 529 he issued an edict forbidding pagans to teach. As a result the ancient Platonic Academy in Athens was closed, ending an existence of more than nine centuries, as its teachers went into retirement or exile.

Those who went into exile included Damascius, the last director of the Academy, along with Isidorus of Miletus, who had been his predecessor, and Simplicius. They and three other scholars from the Academy were given refuge in 531 by the Persian king Chosroes I (r. 531–79), who appointed them to the faculty of the medical school at Jundishapur. The following year the six of them were allowed to come back from their exile, five of them returning to Athens, while Isidorus took up residence in Constantinople.

Justinian appointed Isidorus to be chief of the imperial architects, along with Anthemius of Tralles, their task being to design and build the great church of Haghia Sophia in Constantinople, whose foundation was laid in 532. Anthemius died during the first year of construction, but Isidorus carried the work through to completion, after which Justinian dedicated the church on 26 December 537. Haghia Sophia, which some consider to be the greatest building in the world, still stands today, a symbol of the golden age of the Byzantine Empire under Justinian.

Isidorus and Anthemius studied and taught the works of Archimedes and the Archimedean commentaries of Eutocius of Ascalon. Isidorus was apparently responsible for the first collected edition of at least the three Archimedean works commented upon by Eutocius – *On the Sphere and Cyclinder, On the Measurement of the Circle*, and *On the Equilibrium of Planes* – as well as the commentaries themselves.

The University of Constantinople was closed during the reign of Phocas (r. 602–10), who is generally considered to be the worst emperor ever to rule Byzantine. His successor Heraclius (r. 610–41) reopened the university as an ecumenical academy under the Patriarch Sergius. Philosophical and mathematical studies were directed by Stephen of Alexandria, who was summoned to Constantinople in 612.

Stephen's writings include commentaries on Aristotle, an *Explanation* of the astronomical commentary of Theon of Alexandria, and a commentary on Ptolemy. While in Constantinople he lectured on Plato and Aristotle as well as on the subjects of the quadrivium, that is, arithmetic, geometry, astronomy and music. Later the quadrivium was revived as the foundation of all mathematical instruction in the curriculum of schools in the empire.

By that time the classical Graeco-Roman world had come to an end. Rome had been sacked by the Vandals and Athens utterly destroyed by a Germanic tribe known as the Heruli, while the Platonic school in Alexandria had been closed when the city was captured by the Arabs in 639. That left Constantinople as the only remaining centre of Graeco-Roman culture, though its ties with the classical past had by then become very tenuous. Constantinople only barely survived in 626, when a Turkic tribe called the Avars almost broke through the city walls, while at the same time a Persian invasion swept across Asia Minor as far as the Bosphorus. The empire survived through the heroic efforts of the emperor Heraclius, who in 627 defeated the Persians and drove them out of Asia Minor.

Meanwhile a new and even more formidable power had emerged in Arabia, where the Islamic era began with the flight of the prophet Muhammed from Mecca in 622. The armed might of Islam became evident in 636, when a Byzantine army commanded by the emperor's brother Theodorus was virtually annihilated by the Arabs at the battle of the Yarmuk in Palestine. This opened up all of Syria and Palestine to the Arabs, who captured Jerusalem in 636 and three years later overran Egypt.

Arab forces under the first caliphs went on to conquer Persia in 640, Tripolitania in 647 and northwest Africa in 670. An Arab fleet attacked Constantinople in 674, subjecting the city to an unsuccessful four-year siege. Within the next half-century the armies of Islam conquered Sind and Transoxania and invaded Spain, raiding across the Pyrenees until they were finally stopped by Charles Martel in 732 at the battle of Tours in France.

Mu'awiya assumed the title of caliph at Jerusalem in 661, whereupon he immediately moved to Damascus. This was the beginning of the Umayyad dynasty, whose caliphs ruled mostly from Damascus. After a four-year civil war the Umayyads were overthrown and Abu l-Abbas al-Saffah became caliph in 749, thus founding the Abbasid dynasty, which would last for more than five centuries. Abu l-Abbas was succeeded in 754 by his brother Abu Jafar al-Mansur, who in the years 762 to 755 built Baghdad as his new capital, beginning the most illustrious period in the history of Islam.

Baghdad emerged as a great cultural centre under al-Mansur (r. 754–75) and three generations of his successors, particularly al-Mahdi (r. 775–85), Harun al-Rashid (r. 786–809) and al-Ma'mun (r. 813–33). According to the historian al-Mas'udi (d. 956), Al-Mansur 'was the first caliph to have books translated from foreign languages into Arabic,' including 'books by Aristotle on logic and other subjects, and other ancient books from classical Greek, Byzantine Greek, Pahlavi, Neopersian, and Syriac.'

The translation movement was to a large extent motivated by the desire to educate secretaries needed to administer the Abbasid empire. This is evident in the writings of Ibn-Qutayb (d. 889), whose *Adab al-Katib (Education of the Secretaries)* enumerates the subjects that state secretaries should learn, including arithmetic, geometry and astronomy, as well as practical skills such as surveying, metrology and civil engineering, for which Greek works in science had to be translated into Arabic to provide the necessary textbooks.

The translation program continued under al-Mansur's son and successor al-Mahdi. The new caliph's vizier, Yahya ibn-Khalid ibn-Barmak, is credited by the tenth-century Tunisian scholar Abdallah ibn-abi-Zayd with initiating the Abbasid's policy of importing Greek books from the Byzantine Empire.

The most important intellectual institution in Baghdad under the Abbasids was the famous *Bayt al-Hikma,* or House of Wisdom, which originally seems to have been basically a library. Pahlavi manuscripts were kept there and in the early Abbasid period some of these were translated into Arabic. The chronicler Ibn-an-Nadim notes that the court astrologer Abu-Sahl ibn-Nawbaht was employed by Harun al-Rashid at the *Bayt al-Hikma,* where 'he translated from Persian into Arabic and relied in his scholarship on the books of Iran.' During the reign of al-Ma'mun astronomers and mathematicians were associated with the *Bayt al-Hikma,* which at that time may have served as a research institute as well as a library. Ibn-an-Nadim also reports that the famous mathematician and astronomer Muhammed ibn-Musa al-Khwarizmi (fl. *ca.* 828) 'was employed full-time in the *Bayt al-Hikma* in the service of al-Ma'mun.'

Al-Khwarizmi is renowned for his treatise *Kitab al-jabr wa'l-muqabalah,* known more simply as *Algebra,* for it was from this work that Europe later learned the branch of mathematics known by that name. In his preface the author writes that the Caliph al-Ma'mun 'encouraged me to compose a compendious work on algebra, confining it to the fine and important parts of its calculation, such as people constantly require in cases of inheritance, legacies, partition, law-suits and trade, and in all their dealings with one another, or where surveying, the digging of canals, geometrical computation, and other objects of various sorts and kinds are concerned.'

Another of al-Khwarizmi's mathematical works survives only in a unique copy of a Latin translation entitled *De numero indorum, (Concerning the Hindu Art of Reckoning),* the original Arabic version having been lost. This work, probably based on an Arabic translation of works by the Indian mathematician Brahmagupta (fl. 628), describes the Hindu numerals that eventually became the digits used in the modern Western world. The new notation came to be known as that of al-Khwarizmi, corrupted to 'algorism' or 'algorithm,' which now means a procedure for solving a mathematical problem in a finite number of steps that often involves repetition of an operation.

Al-Khwarizmi is the author of the earliest extant original work of Islamic astronomy, the *Zij al-Sindhind* (a *zij* is an astronomical handbook with tables). This is a set of planetary tables using earlier Indian and Greek astronomical elements, including the epicycle theory. He and Fadil ibn al-Nawbaht are credited with building the first Islamic observatory, which they founded in Baghdad *ca.* 828, during the reign of al-Ma'mun. Al-Khwarizmi also wrote the first comprehensive Islamic treatise on geography, in which he revised much of Ptolemy's work on this subject, drawing new maps.

Euclid's *Elements* were first translated into Arabic during the reign of Harun al-Rashid by the mathematician al-Hajjaj ibn Matar (fl. *ca.* 786–833), under the patronage of the vezir Yahya ibn Khalid ibn Barmak. Al-Hajjaj did an improved and abbreviated version of the *Elements* for Al-Ma'mun, apparently for use as a school textbook.

Al-Mahdi commissioned the translation of Aristotle's *Topics* into Arabic from Syriac, into which it had been translated from Greek. Later the work was translated directly from Greek into Arabic. The motivation for translating the *Topics* was that it taught the art of systematic argumentation, which was vital in discourse between Muslim scholars and those of other faiths and in converting non-believers to Islam, which became state policy under the Abbasids. Aristotle's *Physics* was first translated into Arabic during the reign of Harun al-Rashid, the motivation apparently being its use in theological disputations concerning cosmology.

Harun al-Rashid's son al-Ma'mun continued the translation programme of his predecessors. Al Mas'udi writes of Al Ma'mun's interest in astrology and his patronage of intellectual investigations. 'At the beginning of his reign ... he used to spend time investigating astrological rulings and prognostications, to follow what the stars prescribed, and to model his conduct on that of the past Sassanian emperors .... He had jurists and the learned among men of general culture attend his session; he had such men brought from various cities and stipends for them allocated.'

Islamic astronomy was dominated by Ptolemy, whose works were translated into Arabic and also disseminated in summaries and commentaries. The earliest Arabic translation of the *Almagest* is by al-Hajjaj ibn Matar in the first half of the ninth century. The most popular compendium of Ptolemaic astronomy was that of al-Farghani (d. after 861), who used the findings of earlier Islamic astronomers to correct the *Almagest*. Habash al-Hasib (d. *ca.* 870) produced a set of astronomical tables in which he introduced the trigonometric functions of the sine, cosine and tangent, which do not appear in Ptolemy's works.

Islamic science developed apace with the translation movement, which involved philosophers as well as scientists. The beginning of Islamic philosophy is credited to Yaqub ibn Ishaq al-Kindi (*ca.* 795–866), the Latin Alkindes, famous in the West as the 'Philosopher of the Arabs.' Al-Kindi was from a wealthy Arab family in Kufa, in present-day Iraq, which he left to study in Baghdad. There he worked in the *Bayt al-Hikma*, enjoying the patronage of al-Ma'mun and his immediate successors.

Al-Kindi, though not a translator himself, benefited from the translation movement to become the first of the Islamic philosopher-scientists, founding the Aristotelian movement in Islam. He was a polymath, his treatises including works in geography, politics, philosophy, cosmology, physics, mathematics, meteorology, music, optics, theology, alchemy and astrology. He was the first Islamic theorist of music, following in the Pythagorean tradition. His work on optics follows Theon of Alexandria in studying the propagation of light and the formation of shadows, and his theory of the emission and transmission of light is based on that of Euclid. Al-Kindi's ideas on visual perception, which differed from those of Aristotle, together with his studies of the reflection of light, laid the foundations for what became, in the European renaissance, the laws of perspective. His studies of natural science convinced him of the value of rational thought, and as a result he was the first noted Islamic philosopher to be attacked by fundamentalist Muslim clerics. His *Letter on the Method of Banishing Sadness* says that the cure for melancholia is applying oneself to the only enduring object, the world of the intellect.

The two most famous translators in Baghdad were Hunayn ibn-Ishaq and Thabit ibn Qurra, both of whom were employed by the Banu Musa 'for full-time translation', according to the chronicler Abu-Sulayman al-Sigistani, who says they were paid a salary that put them on a par with the highest officials in the government bureaucracy.

Hunayn ibn-Ishaq (808–873), known in Latin as Jannitus, was born at al-Hira in southern Iraq, the son of a Nestorian apothecary. He went to Baghdad to study under the Nestorian physician Yuhannah Ibn Masawayh (d. 857), personal physician to al Ma'mun and his successors. Hunayn, who at the time knew only Syriac, was disappointed by Ibn Masawayh, who discouraged him when he inquired about Greek medical texts. According to his autobiography, the *Risala*, Hunayn then went away to 'the land of the Greeks' (*bilal-al-Rum*, probably Constantinople) and obtained a sound knowledge of Greek, after which he lived in Basra for a time to learn Arabic. He then moved to Baghdad, where he and his students, who included his son Ishaq ibn-Hunayn and his nephew Hubaysh, made meticulous translations from Greek into both Syriac and Arabic. Their translations included the medical works of Hippocrates and Galen, Euclid's *Elements*, and *De Materia Medica* of Dioscorides, which became the basis for Islamic pharmacology. Ishaq's extant translation of Aristotle's *Physics* is the last and best version of that work in Arabic. His translations included Ptolemy's *Almagest*, while his father Hunayn revised the *Tetrabiblos*. Hunayn also revised an earlier translation of Galen by Yahya ibn al-Bitriq (d. 820); these were synopses that contained Plato's *Republic*, *Timaeus* and *Laws*, the first rendering of the Platonic dialogues into Arabic.

Hunayn was indefatigable in his search for Greek manuscripts, as he writes in regard to Galen's *De demonstratione:* 'I traveled in its search in northern Mesopotamia, all of Syria, Palestine, and Egypt until I reached Alexandria. I found nothing except about half of it, in disorder and incomplete, in Damascus.'

Hunayn was an outstanding physician and wrote two books on medicine, both extant in Arabic, one of them a history of the subject, the other a treatise entitled *On the Properties of Nutrition,* based on Galen and other Greek writers. His other writings include treatises on philosophy, astronomy, mathematics, optics, ophthalmology, meteorology, alchemy and magic, and he is also credited with establishing the technical vocabulary of Islamic science.

Thabit ibn Qurra (*ca.* 836–901) was born in the Mesopotamian town of Harran, a centre of the ancient Sabean cult, an astral religion in which the

sun, moon and five planets were worshipped as divinities. Harran had preserved Hellenic literary culture, and so educated Sabeans like Thabit were
fluent in Greek as well as in Syriac and Arabic. After Thabit established
himself a number of his fellow Sabeans joined him in Baghdad, where
they formed a school of mathematics, astronomy and astrology that lasted
through three generations.

Thabit translated works from both Syriac and Greek into Arabic, his
works including the *Introduction to Arithmetic* by Nicomachus as well as
improved editions of Euclid's *Elements* and Ptolemy's *Almagest*. His descen-
dants, among other works, produced Arabic translations of the writings of
Archimedes and Apollonius of Perge.

Thabit also wrote treatises of his own, including works on physics,
astronomy, astrology, dynamics, mechanics, optics and mathematics. He
wrote a commentary on Aristotle's *Physics* and an original work entitled *The
Nature and Influence of the Stars*, which laid out the ideological foundations
of Islamic astrology. He also wrote a comprehensive work on the construction and theory of sundials.

Thabit revived the erroneous 'trepidation theory' of Theon of
Alexandria. This held that the pole of the heavens oscillated back and
forth, as opposed to the correct theory, first given by Hipparchus, that the
celestial pole precessed in a circular path. Thabit pictured the planets as
being embedded in solid spheres with a compressible fluid between the
orbs and the eccentric circles. His planetary theory included a mathematical analysis of motion, in which he referred to the speed of a moving body
at a particular point in space and time, a concept that is now part of modern kinematics. His contributions in mathematics include calculating the
volume of a paraboloid and giving geometrical solutions to some quadratic
and cubic equations. He also formulated a remarkable theorem concerning so-called 'amicable' numbers, where each number of an amicable pair
is the sum of the proper divisors of the other, the smallest such pair being
220 and 284.

Another prominent figure of the translation movement was Qusta
ibn Luqa, a Greek-speaking Christian from the Lebanon, who worked in
Baghdad as a physician, scientist and translator until his death in 913. His
translations included works of Aristarchus, Hero and Diophantus. He wrote
commentaries on Euclid's *Elements and De Materia Medica* of Diophantus, as
well as original treatises on medicine, astronomy, metrology and optics. His
medical works include a treatise on sexual hygiene and a book on medicine for pilgrims.

The program of translation continued until the mid eleventh century, both in the East and in Muslim Spain. By that time most of the important works of Greek science and philosophy were available in Arabic translations, along with commentaries on these works and the original treatises by Islamic scientists that had been produced in the interim. Thus, through their contact with surrounding cultures, scholars writing in Arabic were in a position to take the lead in science and philosophy, absorbing what they had learned from the Greeks and adding to it to begin an Islamic renaissance, whose fruits were eventually passed on to Western Europe.

The most famous figure in Islamic science is Ibn Sina (980–1037), known in the Latin West as Avicenna, 'Prince of Physicians'. His best known works are the *Canon of Medicine*, and the *Book of* Healing, which also contain chapters on logic, ethics, mathematics, physics, optics, chemistry, biology, botany, geology, mineralogy, meteorology and seismology. Ibn Sina's medicine derived from Galen and his philosophy from Plato and Aristotle. His medical writings were translated into Latin and used as basic texts in Europe's medical schools until the seventeenth century. His *Canon of Medicine* was far ahead of its times in dealing with such matters as cancer treatment, the influence of the environment, the beneficial effects of physical exercise, and the need for psychotherapy, where he recognized the connection between emotional and physical states, including the heartache of unrequited love.

Toledo became a centre for translation from the Arabic to Latin after its recapture from the Moors in 1085 by Alfonso VI, king of Castile and León, the first major triumph of the Reconquista, the Christian reconquest of Al-Andalus, Muslim Spain.

Gerard of Cremona (1114–1187) was by far the most prolific of the Latin translators. His translations included Arabic versions of writings by Aristotle, Euclid, Archimedes, Ptolemy and Galen, as well as works by al-Kindi, al-Khwarizmi, al-Razi, Ibn Sina, Ibn al-Haytham, Thabit ibn Qurra, al-Farghani, al-Farabi, Qusta ibn Luqa, Jabir ibn Hayyan, al-Zarqali, Jabir ibn Aflah, Masha'allah, the Banu Musa and Abu Ma'shar. The subjects covered in these translations include 24 works on medicine; 17 on geometry, mathematics, optics, weights and dynamics; 14 on philosophy and logic; 12 on astronomy and astrology; and 7 on alchemy, divination and geomancy, or predicting the future from geographic features.

More of Arabic science passed to the West through Gerard than from any other source. His translations produced a great impact upon the development of European science, particularly in medicine, where students in the Latin West took advantage of the more advanced state of medical studies in medieval Islam. His translations in astronomy, physics and mathematics were also very influential, since they represented a scientific approach to the study of nature rather than the philosophical and theological attitude that had been prevalent in the Latin West.

By the beginning of the thirteenth century European science was on the rise, stimulated by the enormous influx of Graeco-Arabic works translated into Latin and used at the new universities that sprang up all over Europe, supplanting the cathedral schools of the earlier medieval era.

The earliest of these institutions of higher learning was the university of Bologna, founded in 1088, followed in turn by those of Paris (*ca.* 1150), Oxford (1167), Salerno (1173, a refounding of the medical school), Palenzia (*ca.* 1178), Reggio (1188), Vicenza (1204), Cambridge (1209), Salamanca (1218) and Padua (1222), to name only the first ten, with another ten founded in the remaining years of the thirteenth century. Twenty-five more were founded in the fourteenth century, and another 35 in the fifteenth, so that by 1500 there were 80 universities in Europe, evidence of the tremendous intellectual revival that had taken place in the West, beginning with the initial acquisition of Graeco-Arabic learning in the twelfth century. The curricula at these universities was dominated by the works of Aristotle, reinterpreted for the Christian world view principally by Albertus Magnus (*ca.* 1200–1280) and Thomas Aquinas (*ca.* 1225–1274).

Meanwhile Byzantium had been engaged in a desperate struggle for survival, fighting against the Arabs on their eastern frontiers and in the Mediterranean, while on their European border they tried to repel invasions by the Bulgars who overran all of Greece and penetrated up to the walls of Constantinople before they were driven back. The empire was also riven internally by the famous Iconoclastic Crisis during the years 717 to 845, in which the veneration of icons was banned in the churches of the empire, with those who opposed this policy being imprisoned, tortured and executed. All of these factors made the Iconoclastic period a veritable Dark Age for Byzantium, during which the University of Constantinople was closed and there was little or no discernable intellectual activity in Byzantium.

Byzantium began to revive during the successive reigns of Theophilus (r. 829–42) and his son Michael III (r. 842–67). Michael's uncle, the Caesar Bardas, founded a school of higher studies in the Magnaura Palace, which some modern scholars have viewed as a revival of the University of Constantinople. One of the principal figures of this revival is Leo the Mathematician (*ca.* 790–*ca.* 869), who came to Constantinople during the reign of Theophilus and taught at the Magnaura school. Leo is supposed to have learned mathematics, including the works of Archimedes, from a monk in a monastery on the Aegean island of Andros. Leo's collection of the writings of Archimedes included all of the works now known, excepting *On Floating Problems, On the Method, Stomachion,* and *the Cattle Problem.* Leo also transcribed Ptolemy's *Almagest* as well as the collection of Ptolemy's mathematical and astronomical writings known as the *Little Astronomy.*

One of Leo's students was captured by an Arab army in 830 and ended up at the court of the Abbasid Caliph al-Ma'mun (r. 813–33). The Caliph, who was sponsoring translations of ancient Greek science and mathematics into Arabic, thus learned of Leo's accomplishments and invited him to Baghdad. But the emperor Theophilus kept Leo in Constantinople by appointing him as the head of a new school of philosophy and science, where he had his students copy manuscripts of Archimedes and Euclid. Kurt Vogel, in his article on Byzantine science, writes that 'without Leo, the revival of mathematical studies in the West based on Greek texts is well-nigh inconceivable.'

The University of Constantinople was organized again during the reign of Constantine IX (r. 1042–55), who established faculties of law and philosophy for training lawyers, notaries and high officials in the imperial administration. The leading figure in the university during his reign was Michael Psellus (1018–1078), a high court official who was appointed head of the philosophical faculty, in which he taught classical Greek philosophy, particularly as interpreted by the Neoplatonist school. Most of what is known of Psellus comes from his *Chronographia,* an account of the Macedonian dynasty, beginning with Basil I (r. 867–86) and ending with the empress Theodora (r. 1055–56), a chronicle that reads like a modern historical novel. There Psellus, who was an autodidact in philosophy, writes of how he began his own studies in this field: 'I met some of the experts in the art, and I was instructed by them how to pursue my studies in a methodical way. One passed me to another for tuition, the lesser light to the greater, and he recommended me to a third, and he to Aristotle and Plato. Doubtless my former teachers were well satisfied to take second place to these two.'

Psellus was not an original thinker and his own writings in philosophy and science, which include a commentary on Aristotle's *Physics,* are derivative. Nonetheless, he was very influential in reviving interest in those fields in Byzantium, particularly in Neoplatonist philosophy and mathematics.

This was part of a revival of classical learning in Byzantium that began under the Macedonian dynasty and continued under the Comneni, the next dynasty to rule the empire. This revived Hellenism is evident in the work of the princess Anna Comnena, who in the preface to her *Alexiad*, a history of the reign of her father, Alexius I Comenus (r. 1086–1118), writes that 'I perused the works of Aristotle and the dialogues of Plato and enriched my mind with the quarternion of learning.'

The revival of classical learning in Byzantium is also evident in the number of manuscripts originating in the eleventh and twelfth centuries, including works of Euclid, Archimedes, Apollonius, Hero and Ptolemy. Leonardo of Pisa (*ca.* 1170–after 1240), also known as Fibonacci, the first great mathematician of Western Europe, writes in his *Liber Abaci* that he became acquainted with a number of arithmetical and algebraic problems when he visited Constantinople, evidence of the high level of mathematics in Byzantium at the time.

The first European scholar of the late medieval era to translate the works of Aristotle from Greek to Latin was James of Venice, who flourished in the first half of the twelfth century. His translations include Aristotle's *Prior Analytics, Posterior Analytics, Topics, On the Soul, Parts of Animals, Physics, Metaphysics* and *Sophistical Refutations*. His commentary on the latter work shows that he was aware of Byzantine scholarship on this subject in Constantinople, which was an unrivaled source for the works of Aristotle and other ancient Greek writers. James' translations, together with their revisions, formed the basis for much of Aristotelian studies in Europe until the sixteenth century.

Translations from Greek to Latin were also done in Norman Sicily during the reign of William I (r. 1154–66). The principal translators during his reign was Henricus Aristippus, who became archbishop of Catania in 1156 and four years later was placed in charge of the entire administration of the Sicilian kingdom. He was the first to translate from the Greek two of Plato's dialogues, *Meno* and *Phaedo*, as well as the fourth book of Aristotle's *Meteorology*, works that remained in use until the early Renaissance. Aristippus also served as envoy to the court of Manuel II Comnenus (r. 1143–80) in Constantinople, where the emperor presented him with a beautiful codex of Ptolemy's *Almagest* as a present to King William. The first translation of this manuscript from Greek to Latin was made in Palermo by an anonymous visiting scholar *ca.* 1160. Other works translated from Greek to Latin at the Sicilian court by this scholar include Euclid's *Optica* and *Catoptrica*, the *De Motu* of Proclus and the *Pneumatica* of Hero of Alexandria.

The Dominican monk William of Moerbeke (b. *ca.* 1220–35–d. before 1286), in Belgium, was the most prolific of all medieval translators from Greek into Latin. Thomas Aquinas is said to have suggested to Moerbeke that he complete the translation of Aristotle's works directly from the Greek. Moerbeke says that he took on this task 'in spite of the hard work and tediousness which it involves, in order to provide Latin scholars with new material for study.'

Moerbeke's Greek translations included the writings of Aristotle, commentaries on Aristotle, and works of Archimedes, Proclus, Hero of Alexandria, Ptolemy, Galen, Simplicius and Eutocius. The popularity of Moerbeke's work is evidenced by the number of extant copies of his translations, including manuscripts from the thirteenth to fifteenth centuries, printed editions from the fifteenth century onwards and versions in English, French, Spanish and even modern Greek, done from the fourteenth century through the twentieth. His translations led to a better knowledge of the actual Greek texts of several works, and in a few cases they are the only evidence of lost Greek texts, such as that of Hero's *Catoptrica.*

Thus more than fifteen centuries after the time of Plato and Aristotle their works were being studied again along with those of the great Hellenistic mathematicians and physicists, whose writings had made their way to Latin Europe through both Byzantium and Islam, stimulating a revival of learning in the West that would eventually lead to the emergence of modern science.

CHAPTER 16

THE RENAISSANCE: BYZANTIUM TO ITALY

Constantinople was captured and sacked in 1204 by the army of the Fourth Crusade and the Venetian fleet, after which the Byzantine Empire was reduced to several small states, two of them in Asia Minor. One of these, ruled by the Lascarid dynasty, had its capital at Nicaea, while a branch of the Comneni dynasty reigned from their capital at Trebizond. Then in 1261 the Greeks of Nicaea recaptured Constantinople, which once again became capital of the Byzantine Empire, a state that was much reduced in size and power compared to what it had been in the reign of Justinian. But despite its reduced circumstances, Byzantium flowered in a last renaissance after the recapture of Constantinople, in what was fated to be the final stage of its immensely long history, during which it had preserved the last living links with the classical Graeco-Roman world.

The renaissance had actually begun even before the recapture of Constantinople, during the reign of the Lascarid dynasty in Nicaea in the years 1204–61. Theodore I Lascaris (r. 1204–22), the first of the emperors-in-exile, was succeeded by his son-in-law John III Vatatzes (r. 1222–54), and he in turn by his son Theodore II Lascaris (r. 1254–58). The fourth and last of the dynasty was John IV Lascaris (r. 1258–61), son of Theodore II, who was only seven and one-half years old when his father died on 16 August 1258. The Nicaean nobles appointed Michael Palaeologus as regent, and in December of that year he was made co-emperor as Michael VIII. The young John IV soon disappeared from sight as a virtual prisoner of his co-ruler, and by the time the Greeks recaptured Constantinople in 1261 he was presumed dead. Michael VIII thenceforth reigned as sole emperor until his own death in 1282, beginning the Palaeologus dynasty that would rule Byzantium until Constantinople fell to the Turks in 1453.

John III founded an academy of philosophy in Nicaea and also established schools and libraries at other places in his realm, part of his programme to give his subjects a more comprehensive education, particularly in applied mathematics.

The second director of the academy in Nicaea was Nicephorus Blemmydes (*ca.* 1197–*ca.* 1272), who, after completing his studies in medicine, taught there in the years 1238–48, his pupils including the future emperor Theodore II and the scholar George Acropolites. Blemmydes' only scientific work is the *Epitome physica*, a summary of physics, mathematics and astronomy based on Aristotle, Euclid and Cleomedes, author of an astronomical handbook dating from the late Hellenistic period. The *Epitome* is superficial and unoriginal, but, as David Pingree notes, 'it reawakened an interest in ancient Greek science which had been virtually dead since the time of Michael Psellus in the eleventh century.' His extant works also include an autobiography and a treatise entitled the *Imperial Statue*, a Mirror for Princes that he wrote for Theodore II. He observed at least one lunar eclipse, that of 18 May 1258, and his student George Acropolites recorded a solar eclipse in Nicaea on 3 June 1239.

The science of medicine also flourished at the Byzantine court in Nicaea, as Steven Runciman notes in his work on *The Last Byzantine Renaissance.* 'The Nicaean court physician, Nicholas Myrepsus, wrote a work on *materia medica*, which was for some centuries consulted in the West, as well as in the East. Michal VIII's physician, Demetrius Pepagemus, wrote a book on gout, based mainly on his own observations. He was also the author of a book on falconry, based equally on his own experience and notes.'

Byzantine medicine continued to flourish for a time after the recapture of Constantinople. The last of the great medical writers of Byzantium was John Actuarius (*ca.* 1275–after 1328), chief physician at the court of Andronicus II Palaeologus (r. 1282–1328). According to Runciman, 'He was an authority on diseases of the urine, on which he had much that was new to say. He seems to have been the first doctor to discover the whipcord, *trichocephalus dispar*, in the human intestine; and he was a pioneer in the study of psychosomatic complaints. After his time medicine declined.'

After the recapture of Constantinople Michael VIII Palaeologus reopened the University of Constantinople, appointing George Acropolites to the chair of philosophy. Acropolites also taught mathematics, basing his lectures on Euclid and Nicomachus. John Pediasmus, who wrote commentaries on Ptolemy and Cleomedes as well as treatises on geometry and musical theory, succeeded in the chair of philosophy.

Acropolites' most famous student was the historian George Pachymeres (1242–1310), who also taught at the University of Constantinople. Pachymeres' principal scientific work is the *Handbook on the Four Sciences*, which he used in teaching the quadrivium. The handbook was widely used as a text, for by then the Byzantines had adopted the western Latin system of the seven liberal arts, the trivium and quadrivium. The mathematical section of the handbook, based largely on Euclid and Nicomachus, also covered the mathematics necessary for studying Aristotle. This section also included a partial paraphrase of the *Arithmetica* of Diophantus, which Blemmydes shows that he fully understood, something very unusual for the time. The astronomical section included a discussion of the risings, settings and culminations of prominent constellations, as well as fundamental doctrines of astrology.

A number of scholars from Byzantium went west on diplomatic missions or to teach at European universities. One of the first of the diplomat scholars was the monk Maximos Planudes (1260–1310), who was sent by Andronicus II (r. 1282–1328) on an embassy to Venice in 1296. After his return to Constantinople Planudes taught at the monastery of St Saviour in Chora, where he translated from Latin to Greek a number of books that he had acquired in Italy, including works by Cicero, Ovid, St Augustine and Boethius. The vast number of extant manuscripts of his translations show that they were often used as texts for teaching Greek at universities in Italy, which began with the emergence of Italian humanism and its interest in reviving classical letters.

Planudes is also noted for his mathematical writings. He edited the Greek text of Diophantus and wrote a commentary on the *Arithmetica* as far as Book II, Chapter 5. He is known also to have lectured on Euclid's *Elements*. His treatise on *Arithmetic after the Indian Method*, deals with the so-called Hindu-Arabic numerals, including the use of zero 'in what is termed place notation', that is, where the value of a symbol depends on its place in the number. His treatise also describes an improved method for extracting the square roots of numbers.

Planudes had two notable students at the Chora monastery. One of these was George of Cyprus, later to be Patriarch Gregory II (r. 1283–89), who was inspired by Planudes to study Aristotle and Euclid, which led him to play an important part in the literary revival in late thirteenth-century Byzantium. The other was Manuel Moschopolos, who wrote a thesis on magic squares: a square array of numbers, four or five to a side, which give the same sum added up along any row or column or along the diagonals, where he wrote from the mathematical standpoint rather than the mystical. He is best known for his editions of ancient Greek literature, including Homer, Hesiod, Pindar, Sophocles and Aristophanes, evidence of the revival of Hellenism in the late Byzantine world.

The scholar Manuel Bryennios flourished in Constantinople *ca.* 1300, teaching mathematics, astronomy and, musical theory. His only surviving writing is the three-volume *Harmonika*, the most comprehensive extant codification of Byzantine musical scholarship, based on the work of Ptolemy, Nicomachus, and neo-Pythagorean writers on the numerological theory of music.

The leading figure in the intellectual revival in Byzantium in the thirteenth and fourteenth century was Theodore Metochites (1270–1332), a student of Manuel Bryennios, who was grand logothete, or prime minister, during the reign of Andronicus II Palaeologus (r. 1282–1328), son and successor of Michael VIII. Metochites rebuilt and redecorated the church of St Saviour in Chora, whose restored mosaics and frescoes are among the world's greatest extant treasures of Byzantine art, evidence of the renaissance of Byzantium in its latter years. As well as being a statesman, scholar and patron of the arts, he was the author of works on philosophy, astronomy, theology and literature, citing more than eighty ancient authors in his works. As his student Nikephoros Gregoras wrote of Metochites: 'From morning to evening he was most wholly and eagerly devoted to public affairs as if scholarship was absolutely indifferent to him; but later in the evening, having left the palace, he became absorbed in science to such a degree as if he were a scholar with absolutely no connection with any other affairs.'

The many and varied writings of Metochites include an *Introduction to Astronomy*, based on Ptolemy's *Almagest*. This treatise made Ptolemy's work better known, and, according to David Pingree, 'raised the level of sophistication in Byzantine astronomy to a height it had not attained for centuries.'

Byzantine scholars at the time of Metochites were familiar with Islamic astronomical texts. The source of these texts has been identified as Gregory Chioniades, an astronomer and physician who was born in Constantinople between 1240 and 1250 and died in Trebizond around 1320. One of the important sources of information about his life is George Chrysococces, an astronomer and physician who flourished in Constantinople and Trebizond in the period *ca.* 1335–50. In the introduction to his *Exegesis in the Persian Syntaxis*, written *ca.* 1347, he says that Chioniades went to Persia to study astronomy, and that he 'returned to Trebizond, bearing away from Persia a number of astronomical texts which he translated into Greek. The best of these texts had no commentary; the present *Exegesis* fulfills the need for one.'

More details about the life of Chioniades can be gleaned from his *Confession of Faith* and his 12 surviving letters. After completing his medical studies in Constantinople he became a monk and moved to Trebizond. Then in the early 1290s he went on to Tabriz, capital of the Ilkhanid Mongol kingdom, where he began studying astronomy under the Persian astronomer Shams ad-Din al-Bukhari. Shams dictated to him in Persian the *'Ala'i Tables* of 'Abd al-Karim ash-Shirwani al-Fakhad (*ca.* 1150), which Chioniades rendered roughly into Greek as the *Persian Astronomical Composition*. Chioniades soon afterwards rewrote this in more stylish form as the *Revised Canon*, completed in 1296. Here, according to David Pingree, Chioniades shows that he was becoming familiar with the shorter Arabic version of the Sanjari Tables of 'Abd ar-Rahman al-Khazini (*ca.* 1120), and with the Persian *Ilkhanid Tables* of Nasir ad-Din al-Tusi (1202–1274), both of which he subsequently translated into Greek.

The latter astronomer was famous for an innovation in planetary theory known as the 'al-Tusi couple', a model which has one circle rolling inside another to give a combination of two circular motions, a substitute for the epicycles used by Ptolemy. According to Pingree, Chioniades translated 'an introduction to astronomy that is illustrated by diagrams of the Tusi couple'. He goes on to say that 'Knowledge of the Tusi couple eventually reached the West through a MS of Chioniades' works, and perhaps by other routes as well; it was employed by Copernicus in his planetary models.'

Chioniadis was back in Trebizond by September 1301 and by the following April he was once again in Constantinople, where he taught medicine and astronomy, including the new astronomical theories he had learned in Persia. One of those he taught at that time may have been Manuel Bryennios, the teacher of Theodore Metochites, who writes in his autobiography that he had learned astronomy from someone who had been in Persia. Chioniades may also have been the one who transmitted knowledge of the Hindu-Arabic numbers to Maximos Planudes, his contemporary Then in 1305, with the support of the emperor Alexius II Comnenus (r. 1297–1330) of Trebizond, Chioniades was appointed Orthodox bishop of Tabriz. He remained at his bishopric in Tabriz for at least five years before retiring as a monk in Trebizond, where he spent the rest of his days.

Chrysococces' versions of the *Sanjari Tables*, the *'Ala'i Tables* and the *Ilkhanid Tables* are in his *Exegesis in the Persian Syntaxis*. This was an extremely popular work which, as David Pingree points out, 'influenced several anonymous sets of astronomical tables and canons written in the second half of the fourteenth and the beginning of the fifteenth century as well as the

Tribiblos of Theodore Meliteniotes. Shelemo ben Elihayu of Thessalonica (fl. 1374–86) translated Chrysococces' *Exegesis* into Hebrew. Chrysococces himself made no significant contribution to astronomy.'

The historian and polymath Nikephoros Gregoras was born in Heracleia Pontica *ca.* 1290–94 and died in Constantinople in the period 1358–61. After coming to Constantinople he studied logic and rhetoric with the future Patriarch John XIII Glykys and philosophy and astronomy with Theodore Metochites. He then ran a school at the Chora monastery, where he had access to the rich library of Metochites. His most important work is the *Rhomaike Historia* in 37 books, covering the period 1204–1359. His philosophical writings were more influenced by Plato than Aristotle, and it was his doctrine of a universal soul uniting heaven and earth that inspired George Gemistus Plethon, the last great philosopher of Byzantium.

The scientific writings of Gregoras include treatises on the construction of the astrolabe and calculations of eclipses. His proposals for calendar reform and for the calculation of the date of Easter were not adopted, but they foreshadowed the Gregorian reform of 1582.

The astronomer, mathematician and theologian Isaac Argyros (*ca.* 1305–*ca.* 1373) was a student of Nikephoros Gregoras at the Chora monastery who became the leading Byzantine supporter of Ptolemaic astronomy in the third quarter of the fourteenth century. According to David Pingree:

> He wrote a *Construction of New Tables* and a *Construction of New Tables of Conjunctions and Oppositions* (of the sun and moon), for both of which the epoch is 1 Sept. 1367 ... . Argyros's mathematical works include one on the square roots of nonsquare numbers; a treatise on Hero's *Geometrics* concerning the reduction of nonright to right triangles and other geometrical problems, composed in 1367/8; and a *Method of Geodesy*, also based on Hero. He also wrote scholia to Ptolemy's *Geography* and edited with scholia his *Harmonics*.

The mathematician and astronomer Theodore Meliteniotes (d. 1393) was for many years the head of the patriarchal school in Constantinople. His *Astronomiki Tribiblos* (*Three Books on Astronomy*) 'constitutes the culmination of Byzantine astronomical writings in the fourteenth century,' according to Edmund Fryde, who goes on to remark that 'Meliteniotes praised highly the achievements of Islamic astronomy, while stressing that it built on the foundation of Ptolemaic writings.'

During the last century of Byzantine history, which ended with the Turkish capture of Constantinople in 1453, there was a permanent decline of scholarly activity in Byzantium. Nevertheless Constantinople continued to attract young men looking for an advanced education, as did Mistra in the Peloponnesos, capital of the autonomous Despotate of the Morea, ruled by younger brothers of the reigning Byzantine emperor.

Meanwhile Byzantine scholars were travelling to Italy, some of them on diplomatic missions, others for study, and others, toward the end, fleeing from Byzantium as the tide of Turkish conquest increasingly isolated Byzantium from the West.

The Ottoman Turks established their first capital in 1326 at Bursa, in northwestern Asia Minor, and crossed over into Europe 20 years later, when they captured the city of Callipolis (Gallipoli) on the Dardanelles. The Turkish capture of Callipolis was recorded by the Byzantine scholar Demetrius Cydones, renowned for his translations from Latin into Greek, most notably the *Summa Theologica* of Thomas Aquinas. According to Cydones, the fall of Callipolis began an exodus of Greeks from Byzantium to Italy, Spain and even farther 'towards the sea beyond the Pillars [the Straits of Gibraltar]'.

The renowned Byzantine humanist Manuel Chrysoloras (*ca.* 1350–1417) was sent on a diplomatic mission from Constantinople to Venice in 1390. During his stay in Venice, which ended the following year, Chrysoloras was offered a contract to give Greek lessons in Florence, where he taught from 1396 until 1400. The leading Florentine statesmen and humanists who flocked to his lectures included the chancellor Leonardo Bruni, who is quoted as saying that Chrysoloras inspired him to learn a language that no Italian had understood for 700 years.

The textbook that Chrysoloras wrote for his lessons, the *Erotemata* (*Questions*), was translated into Latin by Guarino of Verona (1374–1460), who studied Greek with him in Constantinople from 1403 to 1408. Guarino went on to teach Greek in Venice, Florence and Ferrara, where he remained for the last 30 years of his life, attracting students from as far away as England. He was also noted for his translations from Greek into Latin, which included Homer, Herodotus, Plutarch and Strabo, whose *Geography* he translated in his latter years.

Scientific ideas were also coming to Byzantium from the West, as evidenced by a treatise on the astrolabe translated into Greek in Constantinople *ca.* 1309 from a Latin version of the Arabic original. Another astronomical work, the *Six Wings*, an anonymous treatise in Hebrew of the thirteenth century, was translated into Greek in Constantinople in the second quarter of the fifteenth century, apparently having made its way from southern France through Venice to Byzantium.

The fall of Thessalonica to the Ottomans in 1430 led the emperor John VIII (r. 1425–48) to seek help from the West, and he proposed to Pope Martin that a council be called to help reconcile the Greek and Latin churches. This eventually gave rise to a council that was convened by Pope Eugenius IV in 1438 at Ferrara, moving to Florence the following year. The council ended on 6 July 1439, when a Decree of Union between the Greek and Latin churches was read in Latin and Greek in the cathedral of Florence, Santa Maria del Fiore, in the presence of the emperor John VIII. But most of the people and clergy of Byzantium rejected the Union, dividing the empire in what were to be the last years of its existence.

The Greek delegates to the Council of Ferrara-Florence included three scholars who would be leading figures in the cultural interchange between Byzantium and Italy. These were George Gemistus Plethon, George Trapezuntios and Bessarion of Trebizond.

George Gemistus Plethon (*ca.* 1355 –1452), whom Sir Steven Runciman called 'the most original of all Byzantine thinkers,' was educated in Constantinople and taught there until *ca.* 1392. He then went to Mistra in the Peloponnesus, which at the time was ruled by the Despot Theodore Palaeologus, second son of the emperor Manuel II (r. 1391–1425). Plethon taught there for the rest of his days, except for a year that he spent as a member of the Byzantine delegation at the Council of Ferrara-Florence. His teaching was dominated by his rejection of Aristotle and his devotion to Plato, who inspired his goal of reforming the Greek world along Platonic lines. His religious beliefs were more pagan than Christian, as evidenced by his treatise *On the Laws*, in which he usually refers to God as Zeus and writes of the Trinity as consisting of the Creator, the World-Mind and the World-Soul. George Trapezuntios writes of a conversation he had at Florence with Plethon, who told him that the whole world would soon adopt a new religion. When asked if the new religion would be Christian or Mohammedan, Plethon replied: 'Neither, it will not be different from paganism.'

While the council was deliberating in Florence Plethon delivered a lecture at the palace of Duke Cosimo de' Medici, the subject being the philosophical and religious differences between Platonism and Aristotelianism, in which he eulogized Plato. Cosimo was so inspired by Plethon that he founded a Platonic Academy in Florence, which became the center of renaissance Platonism.

Plethon's writings also inspired Masilio Ficino (1433–1499), the first of the great Renaissance Platonists.

During his stay in Florence, Plethon recommended the study of Strabo's *Geography* as a supplement to that of Ptolemy. One of those to whom he spoke of this may have been Paolo Dal Pozzo Toscanelli, whom he met in Florence. Toscanelli later passed the suggestion on to Christopher Columbus, who would have read Strabo in Guarino's Latin translation. Columbus, according to the biography written by his son, was directly influenced by two passages of Strabo. These were quotes from Eratosthenes and Posidonius, the first saying 'If the immensity of the Atlantic did not prevent us, we could sail from Iberia to India along the same parallel,' and the second 'If you sail from the west using the east wind you will reach India at a distance of 70,000 stades.'

George Trapezuntios (1395–1486) was born on Crete to a family who had moved there from Trebizond, hence his last name. He was a prolific translator from Greek into Latin, which he studied under Guarino in Venice in 1417–18. He taught in Venice, Vicenza and Mantua before coming to Rome, where he served in the papal bureaucracy under Eugenius IV (r. 1431–47) and then taught under Nicholas V (1447–1465). He severely criticized Plethon for his attack on Aristotelianism, portraying himself as the champion of medieval scholasticism against its humanist critics, and singling out for special praise Albertus Magnus and Thomas Aquinas, which brought him into conflict with Bessarion, among others.

Bessarion (1403–1470) was born into a family of manual labourers at Trebizond. The metropolitan of Trebizond noticed the boy's intelligence and sent him to school in Constantinople. While at the university he met the Italian humanist Francesco Filelfo, who had been inspired to study in Constantinople after attending the classes of Manuel Chrysoloras in Italy.

At the age of 20 Bessarion became a monk and spent some years at a monastery near Mistra, where he studied under Plethon. He then returned to Constantinople and won renown as a professor of philosophy. He was chosen as one of the delegates to the Council of Ferrara-Florence, and was appointed Metropolitan of Nicaea so that he would have appropriate status at the conclave. When the agreement of Union was formally proclaimed on 6 July 1439 in the cathedral in Florence, Cardinal Cesarini read it first in Latin and then Bessarion read it in Greek.

Bessarion's stay in Italy convinced him that Byzantium could only survive in alliance with the West, not only politically, but also by sharing in the cultural life of Renaissance Italy. Disheartened by opposition to the Union in Constantinople, he returned to Florence at the end of 1440, by which time he had already been made a Cardinal in the Roman Catholic Church.

He spent some time travelling on papal diplomatic missions and served as governor of Bologna from 1450 to 1455, but otherwise from 1443 he resided in Rome. He was nearly elected pope in 1455, but he lost out when his enemies warned of the dangers of choosing a Greek, and so the cardinals turned to the Catalan Alfonso Borgia, who was elevated as Callisto IV.

Much of Bessarion's energy was spent trying to raise military support in Europe to defend Byzantium against the Turks, but his efforts came to nought, as the Ottomans captured Constantinople in 1453 and then took his native Trebizond in 1461, ending the long history of the Byzantine Empire. Thenceforth Bessarion sought to find support for a crusade against the Turks, but to no avail.

Bessarion devoted much of his time to perpetuating the heritage of Byzantine culture by adding to his collection of ancient Greek manuscripts, which he bequeathed to Venice, where they are still preserved in the Marciana Library. The group of scholars who gathered around Bessarion in Rome included George Trapezuntios, whom he commissioned to translate Ptolemy's *Almagest* from Greek into Latin. Then in 1459, Trapezuntios published an attack on Platonism, suggesting that it led to heresy and immorality. Bessarion was outraged and wrote a defence of Platonism, published in both Greek and Latin. His aim was not only to defend Platonism against the charges made by Trapezuntios, but to show that Plato's teachings were closer to Christian doctrine than those of Aristotle. His book was favourably received, for it was the first general introduction to Plato's thought, which at the time was unknown to most Latins, for earlier scholarly works on Platonism had not reached a wide audience.

One of Bessarion's diplomatic missions took him in 1460 to Vienna, whose university had become a centre of astronomical and mathematical studies through the work of John of Gmunden (d. 1442), Georg Peurbach (1423–1461) and Johannes Regiomontanus (1436–1476). John had built astronomical instruments and acquired a large collection of manuscripts, all of which he had bequeathed to the university, thus laying the foundations for the work of Peurbach and Regiomontanus.

Peurbach was an Austrian scholar who had received a bachelor's degree at Vienna in 1448 and a master's in 1453, while in the interim he had traveled in France, Germany, Hungary and Italy. He had served as court astrologer to Ladislaus V, king of Hungary, and then to the king's uncle, the emperor Frederick III. His writings included textbooks on arithmetic, trigonometry and astronomy, his best-known works being his *Theoricae novae planetarum (New Theories of the Planets)* and his *Tables of Eclipses*.

Regiomontanus, originally known as Johann Muller, took his last name from the Latin for his native Königsberg in Franconia. He studied first at the University of Leipzig from 1447–50, and then at the University of Vienna, where he received his bachelor's degree in 1452, when he was only fifteen, and his master's in 1457. He became Peurbach's associate in a research programme that included a systematic study of the planets as well as observations of astronomical phenomena such as eclipses and comets.

Bessarion was dissatisfied with the translation of Ptolemy's *Almagest* that had been done by George Trapezuntios, and he asked Peurbach and Regiomontanus to write an abridged version. They agreed to do so, for Peurbach had already begun work on a compendium of the *Almagest*, but it was unfinished when he died in April 1461. Regiomontanus completed the compendium about a year later in Italy, where he had gone with Bessarion. He spent part of the next four years in the cardinal's entourage and the rest in his own travels, learning Greek and searching for manuscripts of Ptolemy and other ancient astronomers and mathematicians.

Regiomontanus left Italy in 1467 for Hungary, where he served for four years in the court of King Mathias Corvinus, continuing his researches in astronomy and mathematics. He then spent four years in Nuremberg, where he set up his own observatory and printing press. One of the works that he printed before his premature death in 1476 was Peurbach's *Theoricae novae planetarum*, reprinted in nearly 60 editions up to the seventeenth century. He also published his own *Ephemerides*, the first planetary tables ever printed, giving the positions of the heavenly bodies for every day from 1475 to 1506. Columbus is said to have taken the *Ephemerides* with him on his fourth and last voyage to the New World, and to have used its prediction of the lunar eclipse of 29 February 1504 to frighten the hostile natives of Jamaica into submission.

Regiomontanus' most important mathematical work is his *De triangulis omnimodis*, a systematic method for analyzing triangles which, together with his *Tabulae directionum*, marked what Carl B. Boyer has called 'the rebirth of trigonometry'.

The astronomical writings of Regiomontanus include the completion of Peurbach's *Epitome of Ptolemy's Almagest*, which he dedicated to Bessarion, a work noted for its emphasis on mathematical methods omitted in other works of elementary astronomy. Copernicus read the *Epitome* when he was a student in Bologna, and at least two propositions in it influenced him in the formulation of his own planetary theory. These propositions seem to have originated with the fifteenth-century Arabic astronomer Ali Qushji, and may have been transmitted to Regiomontanus by Bessarion. If so, this would place Bessarion and Regiomontanus in the long chain that leads from Aristarchus of Samos to Copernicus through the Arabic and Latin scholars of the Middle Ages to the dawn of the Renaissance, which came from Byzantium to Italy, carrying the last breath of the ancient Greek spirit to bring life to the new culture that was being born in the West.

CHAPTER 17

THE SCIENTIFIC REVOLUTION: GREEK SCIENCE REBORN

The European renaissance was followed by a period of intellectual upheaval that has come to be known as the Scientific Revolution. This is generally considered to have begun in 1543 with the publication of the heliocentric theory of Nicolaus Copernicus (1473–1543), entitled *De Revolutionibus Orbium Coelestium* (*The Revolutions of the Heavenly Spheres*) and to have reached its climax with the work of Isaac Newton (1642–1727), particularly his treatise *Philosophicae Naturalis Principia Mathematica* (*The Mathematical Principles of Natural Philosophy*), known more simply as the *Principia*, which appeared in 1687. The works of European thinkers from Copernicus to Newton overthrew the earth-centred Aristotelian world view and led to the Newtonian synthesis that established the foundations of modern science.

The Scientific Revolution was the culmination of the developments that began with the transmission of Graeco-Arabic science to Western Europe. More specifically, it was generated by the revival of ideas that had been conceived by the Greeks when they began to speculate about the nature of the cosmos. This included concepts concerning space, time, motion, mathematics, the atom, light, the celestial bodies and nature and extent of the universe. Pythagorean doctrines such as the harmony of nature, the music of the celestial spheres, the existence of a central fire and the perfect solids were revived in the Renaissance and inspired astronomers as well as poets and playwrights.

Copernicus derived his heliocentric theory from Pythagorean sources as well as from Aristarchus of Samos. He is known to have possessed a copy of George Valla's *Outline of Knowledge*, printed by Aldus Mantius at Venice in 1501, which included two passages by the writer known as pseudo-Plutarch in his *De placitius philosophorum*. The first of these passages concerns the Pythagorean concept of a central fire, about which they believed the earth moves while at the same time rotates on its axis.

> But while some say the earth stands still, Philolaus the Pythagorean held that it is moved about the element of fire in an oblique circle, after the same manner of motion that the sun and moon have. Heraclides of Pontus and Ecphantus the Pythagorean assign a motion to the earth, not progressive, but after the manner of a wheel being carried on its own axis. Thus the earth, they say, turns itself upon its own center from west to east.

Copernicus quotes this passage in the preface to his *De Revolutionibus*. There he says that after reading the passage he 'began to mediate upon the mobility of the Earth.' He continues:

> And although the opinion seemed absurd, nevertheless because I knew that others before me had been granted the liberty of constructing whatever circles they pleased in order to demonstrate astral phenomena, I thought that I too would be readily permitted to test whether or not, by the laying down that the Earth had some movement, demonstrations less shaky than my predecessors could be found for the revolution of the celestial spheres.

Copernicus refers to Aristarchus of Samos thrice in *De Revolutionibus*, twice regarding his predecessor's measurement of the inclination of the ecliptic and once concerning his measurement of the length of the solar year. But nowhere does he mention that Aristarchus had in the mid-third century BC proposed that the sun and not the earth was the centre of the cosmos. Copernicus had referred to the heliocentric theory of Aristarchus in his original manuscript, but deleted it from the edition of *De Revolutionibus* printed in 1543. The suppressed passage had been in the last paragraph of Book One, Chapter 11:

> Though the courses of the Sun and the Moon can surely be demonstrated on the assumption that the Earth does not move, it does not work so well with the other planets. Probably for this and other reasons, Philolaus perceived the mobility of the Earth, a view also shared by Aristarchus of Samos, so some say, not impressed by that reasoning which Aristotle cites and refutes.

The first eight chapters of Book I of *De Revolutionibus* give a greatly simplified description of the Copernican cosmology and its philosophical basis. Copernicus begins with arguments for the spherical nature of the universe; the sphericity of the earth, moon, sun and planets; and the uniform circular motion of the planets around the sun. He shows how the rotation of the earth on its axis, together with its revolution about the sun, can easily explain the observed motions of the celestial bodies. The absence of stellar parallax he explains by the fact that the radius of the earth's orbit is negligible compared to the distance of the fixed stars, using the same argument given by Archimedes in *The Sand Reckoner*.

Chapter 9 is entitled 'Whether many movements can be attributed to the Earth, and concerning the center of the world.' Here Copernicus abandons the Aristotelian doctrine that the earth is the sole source of gravity, and instead takes the first step towards the Newtonian theory of universal gravitation, writing that 'I myself think that gravity or heaviness is nothing except a certain natural appetency implanted in the parts by the divine providence of the universal Artisan, in order that they should unite with one another in their oneness and wholeness and come together in the form of a globe.'

Chapter 10 is entitled 'On the order of the celestial orbital circles.' Here Copernicus removes the ambiguity concerning Mercury and Venus, which in the Ptolemaic model were sometimes placed 'above' the sun and sometimes 'below'.

The Copernican system has Mercury as the closest planet to the sun, followed by Venus, Earth, Mars, Jupiter and Saturn, surrounded by the sphere of the fixed stars, and with the moon orbiting the earth. This model is simpler and more harmonious than Ptolemy's, for all of the planets revolve in the same sense, with velocities decreasing with their distance from the sun, which sits enthroned at the center of the cosmos. As Copernicus writes in the preface to *De Revolutionibus*, in a passage obviously inspired by his Pythagorean beliefs:

> In the center of all the celestial bodies rests the Sun. For who would place this lamp of a very beautiful temple in another or better place than this wherefrom it can illuminate everything at the same time. As a matter of fact, not unhappily do some call it the lantern, others the mind and still others, the pilot of the world .... And so the sun, as if resting on a kingly throne, governs the family of stars which wheel around.

Book Two is a detailed introduction to astronomy and spherical trigonometry, together with mathematical tables and a catalogue of the celestial coordinates of 1,024 stars, most of them derived from Ptolemy, adjusted for the precession of the equinoxes. Book Three is concerned with the precession of the equinoxes and the movement of the earth around the sun. Book Four deals with the motion of the moon around the earth. Books Five and Six study the motions of the planets. Here, as with the motions of the sun, Copernicus used eccentrics and epicycles just as Ptolemy had done, though his conviction that the celestial motions were combinations of circular motion at constant angular velocity made him refrain from using the Ptolemaic device of the equant. Because of the complexity of the celestial motions, Copernicus was forced to use about as many circles as had Ptolemy, and so there was little to choose from between the two theories so far as economy was concerned, and both were capable of giving results of comparable accuracy. The advantages of the Copernican system were that it was more harmonious; it removed the ambiguity about the order of the inner planets; it explained the retrograde motion of the planets as well as their variation in brightness; and it allowed both the order and relative sizes of the planetary orbits to be determined from observations without any additional assumptions.

Copernicus mentions some of the Islamic astronomers whose observations and theories he used in *De Revolutionibus*. But he makes no mention of the Persian astronomer Nasr ad-Din al-Tusi, whose mathematical device for eliminating the deferent, known as the 'al-Tusi couple', Copernicus used in Book III, Chapter 4 of *De Revolutionibus*. Current opinion is that Copernicus was aware of al-Tusi's work, which was certainly known to some of his contemporaries in Western Europe.

Copernicus received many posthumous accolades after the publication of *De Revolutionibus*, but the praise was primarily for his success in giving a mathematical description of the motion of the celestial bodies rather than for his sun-centred cosmology.

The first astronomical tables based on the Copernican theory were due to Erasmus Reinhold (1511–1553), a professor of mathematics at the University of Wittenberg. Reinhold set out to produce a more extensive version of the planetary tables in *De Revolutionibus*, which were published in 1551 as the *Prutenic Tables*, where in the introduction he praises Copernicus but is silent about his heliocentric theory. The *Prutenic Tables* were the first complete planetary tables prepared in Europe for three centuries. They were demonstrably superior to the older tables, which were now out of date, and so most astronomers used the Copernican theory even if they did not acknowledge the sun-centred cosmology he supported. As the

English astronomer Thomas Blundeville wrote in the preface to an astronomy text in 1594: 'Copernicus ... affirmeth that the earth turneth about and that the sun standeth still in the midst of the heavens, by help of which false supposition he hath made truer demonstrations of the motions and revolutions of the celestial spheres, than ever were made before.'

Thomas Digges published the first English translation of the Copernican theory, or at least part of it, in 1576. Digges did a free English translation of chapters 9 through 11 of the first book of *De Revolutionibus*, adding it to his father's perpetual almanac, 'A Prognostication Everlasting'. The section on the heliocentric theory was entitled *Perfit Description of the Celestiall Orbes, according to the most ancient doctrines of the Pythagoreans lately revived by Copernicus and by Geometrical Demonstrations approved*. Digges stated that he had included this excerpt from *De Revolutionibus* 'so that Englishmen might not be deprived of so noble a theory.'

The book was accompanied by a large folded map of the sun-centred universe, in which the stars were not confined to the outermost celestial sphere but were scattered outwards indefinitely in all directions. Digges thus burst the bounds of the medieval cosmos, which till then had been limited by the ninth celestial sphere, the one containing the supposedly fixed stars, which in his model extended to infinity.

The concept of an infinite universe was one of the revolutionary ideas for which the Italian mystic Giordano Bruno (1548–1600) was condemned by the Catholic Church, which had him burned at the stake in Rome on 17 February 1600. At the beginning of his dialogue on *The Infinite Universe and the Worlds*, published in 1584, Bruno has one of his characters say that in this limitless space there are innumerable worlds similar to our earth, each of them revolving around its own star-sun, an idea that he says he derived from Democritus and Lucretius.

Meanwhile astronomy was being revolutionized by the Danish astronomer Tycho Brahe (1546–1601), who in the last quarter of the seventeenth century made systematic observations of significantly greater accuracy than any ever done in the past, all just before the invention of the telescope. He was keenly interested in the new theory of Copernicus, whom he called 'a second Ptolemy.'

Tycho made his first important observation in August 1563, when he noted a conjunction of Saturn and Jupiter. He found that the *Alfonsine Tables* were a month off in predicting the date of the conjunction, and that the *Prutenic Tables* were several days in error. This convinced Tycho that new tables were needed, and that they should be based upon more accurate, precise and systematic observations, which he would make with instruments of his own design in his own observatory.

The first of Tycho's observatories was at Augsburg in Germany, where he lived in the years 1569–71. Tycho returned to Denmark in 1571, and on 11 November of the following year he began observing a nova, or new star, that suddenly appeared in the constellation Cassiopeia, exceeding even the planet Venus in its brilliance. (It is now known that a nova is a star that explodes at the end of its evolutionary cycle, releasing an enormous amount of energy for a few months.) Tycho's measurements indicated that the nova was well beyond the sphere of Saturn, and the fact that its position did not change showed that it was not a comet. This was clear evidence of a change taking place in the celestial region, where, according to Aristotle's doctrine, everything was perfect and immutable.

The nova eventually began to fade, its colour changing from white to yellow and then red, finally disappearing from view in March 1574. By then Tycho had written a brief tract entitled *De nova stella (The New Star)*, which was published at Copenhagen in May 1573. After presenting the measurements that led him to conclude that the new star was in the heavens beyond the planetary spheres.

A spectacular comet appeared in 1577 and Tycho made detailed observations that led him to conclude that it was farther away than the moon, in fact even beyond the sphere of Mercury, and that it was in orbit around the sun among the outer planets. This contradicted the Aristotelian doctrine that comets were meteorological phenomena occurring below the sphere of the moon. He was thus led to reject Aristotle's concept of the homocentric crystalline spheres, and he concluded that the planets were moving independently through space.

Despite his admiration for Copernicus, Tycho rejected the heliocentric theory, both on physical grounds and on the absence of stellar parallax, where in the latter case he did not take into account the argument made by Archimedes and Copernicus that the stars were too far away to show any parallactic shift. Tycho rejected both the diurnal rotation of the earth as well as its annual orbital motion, retaining the Aristotelian belief that the stars rotated nightly around the celestial pole.

Faced with the growing debate between the Copernican and Ptolemaic theories, Tycho was led to propose his own planetary model, which had Mercury and Venus revolving around the sun, which together with the other planets and the moon orbited around the stationary earth. This hybrid theory had been erroneously attributed to Heraclides of Pontus. Tycho believed that his model combined the best features of both the Ptolemaic and Copernican theories, since it kept the earth stationary and explained why Mercury and Venus were never very far from the sun.

In 1600, Tycho moved to Prague, where he set up his instruments and created a new observatory at Benatky Castle, several miles northeast of the city. Soon afterwards he hired an assistant named Johannes Kepler (1571–1630), a young German mathematician who had sent him an interesting treatise on astronomy, the *Mysterium Cosmographicum*. Kepler was a graduate of the University of Tübingen, where in addition to his studies in mathematics, physics and astronomy, Platonism and Pythagoreanism influenced him.

His mathematics lectures were based on the works of Euclid, Archimedes and Apollonius of Perge. (As Kepler later said, 'How many mathematicians are there, who would toil through the *Conics* of Apollonius of Perga?')

Kepler was particularly influenced by his professor of astronomy, Michael Maestlin, from whom he first learned of the heliocentric theory. In the introduction to his first book, the *Mysterium Cosmographicum*, Kepler wrote of his excitement on discovering the work of Copernicus, which he described as 'a still unexhausted treasure of truly divine insight into the magnificent order of the whole world and of all bodies.'

Kepler had learned from his reading of Euclid that there were five and only five regular polyhedra, the so-called Platonic solids, in which all of the faces are equal as well as equilateral – the cube, tetrahedron, dodecahedron, icosahedron and octahedron – and it occurred to him that they were related to the orbits of the earth and the five other planets. He explained the scheme in his treatise, the *Mysterium Cosmographicum*, published in 1596, in which his values for the relative radii of the planetary orbits agree reasonably well with those determined by Copernicus, though there was no physical basis for his theory.

> The earth's orbit is the measure of all things; circumscribe around it a dodecahedron, and the circle containing it will be Mars; circumscribe around Mars a tetrahedron, and the circle containing this will be Jupiter; circumscribe around Jupiter a cube, and the circle containing this will be Saturn. Now inscribe within the earth an icosahedron, and the circle contained in it will be Venus; inscribe within Venus an octahedron, and the circle contained in it will be Mercury.

Kepler sent copies of his treatise to a number of scientists, including Galileo Galilei (1564–1642). In his letter of acknowledgement, dated 4 August

1597, Galileo congratulated Kepler for having had the courage, which he himself lacked, of publishing a work supporting the Copernican theory.

Kepler wrote back to Galileo on 13 October 1597, encouraging him to continue supporting the Copernican theory. 'Have faith, Galilii, and come forward!' he wrote. 'If my guess is right, there are but few of the prominent mathematicians of Europe who would wish to secede from us: such is the power of truth.'

Kepler finally arrived in Prague with his family early in 1600, beginning a brief but extraordinarily fruitful collaboration with Tycho. When Kepler began work at Prague he had hopes that he could take Tycho's data and use it directly to check his own planetary theory. But he was disappointed to find that most of Tycho's data was still in the form of raw observations, which first had to be subjected to mathematical analysis. Moreover Tycho was extremely possessive of his data and would not reveal any more of it than Kepler needed for his work.

Tycho then assigned Kepler the task of analyzing the orbit of Mars, which up to that time had been the responsibility of his assistant Longomontanus, who had just resigned. Kepler later wrote: 'I consider it a divine decree that I came at exactly the time when Longomontanus was busy with Mars. Because assuredly either through it we arrive at the knowledge of the secrets of astronomy or else they remain forever concealed from us.'

Mars and Mercury are the only visible planets with eccentricities large enough to make their orbits significantly different from perfect circles. But Mercury is so close to the sun that it is difficult to observe, leaving Mars as the ideal planet for checking a mathematical theory, which is why Kepler was so enthusiastic at being able to analyze its orbit.

Early in the autumn of 1601 Tycho brought Kepler to the imperial court and introduced him to the Emperor Rudolph. Tycho then proposed to the emperor that he and Kepler compile a new set of astronomical tables. With the emperor's permission, this would be named the *Rudolfine Tables*, and since it was to be based on Tycho's observations it would be more accurate than any done in the past. The emperor graciously consented and agreed to pay Kepler's salary in this endeavour.

Soon afterwards Tycho fell ill, and after suffering in agony for 11 days he died on 24 October 1601. On his deathbed he made Kepler promise that the *Rudolfine Tables* would be completed, and he expressed his hopes that it would be based on the Tychonic planetary model. As Kepler later wrote of Tycho's final conversation with him: 'although he knew I was of the Copernican persuasion, he asked me to present all my demonstrations in conformity with his hypothesis.'

Two days after Tycho's death the Emperor Rudolph appointed Kepler as court mathematician and head of the observatory in Prague. Kepler thereupon resumed his work on Mars, now with unrestricted access to all of Tycho's data. At first he tried the traditional Ptolemaic methods – epicycle, eccentric and equant – but no matter how he varied the parameters the calculated positions of the planet disagreed with Tycho's observations by up to eight minutes of arc. His faith in the accuracy of Tycho's data led him to conclude that the Ptolemaic theory of epicycles, which had been used by Copernicus, would have to be replaced by a completely new theory.

After eight years of intense effort Kepler was finally led to what are now known as his first two laws of planetary motion. The first law is that the planets travel in elliptical orbits, with the sun at one of the two focal points of the ellipse. The second law states that a radius vector drawn from the sun to a planet sweeps out equal areas in equal times, so that when the planet is close to the sun it moves rapidly and when far away it goes slowly. These two laws, which appeared in Kepler's *Astronomia nova (The New Astronomy)*, published in 1609, became the basis for his subsequent work on the *Rudolfine Tables*. Kepler's first two laws of planetary motion eliminated the need for the epicycles, eccentrics and deferents that had been used by astronomers from Ptolemy to Copernicus.

Meanwhile the whole science of astronomy had been profoundly changed by the invention of the telescope. The earliest telescope seems to have appeared in 1604, when a Dutch optician named Zacharias Janssen constructed one from a specimen belonging to an unknown Italian, after which he sold some of them at fairs in northern Europe. After hearing of the telescope, Galileo constructed one in his workshop in 1609, after which he offered it to the Doge of Venice for use in war and navigation. After improving on his original design, he began using his telescope to observe the heavens, and in March 1610 he published his discoveries in a little book called *Siderius nuncius (The Starry Messenger)*.

The book begins with his observations of the moon, which he found to look very much like the earth, with mountains, valleys and what he thought were seas. Seen in the telescope, the planets were pale illuminated discs, whereas the stars remained brilliant points of light. The Milky Way proved to consist of numerous stars, not a nebula reflecting the light of the sun, as some had thought, nor an atmospheric phenomenon, as Aristotle had concluded. He counted more than 90 stars in Orion's belt, where only nine are visible to the naked eye. He discovered four moons orbiting around Jupiter, a solar system in miniature, which he used as an additional argument in favor of the Copernican theory. He called the Jovian moons the 'Medicean Stars' in honour of Cosimo de Medici, the Grand Duke of Tuscany. Cosimo responded by making Galileo his court philosopher and appointing him to the chair of mathematics at the University of Pisa. Galileo had no obligation to teach at the University of Pisa or even to reside in the city, and so after his appointment, in September 1610, he departed to take up residence in Florence.

Galileo sent a copy of the *Siderius nuncius* to Kepler, who received it on 8 April 1610. During the next 11 days Kepler composed his response in a little work called *Dissertatio cum Nuncio sidereal (Answer to the Sidereal Messenger)*, in which he expressed his enthusiastic approval of Galileo's discoveries.

Kepler borrowed a telescope from the Elector Ernest of Cologne at the end of August 1610, and for the next ten days he used it to observe the heavens, particularly Jupiter and its moons. His excitement over the possibilities of the new instrument was such that he spent the next two months making an exhaustive study of the passage of light through lenses, which he published later in 1610 under the title *Dioptrice*, which became one of the foundation stones of the new science of optics.

The death of Rudolph II early in 1612 forced Kepler to leave Prague and take up the post of district mathematician at Linz, where he remained for the next 14 years. During that period he continued his calculations on the *Rudolfine Tables* and published two other major works, the first of which was the *Harmonices Mundi (Harmony of the World)*, which appeared in 1619. The title of this work was inspired by a Greek manuscript of Ptolemy's treatise on musical theory, the *Harmonica*, which Kepler acquired in 1607 and used in his analysis of music, geometry, astronomy and astrology. The most important part of the *Harmonice Mundi* is the relationship now known as Kepler's Third Law of Planetary Motion, which he discovered on 15 May 1618, and presents in Book V. The law states that for each of the planets the square of the period of its orbital motion is proportional to the cube of its distance from the sun (or, strictly speaking, the semi-major axis of its elliptical orbit).

There had been speculations about the relation between the periods of planetary orbits and their radii since the times of Pythagoras, Plato and Aristotle, and Kepler was terribly excited that he had at last, following in the footsteps of Ptolemy, found the mathematical law 'necessary for the contemplation of celestial harmonies.' He wrote of his pleasure 'That the same thought about the harmonic formulation had turned up in the minds of two men (though lying so far apart in time) who had devoted themselves entirely to contemplating nature ... I feel carried away and possessed by an unutterable rapture over the divine spectacle of the heavenly harmony.'

In 1626 Kepler was forced to leave Linz and move to Ulm, where he published the *Rudolfine Tables* in September 1627, dedicating them to the Archduke Ferdinand II. The new tables were far more accurate than any in the past, and they remained in use for more than a century. Kepler used his tables to predict that Mercury and Venus would make transits across the disk of the sun in 1631. The transit of Venus was not observed in Europe because it took place at night. The transit of Mercury was observed by Pierre Gassendi in Paris on 7 November 1631, representing a triumph for Kepler's astronomy, for his prediction was in error by only 10 minutes of arc as compared to 5 degrees for tables based on Ptolemy's model. But Kepler did not live to see his theories vindicated, for he passed away on 15 November 1630.

Meanwhile Galileo had been active in advancing the cause of Copernicanism against the accepted cosmology of Aristotle, which in its reinterpretation by St Thomas Aquinas formed part of the philosophical basis for Roman Catholic theology. At the beginning of March 1616 the Holy Office of the Inquisition in Rome placed the works of Copernicus and all other writings that supported it on the *Index*, the list of books that Catholics were forbidden to read, including those of Kepler. The decree held that believing the sun to be the immovable centre of the world is 'foolish and absurd, philosophically false and formally heretical.' Pope Paul V instructed Cardinal Bellarmine to censure Galileo, admonishing him not to hold or defend Copernican doctrines any longer. On March 3 Bellarmine reported that Galileo had acquiesced to the Pope's warning, and that ended the matter for the time being.

After his censure Galileo returned to his villa at Arcetri outside Florence, where for the next seven years he remained silent. But then in 1623, after the death of Paul V, Galileo took hope when he learned that his friend Maffeo Cardinal Barbarini had succeeded as Pope Urban VIII. Heartened by his friend's election, Galileo immediately proceeded to publish a trea-tise entitled *Il Saggiatore (The Assayer)*, which appeared later that year, dedi-cated to Urban VIII.

Il Saggiatore grew out of a dispute over the nature of comets between Galileo and Father Horatio Grassi, a Jesuit astronomer. This had been stim-ulated by the appearance in 1618 of a succession of three comets, the third and brightest of which remained visible until January 1619. Grassi, who supported the Tychonic model of planetary motion, took the Aristotelian view that the comets were atmospheric phenomena, while Galileo insisted that they were in the celestial region. *Il Saggiatore* was favourably received in the Vatican, and Galileo went to Rome in the spring of 1623 and had six audiences with the Pope. Urban praised the book, but he refused to rescind the 1616 edict against the Copernican theory, though he said that if it had been up to him the ban would not have been imposed. Galileo did receive Urban's permission to discuss Copernicanism in a book, but only if the Aristotelian-Ptolemaic model was given equal and impartial attention.

Encouraged by his conversations with Urban, Galileo spent the next six years writing a book called the *Dialogue Concerning the Chief World Systems, Ptolemaic and Copernican,* which was finally published in February 1632. The book is divided into four days of conversations between three friends: Salviati the Copernican, Sagredo the intelligent sceptic who had been converted to Copernicanism and Simplicio the Aristotelian.

Despite some defects, such as Galileo's mistaken notion of circular inertia, the arguments for Copernicanism were very persuasive and poor Simplicio, the Aristotelian, is defeated at every turn. Simplicio's closing remark represents Galileo's attempt to reserve judgment in the debate, where he says that 'it would still be excessive boldness for anyone to limit and restrict the Divine power and wisdom to some particular fancy of his own.' This statement apparently was almost a direct quote of what Pope Urban had said to Galileo in 1623. When Urban read the *Dialogue* he remembered these words and was deeply offended, feeling that Galileo had made a fool of him and taken advantage of their friendship to violate the 1616 edict against teaching Copernicanism. The Florentine ambassador Francesco Niccolini reported that after discussing the *Dialogue* with Urban, the Pope broke out in great anger and fairly shouted, 'Your Galileo has ventured to meddle with things that he ought not, and with the most grave and dangerous subjects that can be stirred up these days.'

Urban directed the Holy Office to consider the affair and summoned Galileo to Rome. Galileo arrived in Rome in February 1633, but his trial before the court of the Inquisition did not begin until April. There he was accused of having ignored the 1616 edict of the Holy Office not to teach Copernicanism. The court deliberated until June before giving its verdict, and in the interim Galileo was confined to the palace of the Florentine ambassador. He was then brought once again to the Holy Office, where he was persuaded to acknowledge that he had gone too far in his support of the Copernican 'heresy,' which he now abjured. He was thereupon sentenced to indefinite imprisonment and his *Dialogue* placed on the *Index*.

The sentence of imprisonment was immediately commuted to allow him to be confined in one of the Roman residences of the Medici family, after which he was moved to Siena and then, in April 1634, allowed to return to his villa at Arcetri.

After he returned home Galileo took up again the researches he had abandoned a quarter of a century earlier, principally the study of motion. This gave rise to the last and greatest of his works, *Discourses and Mechanical Demonstrations Concerning Two New Sciences, of Mechanics and of Motions,* which he dictated to his disciple Vincenzo Viviani. The work was completed in 1636, when Galileo was 72 and suffering from failing eyesight. Since publication in Italy was out of the question because of the papal ban on Galileo's works, his manuscript was smuggled to Leyden, where the *Discourses* was published in 1638, by which time he was completely blind.

Galileo died at Arcetri on 8 January 1642, 38 days before what would have been his seventy-eighth birthday. The Grand Duke of Tuscany sought to erect a monument in his memory, but he was advised not to do so for fear of giving offence to the Holy Office, since the Pope had said that Galileo 'had altogether given rise to the greatest scandal throughout Christendom.'

Newton was born the year that Galileo died, and his career represents the culmination of the Scientific Revolution, particularly the publication of his *Principia* in 1687. The *Principia* begins with a preface in which Newton outlines the scope and philosophy of his work.

> ... our present work sets forth mathematical principles of natural philosophy. For the basic problem of philosophy seems to be to discover the forces of nature from the phenomena of motions, and then to demonstrate the other phenomena from these forces .... Then the motions of the planets, the comets, the moon, and the sea are deduced from these forces by propositions that are also mathematical. If only we could derive the other phenomena of nature from mechanical principles by the same kind of reasoning!

Book 1 begins with a series of eight definitions, of which the first five are fundamental to Newtonian dynamics. The first effectively defines 'quantity of matter,' or mass, as being proportional to the weight density times volume. The second defines 'quantity of motion,' subsequently to be called 'momentum,' as mass times velocity. In the third definition Newton says that the 'inherent force of matter,' or inertia, 'is the power of resisting by which every body, so far as it is able, perseveres in its state either of rest or of moving uniformly straight forward.' The fourth states that 'Impressed force is the action exerted upon a body to change its state either of resting or of uniformly moving straight forward.'

The fifth through eighth define centripetal force as that by which bodies 'are impelled, or in any way tend, toward some point as to a center.' As an example Newton gives the gravitational force of the sun, which keeps the planets in orbit.

As regards the gravity of the earth, he gives the example of a lead ball, projected from the top of a mountain with a given velocity, and in a direction parallel to the horizon. If the initial velocity is made larger and larger, he says, the ball will go farther and farther before it hits the ground, and may go into orbit around the earth or even escape into outer space (see Figure 16).

The definitions are followed by a *Scholium*, a lengthy comment in which Newton gives his notions of absolute and relative time, space, place and motion. These essentially define the classical laws of relativity, which in the early twentieth century would be superceded by Einstein's theories of special and general relativity. Next come the axioms, now known as Newton's laws of motion, three in number, each accompanied by an explanation and followed by corollaries.

> Law 1: Every body perseveres in its state of being at rest, or of moving uniformly forward, except insofar as it is compelled to change its state of motion by forces impressed .... Law 2: A change of motion is proportional to the motive force impressed and takes place along the straight line in which that force is impressed .... Law 3: To every action there is always an opposite and equal reaction; in other words, the action of two bodies upon each other are always equal, and always opposite in direction.

The first law is the principal of inertia, which is actually a special case of the second law when the net force is zero. The form used today for the second law is that the force F acting on a body is equal to the time rate of change of the momentum p, where p equals the mass m times the velocity v; if the mass is constant then $F = ma$, a being the acceleration, the time rate of change of the velocity. The third law says that when two bodies interact the forces they exert on one another are equal in magnitude and opposite in direction.

The introductory section of the *Principia* is followed by Book 1, entitled 'The Motion of Bodies'. This begins with an analysis of motion in general essentially using the calculus. First Newton analyzed the relations between orbits and central forces of various kinds. From this he was able to show that if and only if the force of attraction varies as the inverse square of the distance from the center of force then the orbit is an ellipse, with the center of attraction at one focal point, thus proving Kepler's second law of motion. Elsewhere in Book 1 he proves Kepler's first and third laws.

The third and final book of the *Principia* is entitled 'The System of the World'. Here Newton states his law of universal gravitation: 'Gravity exists in all bodies universally and is proportional to the quantity of matter in each.' He had already shown that the gravitational force varied as the inverse square of the distance between interacting bodies, whose consequent movement he could then explain through his three laws of motion. He then used his law of universal gravitation and his laws of motion to explain phenomena such as the motion of projectiles and comets, the ebb and flow of the tides, the orbits of the moon and the planets, and the precession of the equinoxes, solving problems that physicists and astronomers had been struggling with for more than two millennia.

This is followed by a General *Scholium,* in which Newton says that mechanism alone cannot explain the universe, whose harmonious order indicated to him the design of a Supreme Being. "This most elegant system of the sun, planets, and comets could not have arisen without the design and dominion of an intelligent and powerful being.'

A second edition of the *Principia* was published in 1713 and a third in 1726, in both cases with a preface written by Newton.

The Pythagorean theory of fluxions was revived by Isaac Newton in his form of the calculus, which he discovered in 1665–66, although he did not publish it until 1687, when it appeared as part of his *Philosophiae Naturalis Principia Mathematica* (*Mathematical Principles of Natural Philosophy*). He published his work on calculus as a purely mathematical thesis in 1704, with the title *Methodus fluxionum et serierum infinitorum* (*Method of fluxions and infinite series*). An English translation done in 1745 reveals the Pythagorean origins of Newton's calculus:

I consider mathematical quantities in this place not as consisting of very small parts, but as described by a continuous motion. Lines are described and therefore generated, not by the apposition of parts, but by the continued motion of points; superficies by the motion of lines; solids by the motion of superficies; angles by the rotation of the sides; portions of time by a continued flux; and so on in other quantities. These geneses really take place in the nature of things, and are daily seen in the motion of bodies.

Meanwhile Newton had in 1704 published his researches on light, much of which had been done early in his career. Unlike the *Principia*, which was in Latin, the first edition of his new work was in English, entitled *Opticks, or a Treatise of the Reflexions, Refractions, Inflexions and Colours of Light*. The first Latin edition appeared in 1706, and subsequent English editions appeared in 1717/18, 1721 and 1730; the last, which came out three years after Newton's death, bore a note stating that it was 'corrected by the author's own hand, and left before his death, with his bookseller.'

Like the *Principia*, the *Opticks* is divided into three Books. At the very beginning of Book I Newton reveals the purpose he had in mind when composing his work. 'My design in this Book,' he writes, 'is not to explain the Properties of Light by Hypotheses, but to propose and prove them by Reason and Experiment.'

The topics dealt with in Book I include the laws of reflection and refraction, the formation of images, and the dispersion of light into its component colours by a glass prism. Other topics include the properties of lenses and Newton's reflecting telescope; the optics of human vision; the theory of the rainbow; and an exhaustive study of colour. Newton's proof of the law of refraction is based on the erroneous notion that light travels more rapidly in glass than in air. This error was due to his belief that light was corpuscular in nature.

Newton's corpuscular view of light stemmed from his acceptance of the atomic theory. He writes of his admiration for 'the oldest and most celebrated Philosophers of Greece ... who made a Vacuum, and Atoms, and the Gravity of Atoms, the first Principles of their Philosophy .... All these things being consider'd, it seems to me that God in the Beginning formed Matter in solid, hard, impenetrable, moveable Particles, of such Sizes and Figures, and with such other Properties and in such Proportions to Space, as much conduced to the End for which he had form'd them.'

Book II begins with a section entitled 'Observations concerning the Reflexions, Refractions, and Colours of thin transparent bodies.' The effects that he studied here are now known as interference phenomena, where Newton's observations are the first evidence for the wavelike nature of light, despite his belief that light was corpuscular.

In Book III the opening section deals with Newton's experiments on diffraction. The remainder of the book consists of a number of hypotheses, not only on light, but on a wide variety of topics in physics and philosophy. The first edition of the *Opticks* had 16 of these Queries, the second 23, the third and fourth 31. It would seem that Newton, in the twilight of his career, was bringing out into the open some of his previously undisclosed speculations, his heritage for those who would follow him in the study of nature.

Newton died in London on 20 March 1727, four days after presiding over a meeting of the Royal Society, of which he had been President since 1703. His body lay in state until April 4, when he was buried with great pomp in Westminster Abbey. Voltaire, writing of Newton's funeral, noted that 'He lived honored by his compatriots and was buried like a king who had done good to his subjects.'

Newton paid tribute to his predecessors when he said that if he had seen farther than Descartes it was 'by standing on the sholders of Giants.' The colossal figures he was referring to can be identified from his works, where he gives credit to his European predecessors, most notably Copernicus, Tycho Brahe, Kepler and Galileo, and to the ancient Greeks, including Pythagoras, Empedocles, Philolaus, Democritus, Plato, Aristotle, Epicurus, Euclid, Archimedes, Apollonius, Aristarchus, Diophantus, Ptolemy and Pappus. Thus the new science created by Newton was, in his opinion, the rebirth and further development of Greek science.

CHAPTER 18

EUREKA! GREEK SCIENCE REDISCOVERED

By Newton's time the rediscovery of ancient Greek scientific manuscripts had long since ceased, and it seemed that the remainder was irretrievably lost, including important works referred to by ancient sources. But at the end of the nineteenth century and the beginning of the twentieth century three lost works of ancient Greek science were rediscovered, one of them by Hero of Byzantium and the other two by Archimedes, the latter two found under most dramatic circumstances.

Hero's principal mathematical work, the *Metrica*, was long lost until its rediscovery by the German scholar Hermann Schöne at Istanbul in 1896, part of a manuscript written around 1100. It is divided into three books, the first two dealing with the mensuration of plane and solid figures, respectively, the third with the division of figures into parts having given ratios to one another. Boyer has pointed out that there are strong resemblances between Hero's results in the *Metrica* and those found in ancient Babylonian problem texts. This has led Michael S. Mahoney to conclude that Hero is 'a vital link in a continuous tradition of practical mathematics from the Babylonian, through the Arabs, to Renaissance Europe.'

Hero's mathematical works seem to have preserved in Byzantium, as evidenced by the rediscovery of his *Metrica* in Istanbul. His mechanical works seem to have been preserved there too, as evidenced by the testimony of Liudprand, Bishop of Cremona, who visited Constantinople on diplomatic missions twice in the mid tenth century. His first visit was in 949, when he had an audience in the Great Palace of Byzantium with the emperor Constantine VII Porphyrogenitus. Liudprand reports that the emperor sat on a great throne of gold and silver that was elevated hydraulically, flanked by golden lions that roared and shaded by a bejewelled tree of gold in which golden birds sang melodiously.

Liudprand's account seems to have inspired William Butler Yeats to write 'Sailing to Byzantium'. 'I have read somewhere,' Yeats writes in a note on this poem, 'that in the Emperor's palace in Byzantium there was a tree made of gold and silver, and artificial birds that sang.' They still sing in the last stanza of the poem, a dying echo of Hero's automated bird-song:

Once out of nature I shall never take
My bodily form from any natural thing,
But such a form as Grecian goldsmiths make
Of hammered gold and gold enamelling
To keep a drowsy Emperor awake;
Or set upon a golden bough to sing
To lords and ladies of Byzantium
Of what is past, or passing, or to come.

In 1900 a Greek sponge boat from the island of Symi anchored off the northern coast of the remote islet of Antikythera to escape a storm. After the storm abated a diver named Elias Stadiatos went down to look for sponges and found the wreck of an ancient ship on the sea-bottom. The antiquities that he and the other divers recovered from the wreck included a bronze statue, now known as the Ephebe of Antikythera, on exhibit in the National Archaeological Museum in Athens. The ship was dated to the first century BC, and is thought to have been on its way from Rhodes to Italy.

Almost overlooked in the objects brought up from the wreck was a wooden box about the size of a book, which when opened proved to contain a complex arrangement of bronze gears and dials, all heavily eroded into shapeless lumps of green metal. The wooden box soon disintegrated into dust, but the bronze gears and dials survived and were eventually subjected to an X-ray analysis to determine their function. The device, now known as the Antikythera Computer, proved to be an elaborate clockwork mechanism, which Derek De Solla Price, historian of science at Yale, showed to be an astronomical device known to the Greeks as a *sphairopoiia*, a mechanism that modelled the motions of the celestial bodies. A more recent analysis by Michael Wright, curator at the Science Museum in London, has shown that the gear system reproduced the epicycle theory for planetary motions derived by Apollonius and used by Ptolemy.

Pappus says that Archimedes wrote a treatise, now lost, called *Peri Sphairopoiias* (On Sphere-Making), describing a celestial globe that he made to represent the motions of the sun and moon and demonstrate both solar and lunar eclipses. Cicero says that after the Roman sack of Syracuse Marcellus took back to Rome two such types of instruments constructed by Archimedes:

> For Gallus told us that the other type of celestial globe [that Marcellus brought back and placed in the Temple of Virtue], which was solid and contained no hollow space, was a very early invention, the first one of that kind having been constructed by Thales of Miletus, and later marked by Eudoxus of Cnidus ... with the constellations which are fixed in the sky .... But this newer kind of globe, he said, on which were delineated the motions of the sun and moon and those five stars which are called the wanderers ... contained more than could be shown on a solid globe, and the invention of Archimedes deserved a special admiration because he had thought out a way to represent accurately by a single device for turning the globe those various and divergent courses with their different rates of speed.

The sphere eventually came into the possession of a grandson of Marcellus, who showed it to the astronomer Gaius Sulpicius Gallus. Gallus used the sphere to predict a lunar eclipse on 21 June 168 B C, and Cicero says that he demonstrated solar eclipses as well, though obviously he could not predict whether these would be visible in Rome. Cicero writes that a device of this type was made by the astronomer Posidonius with whom he had studied in Rome. Thus it would appear that the Antikythera Computer was based on the *sphairopoiia* made by Archimedes, yet another example of his extraordinary genius.

Carl B. Boyer writes in his history of mathematics that 'Unlike the *Elements* of Euclid, which have survived in many Greek and Arabic manuscripts, the treatises of Archimedes have reached us through a slender thread. Almost all copies are from a single Greek original which was in existence in the sixteenth century and itself copied from an original of about the ninth or tenth century.'

One of the most important works of Archimedes, his treatise *On the Method*, was believed to have been lost in late antiquity, and it caused a sensation when it was rediscovered in 1906 by the Danish scholar John Ludwig Heiberg as part of a manuscript now known as Codex C, only to disappear from sight again a few years later until it re-emerged at the end of the twentieth century, under circumstances reminiscent of an Eric Ambler novel.

Early in the sixth century only three of the many works of Archimedes were generally know, those that appeared in the collection edited by Eutocius of Ascalon, namely *On the Equilibrium of Planes, On the Sphere and the Cylinder,* and the incomplete On the *Measurement of a Circle.* Then in the ninth century, Leo the Mathematician added to these the works *On Conoids and Spheroids, On Spirals, On the Quadrature of the Parabola,* the *Lemmata* and *The Sand Reckoner.* Leo's collection, known as Codex A, thus contained all of the works of Archimedes in Greek now known, except *On Floating Bodies, On the Method, Stomachion* and the *Cattle Problem.* This was one of two manuscripts available to William of Moerbeke when he made his translations of Archimedes in 1269.

The other, known as Codex B, also called the Codex Mechanicorum, which contained only the mechanical works – *On the Equilibrium of Planes, On the Quadrature of the Parabola,* and *On Floating Bodies* (and possibly *On Spirals*) – is last referred to in the early fourteenth century and then disappeared. Thus, as Marshall Claggett remarks, Codex A 'was the source, directly or indirectly, of all the Renaissance copies of Archimedes.'

Claggett also notes that it seems unlikely that Arab mathematicians possessed any collection of the works of Archimedes as complete as Codex A. According to Claggett, the writings of Archimedes available to the Arabs consisted of the following works: *On the Sphere and the Cylinder,* in an early ninth-century translation revised in turn by Ishaq ibn Hunayn and Thabit ibn Qurra and reedited by Nasir ad-Din al-Tusi; *On the Measurement of the Circle,* translated by Thabit ibn Qurra and reedited by Al-Tusi; a fragment of *On Floating Bodies*; possibly *On the Quadrature of the Parabola,* as evidenced by research on this work by Thabit ibn Qurra; some indirect material of *On the Equilibrium of Planes,* as indicated in Greek mechanical works translated into Arabic; and other writings attributed to Archimedes by Arab mathematicians for which there is no extant Greek text, such as the *Book on Lemmas,* the *Book on the Division of the Circle into Seven Equal Parts* and *On the Properties of the Right Triangle.*

Western Europe acquired its knowledge of Archimedes solely from Byzantium and Islam, for there is no trace of the earlier translations that Cassiodorus attributes to Boethius. The translation of Archimedean texts from the Arabic began in the twelfth century with *On the Measurement of the Circle,* a defective rendering that may have been done by Plato of Tivoli. A much superior translation of the same work was done by Gerard of Cremona, using an Arabic text due to Thabit ibn Qurra. The earliest-known Arabic translations of Archimedes are those of Thabit ibn Qurra. These comprise all the works of Archimedes that have not been preserved in Greek, including *The Book of Lemmas, On Touching Circles,* and *On Triangles.*

The texts used by William of Moerbeke in his 1269 translations – Codices A and B – had come to the papal library in the Vatican from the collection of the Norman kings of the Two Sicilies. William translated all the works included in Codices A and B, except for the *Sand Reckoner* and Eutocius' *Commentary on the Measurement of the Circle.* William's translations did not include *On the Method, The Cattle Problem,* and the *Stomachion,* since these works were not in Codices A and B.

A new Latin translation of the works of Archimedes was done ca. 1450 by James of Cremona, sponsored by Pope Nicholas V. James worked entirely from Manuscript A, and so his translation did not include *On Floating Bodies,* but it did have the two works in Codex A omitted by William of Moerbeke, namely *The Sand Reckoner* and Eutocius' *Commentary on the Measurement of the Circle.* Soon after James completed his translation the pope sent a copy to Nicholas of Cusa, who made use of it in his *De mathematicis complementis,* written in 1453–54. There are at least nine extant copies of this translation, one of which was corrected by Regiomontanus.

Codex A itself was copied several times, one copy being made by Cardinal Bessarion in the period 1449–68, and another by the humanist Georgio Valla, who used it in his *Outline of Knowledge,* printed at Venice in 1501. Copernicus, as we have learned, had a copy of the *Outline of Knowledge,* in which he would have read Archimedes' account in the *Sand Reckoner* of the heliocentric theory proposed by Aristarchus of Samos, which preceded the Copernican theory by 18 centuries.

Interest in Archimedes intensified from the mid sixteenth century onwards, and his influence can be seen in the works of Commandino, Simon Stevin, Kepler, Galileo, Torricelli, Leibnitz, Newton and many others. Translations were made into Italian, French and German, and a new Latin edition was published at London in 1675 by Isaac Barrow, Newton's predecessor as Lucasian professor of geometry at Cambridge. At the end of the eighteenth century, the Italian mathematician Joseph Torelli (1721–1781) prepared a new edition of the Greek text with Latin translation that was published posthumously by Abram Roberson at Oxford. Nevertheless a number of Archimedean writings remained missing, most notably the work *On the Method,* the existence of which was known only from references by Hero of Alexandria and the tenth-century Byzantine writer Suidas, who says that Theodosius of Bithynia write a commentary on it, though that was also lost.

The manuscripts that Heiberg discovered were part of a palimpsest, in this case a Euchologion, or prayer book, made up from recycled parchment leaves whose original contents had been scraped away and then written over with the new liturgical document. Heiberg's attention had been drawn to the Euchologion through a report published in 1899 by the Greek scholar A. Papadopoulos-Kerameus, a catalogue description of a manuscript collection in Istanbul belonging to the Metochion of the Holy Sepulchre, the daughter-house of a famous monastery in Jerusalem. Papadopoulos-Keramus had noted that the underlying script of the palimpsest MS 355 included a mathematical text, of which he printed a few lines in his catalogue. Heiberg, who at the time was revising his edition of Archimedes, recognized the lines as being from an Archimedean work. He went to Istanbul and examined the palimpsest, first in 1906 and then again two years later, when he photographed the manuscript using the newly invented ultraviolet lamp. He reported on his discovery in 1907 in a long article in the scholarly journal *Hermes*, and then in the years 1910–15 he incorporated his findings in the second edition of his three-volume opus on the works of Archimedes, upon which all subsequent Archimedean studies have been based. Meanwhile T. L. Heath translated *On the Method* into English, including it as a supplement to a new edition of his book, *The Works of Archimedes*, published in 1912, which I used when I first began studying Archimedes.

Papadopoulos-Kerameus noted that the palimpsest contained a sixteenth-century inscription recording that it belonged to the ancient Palestinian monastery of St Savas, known in Arabic as Mar Saba, founded in 483 a few miles east of Bethlehem on the west bank of the Jordan. The monastery had a renowned scriptorium for the copying and preservation of ancient manuscripts, of which its collection included more than a thousand works. Mar Saba was in ruins in 1625 when it was purchased by the Greek Orthodox Patriarchate of Jerusalem, which began a restoration in 1688. It has been suggested that in the early nineteenth century the Euchologion and other ancient manuscripts in Mar Saba were taken for safekeeping to Istanbul; there they were preserved in the Jerusalem patriarchate's Metochion of the Holy Sepulchre.

The German Biblical scholar Constantine Tischendorf visited the Metochion in the early 1840s. He described the Metochion in his *Reise in den Orient* (Leipzig, 1846), where he says he found nothing of particular interest except a palimpsest whose pages included some mathematics. He appears to have stolen a page from the Euchologion, for a leaf from the palimpsest was sold from his estate in 1879 to the Cambridge University

Library. Professor Nigel Wilson of Lincoln College Oxford examined this leaf in 1971 and identified it as being part of what by then had come to be known as the Archimedes Palimpsest.

The palimpsest disappeared from the Metochion not long after Heiberg's discovery, probably stolen in the chaos surrounding the fall of the Ottoman Empire and the creation of the new Republic of Turkey in 1923. Early in the 1920s the palimpsest was acquired by Mr. Marie Louis Sirieix, a French businessman and civil servant. In 1946 Sirieix gave the palimpsest as a wedding present to his daughter Mme. Anne Guersan, who had the Euchologion restored, and, as it appears, 'embellished', by the addition of what proved to be forged images of the four Evangelists. Nigel Wilson stated that the images were 'a disastrously misguided attempt to embellish the manuscript, presumably to enhance its value in the eyes of a prospective purchaser.' In any event, the Guersan family put the palimpsest up for sale, and on 29 October 1998 it was auctioned at Christies' in New York, where where an anonymous buyer purchased it for two million dollars. The Jerusalem Patriarchate contested the auction in a law-suit in New York, but the court ruled that the sale was legal.

Meanwhile the anonymous buyer deposited the palimpsest with the Walters Art Museum in Baltimore, Maryland, in January 1999, providing funds for conservation, imaging and scholarly study of the manuscript. A team of scientists from the Rochester Institute of Technology and Johns Hopkins University has used computer processing of digital images of the underlying text of the palimpsest photographed in ultraviolet, infrared and visible light. Then in May 2005 the palimpsest was irradiated with highly focused X-rays produced at the Stanford University Linear Accelerator Center in Menlo Park, California, which made it possible to read parts of the underlying text that had previously been undecipherable.

In 2002, Professor John Lowden of the Courtwald Institute in London deciphered a colophon on the palimpsest giving the date 13 April 1229, when the Euchologion was dedicated after the recycling of the ancient manuscripts on which it was written. The palimpsest, now referred to as Codex C, contains parts of seven treatises by Archimedes as well as pages of four other works, including those of the fourth-century BC Attic orator Hyperides. The Archimedean writings include an almost complete text of the previously unknown work *On the Method*; a substantial part of *On Floating Bodies*, whose original Greek text had been lost; a page from the *Stomachion*, another unknown work of Archimedes; and fragments of *On the Sphere and the Cylinder*, *On Spirals*, *Measurement of the Circle* and *On the Equilibrium of Planes*.

Thus Codex C overlaps with Codices A and B for several works: together with A, it has a text of *On Spirals, On the Sphere and the Cylinder* and *Measurement of the Circle*; along with B, it has a text of *On Floating Bodies*. Studies have shown that the Archimedean texts in the palimpsest, Codex C, were written in the second half of the tenth century, almost certainly in Constantinople.

The treatise *On Floating Bodies* was previously known only from the Latin translation done in 1269 by William of Moerbeke, the Greek original having been lost. The text of this thesis in the Archimedes palimpsest has considerable lacunae, so that William's translation is still used to give the undecipherable or missing parts of the Greek text.

Only a single page of the *Stomachion* was used in the palimpsest, the first page of the thesis, which became the last page in the Euchologion. Otherwise, the only source for this thesis is a brief passage in an Arabic text published in Berlin in 1899, said to derive from a work by Archimedes entitled *Stomachion*.

The Archimedes Palimpsest presently comprises 174 pages, three less that when Heiberg examined it, the missing pages probably removed when the Euchologion was stolen from the Metochion. All but 15 pages of the underlying text of the palimpsest have been deciphered, and these are now being analyzed at the Stanford Linear Accelerator Center. It takes about 12 hours to scan one page using an X-ray beam about the width of a human hair. After each new page is analyzed it is posted online for the general public to examine. And so in a sense we are receiving a message that has been lost for more than two thousand years:

> Archimedes to Eratosthenes greeting! On an earlier occasion I sent you some of the theorems found by me, the propositions of which I had written down, urging you to find the proofs which I did not yet communicate at that time. The propositions of the theorems I sent you were the following:

Along with the *Method of Solving Mechanical Problems* we now have the original Greek text of *On Floating Bodies*, in which discovered the law of buoyancy that led him to shout '*Eureka!*', uncovered from a palimpsest that connects the time of Archimedes with our own through the underlying layers of history.

Such is the heritage of Greek science and philosophy that began with the first physicists at Miletus and flourished in the groves of Academe and Apollo in Athens and the Library and Museum in Alexandria, creating the most enduring and powerful of all the forces that have shaped the modern world.

NOTES

ABBREVIATION

DSB: Dictionary of Scientific Biography

CHAPTER 1

'Many are the ...', Strabo, 14.1.6
'had the good fortune ...', Herodotus, 1.142
'the wonders of Ionia ... , Pausanias, vol. 1, p. 245
Yet in Delos ... , *Hesiod, the Homeric Hymns and Homerica*, p. 335
'Seven wealthy towns ...', Burr, p. 73
'the son of Meles, ...', *Hesiod, the Homeric Hymns and Homerica*, p. 567
'He dwelt near Helicon ...', Hesiod, *Works and Days*, pp. 639–40
'the Egyptians by ...', Herodotus, 2.4
'knowledge of the sun-dial ...', Herodotus, 2.109
'When the Pleiades, ...', Hesiod, *Works and Days*, pp. 383–4
'Herodotus of Halicarnassus, his Researches ...', Herodotus, 1.1
'a Milesian and therefore ...', Diogenes Laertius, 1.13
'the first founder ...', Aristotle, *Metaphysics A*, 983b20
'first went to Egypt ...', Heath, *History of Greek Mathematics*, vol. 1, p. 128
Most of the earliest ... , Aristotle, *Metaphysics A*, 983b6ff
'from the observation ...', Ibid., 983b20ff
'Others say that ...', Aristotle, *On The Heavens*, 294a28
'Okeanos, whence the Gods ...', Homer, *The Iliad*, xiv. 201
'Okeanos, whence is risen ...', Ibid., xiv. 246
'the first of the Greeks ...', Guthrie, vol. 1, p. 72
'Anaximander named the *arche* ...', Ibid., p. 76
Anaximander of Miletus, son ... , Ibid., p. 100
According to Anaximander, the ... , Ibid., p. 93
The moon is essentially ... , Ibid., pp. 93–4
'is similar to the drum ...', Long, p. 351
'The earth hangs freely, ...', Guthrie, vol. 1, p. 98
'He says moreover ...', Ibid., p. 102
'Wind is a flow ...', Ibid., p. 105
'When it is imprisoned ...', Ibid., p. 106
'solstices, times, seasons ...', Ibid., p. 74

'Those who followed him ...', Ibid., p. 74

Anaximenes of Miletus, son ... , Ibid., p. 121

After Anaxinander his pupil ... , Ibid., p. 122

It [the earth] does not ... , Ibid., p. 133

'Anaximenes of Miletus, son ...', Ibid., p. 131

'Exiled from his country, ...', Ibid., p. 363

'Seven and sixty years ...', Edmonds, *Elegy and Iambus*, p. 199

'But they learned useless ...', Ibid., p. 195

'Xenophanes asserted ... that all ...', Guthrie, vol. 1, p. 377

'God is one, greatest ...', Ibid., p. 374

'ascribed to the gods ...', Ibid., p. 371

'Ethiopians imagine their gods ...', Ibid., p. 371

'Xenophanes says that ...'. Ibid., p. 391

'She whom they call ...', Edmonds, *Elegy and Iambus*, p. 211

'Certain truth has no man ...', Guthrie, vol. 1. p. 395

'Such things should be ...'. Edmonds, *Elegy and Iambus*, p. 205

CHAPTER 2

'The history of Pythagoreanism ...', Guthrie, vol. 1, p. 146

"It was in his ...', Strabo 14.1.16

'laid down a constitution ...', Diogenes Laertius, 8.3

'A great reputation ...', Long, p. 70

They preserved their original ...', Guthrie, vol. 1, p. 180

'Pythagoras was especially ...', Plato, *Republic*, 600b

'The divine Pythagoras', Long, p. 67

'About no one else ...', Ibid., p. 67

The science, therefore ... , Heninger, p. 28

What he said to ... , Guthrie, vol. 1, p. 186

'Stop, do not beat ...', Ibid., p. 157

'The wise men,' he says, ...', Ibid., p. 209

'His teaching took two ...', Ibid., p. 192

The Pythagoreans, because they ...', Aristotle, *Metaphysics*, 1090a20

'The philosophy of the ...', Guthrie, vol. 1, p. 192

'Pythagoras, who came ...', Heath, *History of Greek Mathematics*, vol. 1, p. 141

'discovered the construction ...', Guthrie, vol. 1, p. 268

'The bodies in the ...', Ibid., p. 267

'There being five ...', Ibid., p. 267

But some say ... , Ibid., pp. 263–4

'By him who ...', Ibid., p. 225

'magical arts and Pythagorean ...', Thorndike, vol. 1, p. 370

'a harmonia and ...', Guthrie, vol. 1, p. 220

'saw that the ...', Kirk and Raven, p. 237

'Pythagoras ... discovered that ...', Guthrie, vol. 1, p. 222

'was something perfect ...', Aristotle, *Metaphysics*, 986a8

Alcmaeon says that ... , Ibid., 986a31

'Not without cause …', Heninger, p. 104

The Pythagoreans define … , Ibid., p. 104

'For instance, they regarded …', Aristotle, *Metaphysics*, 986a3

Philolaus teaches that … , Guthrie, vol. 1, p. 284

'Heraclides of Pontus and …', Ibid., p. 325

'Some of the Pythagoreans, …', Ibid., p. 285

They said too … , Ibid., p. 296

'Pythagoras, Archytas, Plato …', Heninger, p. 181

'To meet the difficulty …', Aristotle, *On the Heavens*, 290b25

How sweet the moonlight … , Shakespeare, *The Merchant of Venice*, V, i, 54–65

'Much learning does not …', Guthrie, vol. 1, p. 157

'prince of cheats', Ibid., p. 417

'made a wisdom …', Ibid., p. 417

'The Lord [Apollo] whose … , Kirk and Raven, p. 211

'Disease it is that …', Long, p. 94

'What I understand …', Guthrie, vol. 1, p. 412

'He was no man's …', Diogenes Laertius, 9.5

'*Panta rhei*', Guthrie, vol. 1, p. 450n1

'Heraclitus somewhere says …', Kirk and Raven, p. 197

'strife' … 'tension' … 'Opposites', Freeman, p. 113

'They do not grasp …', Guthrie, vol. 1, p. 439

'Invisible *harmonia* is …', Ibid., pp. 440–1

'Nature loves concealment', Ibid., p. 441

'God is day night, …', Kirk and Raven, vol. 1, p. 191

'Evil witnesses are eyes …' Ibid., p. 180

'the Logos which …', Guthrie, vol. 1, p. 419

'everything comes to pass …', Ibid., p. 419

Although this Logos …', Ibid., p. 424

Listening not to me … , Ibid., p. 425

One must follow … , Ibid., p. 425

One must speak … , Ibid., p. 425

'is both human thought …', Ibid., p. 428

'This world-order [*kosmos*], the same …', Ibid., p. 454

First, as Aristotle said …', Ibid., p. 466

'a spark of the …', Ibid., p. 481

'the limits of soul …', Ibid., p. 481

'A man's character …', Ibid., p. 482

'Here we leave this …', Ibid., pp. 486–7

CHAPTER 3

'Though he was a pupil …', Guthrie, vol. 2, p. 3

'The lines of Parmenides …', Ibid., p. 3

'Either a thing is …', Kirk and Raven, p. 269

'What is does not come …', Guthrie, vol. 2, p. 31

'It was not in …', Ibid., p. 26

'Nor is it divisible, …', Ibid., p. 31

But unmoved, in the … , Ibid., p. 34

But since there is no …'. Ibid., p. 43

'let custom, born of …', Kirk and Raven, p. 271

Then gin I thinke …', Spenser, *The Faerie Queene*, 7, viii, 2–7

'preferring it to …', Guthrie, vol. 2, p. 80

I see Parmenides, that …', Plato, *Parmenides*, 128a

In his book, in which … , Lee, p. 19

Friends who inhabit … , Guthrie, vol. 2, p. 137

'Fools, for they have no …', Ibid., p. 139

'Nor is any part …', Ibid., p. 139

'Of the All, none …', Ibid., p. 139

'Come now, observe with …', Ibid., p. 139

'roots of everything', Ibid., p. 141

'spring of mortal things', Ibid., p. 141

'Fire and water and …', Ibid., p. 141

'all these are equal …', Ibid., p. 142

'from these sprang …', Kirk and Raven, pp. 328–9

'the elements are continually …', Ibid., pp. 329–30

'When the whole is …', Guthrie, vol. 2, p. 156

'the groundwork bee …', Spenser, *The Fairie Queene*, 7, vii, 25–6

'To thousand sorts of Change … ,' Ibid., 7, vii, 27–33

'Empedocles, and any other …', Guthrie, vol. 2, p. 195

'a narrow-necked vessel …', Ibid., p. 221

'the way that all …', Ibid., p. 220

It is as when a girl … , Ibid., pp. 220–1

'All things were together, then …', Ibid., p. 272

But the man who … , Plutarch, *Pericles*, IV, 4

'We must suppose, …', Kirk and Raven, p. 378

'the sun, the moon …', Ibid., p. 391

The rest have a portion … , Guthrie, vol. 2, pp. 273–4

'Anaxagoras' recent assertion …', Ibid., p. 306

'an incandescent stone', Ibid., p. 307

'larger than the Peloponnese', Ibid., p. 307

'Similar segments of circles …', Boyer, p. 72

But Leucippus thought he … , Guthrie, vol. 2, p. 390

Leucippus and his associate … , Ibid., p. 392

'Democritus claims that …', Ibid., p. 393

'They are differentiated by …', Ibid., p. 393

'so small as to …', Ibid., p. 394

'Leucippus and Democritus, who …', Ibid., p. 397

'but from what cause, …', Ibid., p. 397

'They are wrong, and ... ,' Ibid., p. 397
'some are irregular, some ...', Ibid., p. 405
These atoms, separate from ... , Ibid., p. 405
animals, plants, cosmic systems ... , Ibid., p. 404
there are innumerable worlds ... , Ibid., p. 405
Many bodies [atoms] of all sorts ... , Ibid., pp. 406–7
'Nothing occurs at random, but ...', Ibid., p. 415
'Democritus, ignoring the final ...', Ibid., p. 415
'glens and valleys', Ibid., p. 421
'earth was borne ...', Ibid., p. 422
'Democritus says the soul ...', Ibid., p. 430
'that the soul is mortal ...', Ibid., p. 434
'I covered more territory ...', Ibid., p. 387
'I came to Athens and ...', Ibid., p. 349
'avoid all possible disturbances ...', Ibid., p. 493
'The telos [*goal*], he ...', Ibid., pp. 492–3

CHAPTER 4

'open to the world', Thucydides, 2.39
'love of the things of the mind', Ibid., 2.40
'the school of Hellas', Ibid., 2.41
'Mighty indeed, ...' Ibid., 2.41
'This is what Pericles ...', Plato, *Phaedrus*, 270a
'from his youth', Guthrie, vol. 4, p. 13
'to visit the prophets', Ibid., p. 15
'first came to Italy and Sicily', Ibid., p. 17
'who maddened my soul ...', Ibid., p. 43
'from a waterless ...', Plutarch, 'Cimon', XIII, 8
'You will spend your ...', Aristophanes, *The Clouds*, 1008ff
'the olive grove of Academe ...', Milton, *Paradise Regained*, 4, 244ff
'what we have in mind ...', Plato, *Laws*, I, 643e
'the philosophers make it ...', Guthrie, vol. 4, p. 21
'but that they might ...', Ibid., p. 21
'Let no one ignorant ...', Boyer, p. 93
'we must require those ...', Plato, *Republic*, VII, 529d
'the mere corruption and ...', Boyer, p. 95
'the awkward cylinders of ...', Guthrie, vol. 5, p. 449
'Well, Socrates, I think ...', Plato, Theaetatus, 143e, 144d
'I do not believe ...', Lloyd, *Early Greek Science: Thales to Aristotle*, p. 54
'This magnificent hope ...', Plato, *Phaedo*, 98c
'I was delighted with ...', Ibid., 98c
'Zeno and Parmenides ...', Plato, *Parmenides*, 127b–c
So anyone who is a ... , Plato, *Timaeus*, 46d–e

'along the lines of …', Ibid., 59d

'is not in sole …', Guthrie, vol. 4, p. 255

'Hence the god set …', Plato, *Timaeus*, 31b

our ability to see …', Ibid., 47a

'given for the same purpose …', Ibid., 47d

'if the earth is a sphere …', Plato, *Phaedo*, 109a

'The Spindle of Necessity', Plato, *Republic*, X, 617b

'above on the rims …', Ibid., 617b

Such was … god's design … , Plato, *Timaeus*, 38c–d

'cooperate in producing …', Ibid., 38e

Some bodies would … , Ibid., 38e

'let's study astronomy …', Plato, *Republic*, VII, 530b–c

'on what hypotheses …', Guthrie, vol. 5, p. 450

The Sun passes through … Evans, p. 149

'Magnitudes are said to …', Heath, *The Thirteen Books of Euclid's Elements*, vol. II, p. 114

If from any magnitude …', Heath, *The Thirteen Books of Euclid's Elements*, vol. III, p. 14

Finally Heraclides Ponticus, when …', Lloyd, *Early Greek Science: Thales to Aristotle*, p. 95

'containing earth and air …', Guthrie, vol. 5, p. 485

CHAPTER 5

'a man of taste and …', Guthrie, vol. 6, p. 27

'He deliberately turned his …', Ibid., p. 28

'he chose a public …', Diogenes Laertius, 5.2

The lectures of the philosopher …', Guthrie, vol. 6, p. 41

It remains to treat …', Aristotle, *On the Parts of Animals*, 645a5–17

'Aristotle that hath …', quoted by Guthrie, vol. 6, p. ix

Now action is for … , Aristotle, *Physics*, 199a11–15

'he neglected theological principles …', Guthrie, vol. 6, p. 94

'Those who have spent …', Aristotle, *On Generation and Corruption*, 316a6

This then appears … , Aristotle, *Generation of Animals*, 760b28

'For my definition of …', Aristotle, *Physics*, 192a31

The elements are four, …', Aristotle, *On Generation and Corruption*, 330a30–b7

Air, for example, will … , Aristotle, Ibid., 331a2–b1

The Universe then is a …', Aristotle, *On the Universe*, 391b9–18

'the simple bodies, since …', Aristotle, *On Generation and Corruption*, 330b31

'A given weight moves …', Aristotle, *On the Heavens*, 273a30–b2

'If everything that is …', Aristotle, *Physics*, 266b28–30

'a mover that is …', Ibid., 259b33

Of the stars …', Aristotle, *On the Heavens*, 392a5–30
After the ethereal and … , Ibid., 392a31–b13
Next to the aerial … , Aristotle, *On the Heavens*, 392b14–35
Thus the five elements, … , Aristotle, Ibid., 393a1–9
'those mathematicians who …', Aristotle, Ibid., 297b32–298a16
We have, then, first … , Aristotle, *Parts of Animals*, 645b21–26
Nature proceeds little by little … , Aristotle, *History of Animals*, 588b4–18
'the philosophy of human nature.' Aristotle, *Nicomachean Ethics*, 1181b15
If happiness is activity … , Aristotle, Ibid., 1177a11–17
'When the Athenians rose …', Aristotle, *Fragments*, F667R (*Vita Aristotelis Marciana* 184.91)

CHAPTER 6

'that had been obtained …', Diogenes Laertius, 5.39
The garden and walk … , Ibid., 5.39
'We must,' he says, 'set …', Theophrastus, *Metaphysics*, 11a1 ff
'Everything that burns …', Lloyd, *Greek Science After Aristotle*, p. 10
In considering the distinctive … , Theophrastus, *Enquiry into Plants*, I. 1. 1
'As is said, of some … , Ibid., IX, 9. 2
It remains to speak … , Theophrastus, *Causes of Plants*, I.6.1–2
'the kinds of stones …', Aristotle, *Meteorology*, 378a21
Of the things formed …', Theophrastus, *On Stones*, 1
All these [stones] must … , Ibid., 2–3
'The effects of plasters …', Theophrastus, *Concerning Odours*, 59–60
It is a sign if … , Theophrastus, *Concerning Weather Signs*, 16
Flattery might be understood … , Theophrastus, *Characters*, II, 1–3
'At a regular hour …', Ibid., Introduction, p. 8
'a distinguished man …', Diogenes Laertius, 5.58
'Everything that exists …', H. B. Gottschalk, 'Strato of Lampsacus', *DSB*, 13, 92
'frees God from …', quoted by Clagett, *Greek Science in Antiquity*, p. 69
'void can exist …', H. B. Gottschalk, 'Strato of Lampsacus', *DSB*, 13, 92
For in his treatise … , Cohen and Drabkin, pp. 211–12
All sounds, whether articulate … , Aristotle, *On Things Heard*, 800a11
'bear in mind …', Lloyd, *Greek Science After Aristotle*, p. 21
One further point … , Lucretius, II, 216–25
Again, if all motion … , Ibid., 251–60
'Chrysippus … supposes the whole …', Sambursky, *The Physical World of the Greeks*, p. 134
'Those who have most …', Ibid., p. 135
The Stoics say that air … , Ibid., p. 138
'Without one binding tension …', Ibid., p. 138
According to Chrysippus … , Ibid., p. 138

Chrysippus distinguishes between ... ., Ibid., p. 145
The results of these ... , Ibid., p. 174

CHAPTER 7

'The Museum is also ...', Strabo, *Geography*, XVII. 1. 8
'had at his disposal ...', Mostafa El-Abbadi, 'The Alexandria Library in History',
    Hirst and Silk, p. 171
'the beautiful city of ...', Robert Barnes, 'Cloistered Bookworms',
    MacLeod, p. 66
'first library and another ...', Ibid., p. 66
'most fair and well disposed ...'. Bulmer-Thomas, 'Euclid: Life and
    Works', *DSB*, 4, 415
'This wonderful book, ...', Heath, *Greek Mathematics*, p. 204
Euclid, who was not ... , Cohen and Drabkin, p. 37
'On a given finite ...', Heath, *The Thirteen Books of Euclid's Elements*, vol. I,
    p. 241
'in any right-angled triangle ...', Bulmer-Thomas, 'Euclid: Life and
    Works', *DSB*, 4, 418
'is interesting historically ...', Ibid., 4, 417
'to a given [straight] line ...', Ibid., 4, 417
'Euclid used instead ...', Boyer, p. 119
'It is impossible not ... , Bulmer-Thomas, 'Euclid: Life and Works',
    DSB, 4, 419
If a straight line be ... .', Boyer, p. 122
'tangent' as 'a straight line ...', Heath, *Greek Mathematics*, pp. 221–2
There is no book ...', Bulmer-Thomas, 'Euclid: Life and Works',
    DSB, 4, 419
'In right-angled triangles ...', Boyer, p. 128
'even, odd, even-times ... , ...', Heath, *Greek Mathematics*, p. 235
'that which is equal ..., Boyer, p. 126
'in continued proportion', Bulmer-Thomas, 'Euclid: Life and Works',
    DSB, 4, 421
'the products of two ...', Heath, *Greek Mathematics*, p. 239
'a number can be ...', Bulmer-Thomas, 'Euclid: Life and Works', *DSB*, 4, 421
'Book X of the *Elements* ...', Boyer, p. 128
'the famous proposition ...', Heath, *Greek Mathematics*, p. 242
'If the lesser of two unequal ...', Bulmer-Thomas, 'Euclid: Life and Works',
    DSB, 4, 422
'The sphere is defined, ...', Heath, *Greek Mathematics*, p. 247
Book XII applies the method ...', Bulmer-Thomas, 'Euclid: Life and
    Works', *DSB*, 4, 422
'fruitful Praeface ... manifolde ...', quoted by Freely, *Aladdin's Lamp*, pp. 124–5
'The *editio princeps* of ...', Heath, *Greek Mathematics*, p. 254

'The circle of the zodiac …', Bulmer-Thomas, 'Hypsicles of Alexandria', *DSB*, 6, 615
'let the name horizon …', Heath, *Greek Mathematics*, p. 266
'it may have been intended …', Ibid., p. 267
'the figure formed by …', Ibid., p. 267

CHAPTER 8

Now you are aware … , Heath, *The Works of Archimedes*, pp. 221–2
'the school of Aristarchus', Toomer, *Ptolemy's Almagest*, p. 137
'he too made the earth …', Heath, *Aristarchus of Samos*, p. 307
That the moon receives … , Ibid., p. 353
The distance of the sun … , Heath, *Aristarchus of Samos*, pp. 353, 355
'When the sun is totally eclipsed …', Ibid., p. 383
'Aristarchus discovered that …', Heath, *The Works of Archimedes*, p. 223
Proposition 10 … , Heath, *Aristarchus of Samos*, pp. 385–411
Distance of Sun … , Evans, pp. 71–3
'seems to be the ultimate …', Heath, *Aristarchus of Samos*, p. 325
'Aristarchus said that colours …', Ibid., p. 300
'determined the year …', Copernicus, p. 157
'We are told by …', Heath, *Aristarchus of Samos*, p. 314
'it is difficult to believe …', Ibid., p. 316
'was a mathematician among …', Dicks, 'Eratosthenes', *DSB*, 4, 389
'the summer tropic … must pass …', Strabo, II.5.6
'On the most probable …', Dicks, 'Eratosthenes', *DSB*, 4, 390
Sophocles, the tragic poet, … , Evans, p. 41
With all the natural numbers … , Boyer, p. 179

CHAPTER 9

'is said to have …', Claggett, 'Archimedes', *DSB*, 1, 213
… tracked out his grave … , Ibid., 213
fixed upon a three-masted … , Ibid., 213
'if there were another …', Ibid., 213
'Give me a place …', Ibid., 213
'diversions of a geometry …', Plutarch, *Marcellus*, XIV, 4
And yet Archimedes possessed … , Ibid., 4
I thought it might … , Dijksterhuis, p. 314
'Of unequal magnitudes, …', Heath, *Greek Mathematics*, p. 294
If a straight line one … , Ibid., p. 317
When Archimedes was turning … , Vitruvius, 9, 3
'is a kind of game, …', Dijksterhuis, p. 409
'it consisted of fourteen …', Ibid., p. 410
Many scientific problems … , Lindberg, *The Beginnings of Modern
  Science*, p. 110

NOTES

CHAPTER 10

'three mathematicians stood …', Boyer, p. 157

'If a straight line, …', Ibid., p. 182

The first four books … , Toomer, 'Apollonius of Perga', *DSB*, 1, 185

'All belong to "higher geometry", … , Ibid., 187

'can be reduced to …', Ibid., 188

'To draw through …', Ibid., 188

'might be called …', Boyer, p. 159

'he proved that …', Heath, *Greek Mathematics*, p. 375

'Several other writers …', Heath, *Greek Astronomy*, p. 116

'to set out the details', Ibid., p. 117

'not less than …', Evans, p. 259

'from Babylonian and …', Toomer, 'Hipparchus', *DSB*, 15, 211

'a *terminus post quem* …', Ibid., 212

5 (1) The moon at mean distance … , Ibid., 212

'four-cubit diopter', Ibid., 219

'The object of the propositions …', Heath, *Greek Mathematics*, p. 394

'of things on land …', Strabo, *Geography*, 1.1.1

'inhabitants are more …', Ibid., 4.5.4

Notable men were … , Ibid., 14.10,7

'on the borders of …', Ibid., 11.5.1

The Amazons spend … , Ibid., 11.5.1

'the spread of the empires …'. Ibid., 1.2.1

CHAPTER 11

'diversions of a geometry …', Plutarch, *Marcellus*, XIV, 4

'when he had gone …', Diogenes Laertius, IV, 37

Methods of making … ,Vitruvius, IX, 8, 2

'As the weight fell …', Ibid., IX 8, 3

'Ctesibius, observing that …', Ibid, IX, 8, 4

A regular flow … , Ibid., IX, 8, 5

The hours are marked … , Ibid., IX, 8, 6

'which raises water …', Ibid., X, 7, 1

'This, however,' he writes, … , Vitruvius, X, 7, 4

'almost certainly taken …', Drachmann, 'Philo of Byzantium',
    DSB, 10, 587

'consists of descriptions …', Ibid., 588

I say, then, that … , Cohen and Drabkin, p. 256

Hence we shall prove … , Ibid., p. 256

We may make … , Ibid., pp. 346–7

'its construction is similar …', Lewis, p. 356

'All the technical …', Drachmann, 'Hero of Alexandria', *DSB*, 311

'Byzantine schoolbooks with ...', Ibid., 311

'all the rest are ...', Ibid., 311

'Sacrificial Vessel which ...', Hero, Chapter 21

These sounds are produced ... , Hero, Chapter 14

'Now both Hero and Philo ...', Cohen and Drabkin, p. 224

'In this and similar ...', Ibid., p. 232

'If one mirror ... .', Ibid., p. 267

'is a valuable ...', Mahoney, 'Hero of Alexandria: Mathematics', *DSB*, 1, 315

CHAPTER 12

'anatomy and physiology, ...', Sarton, *Galen of Pergamon*, p. 27

'One of his Roman ...', Ibid., p. 37

'on watching and vigilance ...', Ibid., p. 32

'What gained Asclepiades ...', Ibid.,, p. 168

'a mixture of Stoicism ...', Nutton, p. 203

Galen's duty was ...', Ibid., p. 223

'cannot have been written ...', Ibid., p. 226

'a strong tradition ...', Ibid., p. 226

His physiological theories ... , Wilson, Leonard G., 'Galen: Anatomy
   and Physiology', *DSB*, 5, 233–4

'Later Galenists ...', Nutton, p. 234

Galen also observed ... , Wilson, Leonard G., 'Galen: Anatomy and Physiology',
   DSB, 5, 235

Make it your serious ... , Irby-Massie and Keyser, p. 324

All this will be ... , Ibid., p. 325

'the belief that blood ...', Lloyd, *Greek Science After Aristotle*, p. 147

Having made his observations ... , Nutton, p. 238

'encompassed one's whole ...', Ibid.,, p. 241

'Most of Galen's ...', Ibid., p. 241

'If dietetics failed, ...', Ibid., p. 242

'all formed part ...', Ibid., p. 242

Galen's pharmacalogical writings ... , Nutton, pp. 246–7

'discusses over 600 plants, ...' Riddle, 'Dioscorides', *DSB*, 4, 119

'led a soldier's life', Cohen and Drabkin, p. 511

'since modern subspecies ...', Riddle, 'Dioscorides', *DSB*, 4, 119

'book I (129 items), ...', Ibid, 120

Now it is obvious ... , Cohen and Drabkin, p. 512

'both in the storing ...', Ibid., p. 512

We ought to gather ... , Ibid., p. 512

Cannabis: a plant useful ... , Irby-Massie and Keyser, pp. 275–6

'If you have not ...', Riddle, 'Dioscorides', *DSB*, 4, 121

'What remains for consultation ...', Nutton, p. 7

NOTES

CHAPTER 13

'the only place mentioned ...', Toomer, 'Ptolemy', *DSB*, 11, 186–7
'As is implied ...', Ptolemy' *Almagest*, p. 1
'by the early fourth ...', Ibid., p. 2
'What Ptolemy has done ...', Ibid., pp. vi–vii
'in the middle of ...', Ibid., p. 41
'Ptolemy's own chronological ...', Ibid., p. 9
'For that is the era ...', Ibid., p. 166
Having set the instrument ... , Ibid., p. 62
'it is likely that ...', Toomer, 'Ptolemy', *DSB*, 11, 189
Since the sun travels ... , Ibid., 191
'from Babylonian and ...', Ibid., 191
(1) In 126,007 days, ... , Ibid., 191
'is able to construct ...', Ibid., 191
'a "crank" mechanism that "pulls in"... , Ibid, 193
'is easily derived ...', Ibid., 194
'below the sun ... above the sun ...', Ptolemy's *Almagest*, p. 420
'Now it is our ...', Ibid., p. 420
Ptolemy eventually reaches ... , Toomer, 'Ptolemy', *DSB*, 11, 196
'The epoch is changed ...', Ibid., 196
'This method of determining ...', Ibid., 197 .
'It is an explanation ...', Ibid., 196
'Since the work explains ...', Ibid., 198
'we shall dismiss ...', Lloyd, *Greek Science After Aristotle*, pp. 130–1
There follows a remarkable ... , Toomer, 'Ptolemy', *DSB*, 11, 200
'we have found no ...', Lloyd, *Greek Science After Aristotle*, p. 134
'it deals with the mathematical ...', Toomer, 'Ptolemy', *DSB*, 11, 201
'Kepler intended to publish ...', Ibid., 201

CHAPTER 14

'he fled from the gloom ...', Morford, p. 25
'Live unnoticed', Furley, 'Lucretius', *DSB*, 8, 536
'To measure the angle ...'
'this very superstition ...', Lucretius, *De Rerum Natura*, 1, 82–3
'Nothing is ever produced ...', Ibid., 1, 150–1
'time by itself ...', Ibid., 1, 459–61
'What can be a surer ...', Ibid., 1, 699–700
'at quite indeterminate ...', Lucretius, *De Rerum Natura*, 2, 218–20
'that by perusing ...', Pliny the Elder, 1, 17
'a diffuse and learned ...', Eicholz, 'Pliny', *DSB*, 11, 19
'counted the stars ...', Seneca, VII, 25
'there are many nations ... , Ibid, VII, 25

'the day will come …', Ibid., VII, 25

'It is enough for Christians …', Claggett, *Greek Science in Antiquity*,
  pp. 132-3

'a handbook on those …', Boyer, p. 200

'God granted him …', Cohen and Drabkin, p. 27

Although Diophantus knew … , Vogel, 'Diophantus of Alexandria',
  DSB, 4, 111

'It is impossible to divide …', Heath, *Diophantus of Alexandria*, pp. 145-6

'which this margin …', Boyer, p. 354

While it covers … , Heath, *Greek Mathematics*, pp. 435-6

'the comparison of the …', Ibid., p. 448

'sagacity of bees …', Ibid., p. 448

Presumably because they … , Ibid., p. 448

'Books VI and VIII …', Boyer, p. 211

'The Collection of Pappus …', Ibid., p. 211

'I therefore swear …', Bulmer-Thomas …', 'Pappus of Alexandria', *DSB*, 10, 301

'philosophy and magic …', Thorndike, vol. 1, p. 290

'On the inner side …', Mostafa El-Abadi, 'The Alexandria Library in History', in
Hirst and Silk, pp. 173-4

'The most notable of …', Toomer, 'Theon of Alexandria', *DSB*, 13, 322

'certain ancient astrologers', Carmody, pp. 45-6

'With the revival of learning …', Morrow, 'Proclus', *DSB*, 11, 161-2

What then has Athens … , Lloyd, *Greek Science After Aristotle*, p. 168

CHAPTER 15

'a man eloquent and …', Clagett, *Greek Science in Antiquity*, p. 181

'their valuable methods …', Boyer, p. 238

'I only wish …', Ibid., p. 238

'Though I am a …', Runciman, *The Last Byzantine Renaissance*, p. 22

'is eternal and not subject …', Aristotle, *On the Heavens*, 270b1

'the stars are neither … ,' Ibid., 268a34

'Besides, the sun, which …' Aristotle, *Meteorology*, 341a36

'The sun is not …', Sambursky, 'John Philoponus', *DSB*, 7, 134

'However, if one abstracts …', Ibid., 135

The monotheistic dogma … , Ibid., 135

'if one lets fall …', Ibid., 135

'some incorporeal kinetic power …', Ibid., 136

'an incorporeal kinetic …', Ibid., 136

'If we pass a wet …', Ibid., 137

'the body struck must …', Ibid., 137

'was the first caliph …', Gutas, *Greek Thought, Arabic Culture*, p. 30

'he translated from Persian …', Ibid., p. 55

'was employed full time …', Ibid., p. 55

NOTES

'encouraged me to compose ...', Ibid., p. 113

'At the beginning ...', Ibid., pp. 77–8

'for full-time translation ...', Ibid., p. 133

'the land of the ...', Anawati, 'Hunayn ibn Ishaq', *DSB*, 15, 230

'I traveled in its search ...', Ibid., 230

'without Leo, the revival ...', Vogel, 'Byzantine Science', in *The Cambridge Medieval History*, new edition, Vol. IV, Part II, p. 265

'I met some of the ...', Psellus, p. 127

'I perused the works ...', Hussey and Hart, 'Byzantine Theological Speculation and Spirituality', in *The Cambridge Medieval History*, new edition, Vol. IV, Part II, p. 194

'in spite of the hard ...', Minio-Paluello, 'William of Moerbeke', *DSB*, 9, 435

CHAPTER 16

'it reawakened an interest ...', Pingree, 'Gregory Chioniades and Palaeologan Astronomy', *Dumbarton Oaks Papers* 18 (1964), 135

'The Nicaean court physician ...', Runciman, *The Last Byzantine Renaissance*, p. 91

'He was an authority ...', Ibid., p. 92

'in what is termed ...', Fryde, p. 341

'From morning to evening ...', Freely, *Istanbul, The Imperial City*, p. 159

'raised the level ...', Pingree, 'Gregory Chioniades and Palaeologan Astronomy', *Dumbarton Oaks Papers* 18 (1964), 137

'returned to Trebizond ...', Ibid., 141

'an introduction to astronomy ...', Pingree, *Oxford Dictionary of Byzantium*, p. 423

'Knowledge of the Tusi couple ...', Ibid., p. 423

'influenced several anonymous ...', Ibid., p. 453

He wrote a *Construction* ...', Ibid, p. 166

'constituted a culmination ...', Fryde, p. 350

Meliteniotes praised highly ... , Ibid., p. 351

'towards the sea ...', Vasiliev, vil. II, p. 623

'the most original ...', Runciman, *The Last Byzantine Renaissance*, p. 2

'Neither, it will not ...', Nigel Wilson, *From Byzantium to Italy: Greek Studies in the Italian Renaissance*, p. 56

'If the immensity ...', Ibid., p. 56

'If you sail ...', Ibid., p. 56

'The rebirth of trigonometry.', Boyer, p. 108

CHAPTER 17

But while some say ... , Heninger, p. 28

'began to mediate ...', Copernicus, *De Revolutionibus*, p. 4

And although the opinion ... , Ibid., p. 4

Though the courses …', Africa, 'Copernicus' Relation to Aristarchus and Pythagoras', p. 407

I myself think … , Copernicus, *De Revolutionibus*, pp. 19–20

In the center of all … , Ibid., pp. 25–6

'Copernicus … affirmith that …', Kuhn, *The Copernican Revolution*, p. 186

'so that Englishmen might not …', Gingerich, *The Book Nobody Read*, p. 119

'a second Ptolemy', Dryer, *Tycho Brahe*, p. 74

'How many mathematicians …', A. R. Hall, *The Scientific Revolution*, p. 126

'a still unexhausted treasure …', Caspar, *Kepler*, p. 64

The earth's orbit …', Gingerich, 'Johannes Kepler, *DSB*, 7, 290

'Have faith, Galilii, …', Koestler, *The Sleepwalkers*, p. 364

'I consider it a divine …', Caspar, *Kepler*, p. 131

'Although he knew …', Ferguson, *Tycho and Kepler*, p. 284

'necessary for the contemplation …', Caspar, *Kepler*, p. 296

'That the same thought …', Ibid., pp. 276–7

'foolish and absurd …', Armitage, *Copernicus and Modern Astronomy*, p. 189

'It would still be …', Galileo, *Dialogue Concerning the Two Chief Systems, Ptolemaic and Copernican*, p. 464

'Your Galileo has …', De Santillana, *The Crime of Galileo*, p. 191

'had altogether given …'. Koestler, *The Sleepwalkers*, p. 503

our present work … , Newton, *Principia*, p. 382

'quantity of matter', Ibid., p. 403

'quantity of motion, Ibid., p. 404

'inherent force of matter', Ibid., p. 404

'Impressed force', Ibid., p. 405

'are impelled, or in …', Ibid, p. 405

Law 1: Every body … , Ibid., pp. 416–17

'Gravity exists in all …', Ibid., p. 810

'This most elegant …', Ibid., p. 940

I consider mathematical … , Guthrie, vol. 1, p. 264n1

'corrected by the …', Newton, *Opticks*, p. lxxvii

'My design in …', Ibid., p. 1

'the oldest and most …', Newton, *Opticks*, p. 369

'He lived honored …', Voltaire, *Letters on England*, p. 69

'by standing on the …', Sullivan, *Isaac Newton, 1642–1727*, p. 150

CHAPTER 18

'a vital link in …', Mahoney, 'Hero of Alexandria: Mathematics', *DSB*, 1, 314

'I have read …', quoted by Freely, *Istanbul, The Imperial City*, p. 112

Once out of nature … , Yeats, *The Collected Works*, p. 164

NOTES

For Gallus told us ...', Cicero, *The Nature of the Gods*, II, 87–9
'Unlike the *Elements* ...', Boyer, p. 136
'was the source, directly ...', Claggett, 'Archimedes,' *DSB*, 1, 223
'a disastrously misguided attempt ...', Lowden, 'Archimedes into Icon',
    p. 236
Archimedes to Eratosthenes ... , Dijksterhuis, p. 313

BIBLIOGRAPHY

Aaboe, Asger, *Episodes from the Early History of Mathematics*, New York, 1964

Africa, Thomas W., 'Copernicus' Relation to Aristarchus and Pythagoras', *Isis* 52, No. 3 (Sept. 1961), 403–9

Allan, D. J., 'Plato', *DSB*, 11, 443–6

Aristophanes, translated by Benjamin Bickley Rogers, 3 vols., London, 1978

Aristotle, *The Complete Works*, edited by Jonathan Barnes, 2 vols., Princeton, 1984

Armitage, Angus, *Sun Stand Thou Still; The Life and Works of Copernicus the Astronomer*, New York, 1947

———, *Copernicus and Modern Astronomy*. New York, 2004

Armstrong, A. H. (ed.), *The Cambridge History of Later Greek and Early Medieval Philosophy*, Cambridge, 1967

Bailey, Cyril, *The Greek Atomists and Epicurus*, Oxford, 1964

Baker, Robert H., *Astronomy: an Introduction*, New York, 1930

Barnes, Jonathan, *The Presocratic Philosophers*, London, 1982

———, *Aristotle*, Oxford, 1982

——— (ed.), *The Cambridge Companion to Aristotle*, Cambridge, 1995

Becker, Adam H., *Fear of God and the Beginning of Wisdom, The School of Nisibis and the Development of Scholastic Culture in Late Antique Mesopotamia*, Philadelphia, 2006

Bevan, Edwyn, *The House of Ptolemy: A History of Egypt under the Ptolemaic Dynasty*, Chicago, 1968

Boardman, John, *The Greeks Overseas*, Baltimore, 1964

Boyer Carl B., *A History of Mathematics*, New York, 1968

Bulmer-Thomas, Ivor, 'Euclid: Life and Works', *DSB*, 4, 414–37

———, 'Eutocius of Ascalon', *DSB*, 4, 488–91

———, 'Hippocrates of Chios', *DSB*, 6, 410–18

———, 'Hypsicles of Alexandria, *DSB*, 6, 616–17

———, 'Isidorus of Miletus', *DSB*, 7, 28–30

———, 'Menelaus of Alexandria', *DSB*, 9, 296–302 and 15, 420–1

———, 'Pappus of Alexandria, *DSB*, 10, 293–304

———, 'Theodosius of Bithynia', *DSB*, 13, 319–21

BIBLIOGRAPHY

Bunbury, E. U., *A History of Ancient Geography among the Greeks and Romans from the earliest days to the fall of the Roman Empire*, 2 vols., New York, 1959

Bunt, Lucas, Philip S. Jones, and Jack D. Bedient, *The Historical Roots of Elementary Mathematics*, New York, 1988

Burnet, John, *Greek Philosophy, Thales to Plato*, London, 1981

Burr, A. R., *The Pelican History of Greece*, Harmondsworth, 1966

Butterfield, Herbert, *The Origins of Modern Science, 1300–1800*. New York, 1957

Cambridge Medieval History, Vol. 4, Part II, edited by J. M. Hussey, Cambridge, 1967

Carmody, Francis J., *The Astronomical Works of Thabit Ibn Qurra*, Berkeley, 1960

Caspar, Max, *Kepler*, translated by C. Doris Hellman, New York, 1962

Casson, Lionel, *Libraries of the Ancient World*, New Haven, 2001

Claggett, Marshall, *Archimedes in the Middle Ages*, Madison, Wisconsin, 1964

———, *Greek Science in Antiquity*, Mineola, New York, 2001

———, 'Archimedes', *DSB*, 1, 213–31

Cohen, Morris and I. E. Drabkin, *A Source Book in Greek Science*, Cambridge, Mass., 1958

Cook, John M., *The Greeks in Ionia and the East*, New York, 1963

Copernicus, Nicolaus, *De Revolutionibus* (*On the Revolutions of the Celestial Spheres*), translated by Glen Wallis, edited by Stephen Harking, Philadelphia, 2002

Crombie, A. C., *Medieval and Early Modern Science*, 2 vols., 2nd ed., Cambridge, Mass., 1963

———, (ed.), *Scientific Change; historical sketches in the intellectual, social and technical conditions for scientific discovery and technical invention from antiquity to the present*, New York, 1963

Cuomo, Serafina, *Ancient Mathematics*, London, 2001

———, *Technology and Culture in Greek and Roman Antiquity*, Cambridge, 2007

Dannenfeldt, Karl, H., 'Callinicos of Heliopolis', *DSB*, 3, 20–1

———, 'Hermes Trismegistus', *DSB*, 6, 305–6

———, 'Stephanus of Alexandria', *DSB*, 13, 37

De Santillana, Giorgio, The Crime of Galileo, Chicago, 1955

De Santillana, Giorgio, *The Origins of Scientific Thought: from Anaximander to Proclus 600 BC to AD 300*, Chicago, 1961

Dicks, D. R., *Early Greek Astronomy to Aristotle*, Ithaca, New York, 1970

———, 'Cleomedes', *DSB*, 3, 318–20

———, 'Eratosthenes', *DSB*, 4, 388–93

———, 'Hecataeus of Miletus', *DSB*, 6, 212–13

Dictionary of Scientific Biography (DSB), 16 vols., edited by Charles Coulston Gillespie, New York, 1970–80

Dijksterhuis, F. J., *Archimedes*, Princeton, 1987

Diogenes Laertius, *Lives of Eminent Philosophers*, 2 vols., translated by H. D. Hicks, Cambridge, Mass., 1925

Dowden, Ken, 'The Epic Tradition in Greece', in Robert Fowler (ed.), *The Cambridge Companion to Homer*, pp. 188–205

Drachmann, A. G., *The Mechanical Technology of Greek and Roman Antiquity*, Copenhagen, 1963

———, 'Ctesibius', *DSB*, 3, 491–2

———, 'Hero of Alexandria', *DSB*, 6, 310–14

———, 'Philo of Byzantium', *DSB*, 10, 586–9

Drake, Stillman (translator), *Discoveries and Opinions of Galileo*, Garden City, New York, 1952

———, 'Galileo Galilei', *DSB*, 5, 237–248

Dreyer, J. L. E., *A History of Astronomy from Thales to Kepler*, New York, 1953

———, *Tycho Brahe*, New York, 1963

Edmonds, J. M. (tran. and ed.), *Lyra Graeca*, 3 vols., London, 1928

——— (tran and ed.), *The Characters of Theophrastus*, London, 1929

———, *Elegy and Iambus* (tran. and ed.), 2 vols., Cambridge, Mass., 1951

Eicholz, David E., 'Pliny', *DSB*, 11, 38

Evans, James, *The History and Practice of Ancient Astronomy*, Oxford, 1998

Farrington, Benjamin, *Greek Science: its meaning for us*, Baltimore, 1953

Ferguson, Kitty, *Tycho and Kepler: The Unlikely Partnership That Forever Changed Our Understanding of the Heavens*, New York, 2002

Folkerts, Menso, 'Regiomontanus' Role in the Transmission and Transformation of Greek Mathematics', Ragep, F. Jamil, and Sally P. Ragep with Steven Livesey (eds.) *Tradition, Transmission, Transformation*, pp. 89–113

Fowler, D. H., *The Mathematics of Plato's Academy: a new reconstruction*, New York, 1990

Fowler, Robert (ed.), *The Cambridge Companion to Homer*, Cambridge, 2004

Freely, John, *Istanbul, The Imperial City*, London, 1996

———, *The Emergence of Modern Science, East and West*, Istanbul, 2004

———, *The Western Shores of Turkey*, London, 2004

———, *Aladdin's Lamp: How Greek Science Came to Europe Through the Islamic World*, New York, 2009

———, *Children of Achilles: The Greeks in Asia Minor Since the Days of Troy*, London, 2009

Freeman, Kathleen, *The Presocratic Philosophers*, Oxford, 1953

Fried, Michael N. and Sabatai Unguru, *Apollonius of Perga's Conica: text, context, subtext*, Leiden and Boston, 2001

Fritz, Kurt von, 'Philolaus of Croton', *DSB*, 10, 589–91

———, 'Pythagoras of Samos', *DSB*, 11, 219–25

———, 'Zeno of Elea', *DSB*, 607–12

Fryde, Edmund, *The Early Palaeologan Renaissance, 1261 – ca. 1360*, Leiden, 2000

Furley, David J., 'Epicurus', *DSB*, 4, 381–2

———, 'Heraclitus of Ephesus', *DSB*, 6, 289–91

———, 'Lucretius', *DSB*, 8, 536–9

———, 'Zeno of Citium', *DSB*, 14, 605–6

Gade, John A., *The Life and Times of Tycho Brahe*, Princeton, 1947

Geymont, Ludovico, *Galileo, a biography and inquiry into his philosophy of science*, New York, 1965

BIBLIOGRAPHY

Galilei, Galileo, *Dialogue Concerning the Two Chief Systems, Ptolemaic and Copernican*, translated by Stillman Drake, Berkeley, 1967

Geanakoplos, Dino John, *Greek Scholars in Venice: Studies in the Dissemination of Greek Learning from Byzantium to Western Europe*, Cambridge, Mass., 1962

Gingerich, Owen, *The Book Nobody Read: Chasing the Revolutions of Nicolaus Copernicus*, New York, 2004

———, 'Johannes Kepler', *DSB*, 289–312

Goldstein, Bernard R. and Alan C. Bowen, 'A New View of Early Greek Astronomy', *Isis* 74, no. 3 (Sept. 1983): 330–40

Gottschalk, H. B., 'Strato of Lampsacus', *DSB*, 13, 91–5

Grant, Edward, *Physical Science in the Middle Ages*, New York, 1971

Grant, Michael, *The Rise of the Greeks*, London, 1987

Gregory, John, *The Neoplatonists: A Reader*, London, 1999

Grene, Marjorie, *A Portrait of Aristotle*, Chicago, 1963

Gutas, Dimitri, *Greek Thought, Arabic Culture: the Graeco-Arabic Translation Movement in Baghdad and Early Abbasid Society*, London, 1998

———, *Greek Philosophers in the Arabic Tradition*, Aldershot, UK, 2000

Guthrie, W. K. C., *A History of Greek Philosophy*, 6 vols., Cambridge, 1962–81

Hall, A. Rupert, *The Scientific Revolution, 1500–1800*, Boston, 1956

Hammond, N. G. L., *A History of Greece to 322 BC*, Oxford, 1967

Hammond, N. G. L. and H. H. Scullard (eds.), *The Oxford Classical Dictionary*

Haskins, Charles Homer, *The Rise of Universities*, New York, 1923

———, *Studies in the History of Mediaeval Science.* Cambridge, 1924.

———, *The Renaissance of the Twelfth Century.* New York, 1957

Heath, T. L., *The Works of Archimedes*, New York, 1912

———, *A History of Greek Mathematics*, 2 vols., Oxford, 1921

———, *Mathematics in Aristotle*, Oxford, 1949

———, *The Thirteen Books of Euclid's Elements*, 3 vols. New York, 1956

———, *Aristarchus of Samos, the ancient Copernicus*, Oxford, 1959

———, *Greek Mathematics*, New York, 1963 (QA22.H43)

———, *Diophantus of Alexandria: a study in the history of Greek algebra*, New York, 1964

———, *Greek Astronomy*, New York, 1991

Heiberg, J. L., *Mathematical and Physical Sciences in Classical Antiquity*, translated by D. C. Macgregor, London, 1922

Heidel, W. H., *The Heroic Age of Science*, Baltimore 1933

Hellman, C. Doris and Noel M. Swerdlow, 'Georg Peurbach', *DSB*, 15, 473–9

Heninger, S. K., *Touches of Sweet Harmony: Pythagorean Cosmology and Renaissance Poetics*, San Marino, California, 1974

Henry, John, *The Scientific Revolution and the Origins of Modern Science*, New York, 2002

Hero of Alexandria, *The Pneumatics*, translated for and edited by Bennet Woodcroft, London, 1851

Herodotus, *The Histories*, translated by Aubrey de Sélincourt, Harmondsworth, 1954

Hesiod, the Homeric Hymns and Homerica, translated by Hugh G. Evelyn-White, London, 1926

Hesiod, *Theogony and Works and Days*, translated by Dorothea Wender, New York, 1973

Hirst, Anthony, and Michael Silk, *Alexandria, Real and Imagined*, Aldershot, U.K., 2004

Homer, *The Iliad*, translated by Richmond Lattimore, Chicago, 1951

Hussey, Edward, *The Presocratics*, New York, 1973

Hussey, Joan and T. A. Hart, 'Byzantine Theological Speculation and Spirituality', in *Cambridge Medieval History*, Vol. 4, Part II, pp. 185–205

Huxley, G. L., *Anthemius of Tralles: a study in late Greek geometry*, Cambridge, Mass, 1959

———, *The Early Ionians*, London, 1966

———, 'Anthemius of Tralles', *DSB*, 1, 169–70

———, 'Autolycus of Pitane', *DSB*, 1, 338–9

———, 'Eudoxus of Cnidus', *DSB*, 4, 465–7

———, 'Theon of Smyrna', *DSB*, 13, 325–6

Ierodiakonou, Katerina (ed.), *Byzantine Philosophy and its Ancient Sources*, Oxford, 2002

Irbie-Massie, Georgia L and Paul T. Keyser, *Greek Science of the Hellenistic Era: a sourcebook*, London, 2002

Joly, Robert, 'Hippocrates of Cos', *DSB*, 6, 418–31

Jones, A., 'On Babylonian astronomy and its Greek metamorphoses', in *Tradition, Transmission and Transformation*, ed. F. Jamil Ragep, and Sally P. Ragep, 139–55

Kahn, Charles H., *Pythagoras and the Pythagoreans; A Brief History*, Indianapolis, ca. 2001

Kerferd, G. B., 'Democritus', *DSB*, 4, 30–5

———, 'Leucippus', *DSB*, 8, 269

Kingsley, Peter, *Ancient philosophy, mystery and magic: Empodocles and Pythagorean tradition*, Oxford, 1995

Kieffer, John S., 'Callippus', *DSB*, 3, 21–3

Kirk, G. S. and J. E. Raven, *The Presocratic Philosophers: a critical history with a selection of texts*, Cambridge, 1983

Klein, Jacob, *Greek Mathematical Thought and the Origin of Algebra*, tran. by Eva Brann, Cambridge, Mass., 1968

Kline, Morris, *Mathematical Thought from Ancient to Modern Times*, 3 vols., New York, 1990

Koestler, Arthur, *The Sleepwalkers: A History of Man's Changing Vision of the Universe*, London, 1959

Koyré, Alexandre, *From the Closed World to the Infinite Universe*, New York, 1958

———, *Newtonian Studies*, Cambridge, Massachusetts, 1965.

———, *The Astronomical Revolution: Copernicus, Kepler, Borelli*, tran. R. E. W. Madison, Ithaca, New York, 1973

Kramer, Edna E., 'Hypatia', *DSB*, 6, 615–16

BIBLIOGRAPHY

Kraut, Richard (ed.), *The Cambridge Companion to Plato*, Cambridge, 1992

Kudlien, Fridolf, 'Aëtius of Amida', *DSB*, 1, 68–9

———,'Galen', *DSB*, 5, 227–33

Kuhn, Thomas S., *The Copernican Revolution: Planetary Astronomy in the Development of Western Thought*, Cambridge, Mass., 1957

Lee, H. D. P., *Zeno of Elea*, Cambridge, 1936

Lewis, Michael, 'Theoretical Hydraulics, Automata and Water Clocks', in Wikander, Örjan, *Handbook of Ancient Water Technology; Technology and Change in History*, 2, Leiden, 2000, pp. 343–369

Lindberg, David C., *The Beginnings of European Science: The European Scientific Tradition in Philosophical, Religious and Institutional Context*, Chicago, 1992

Lloyd, G. E. R., *Polarity and Analogy: two types of argumentation in early Greek thought*, Cambridge, 1966

———, *Aristotle, the Growth and Structure of his Thought*, London, 1968

———, *Early Greek Science, Thales to Aristotle*, London, 1970

———, *Greek Science After Aristotle*, London, 1973

———, (ed.), *Hippocratic Writings*, New York, 1983

———, *Adversaries and Authorities: investigation into ancient Greek and Chinese science*, Cambridge, 1996

Long, A. A. (ed.), *The Cambridge Companion to Early Greek Philosophy*, Cambridge, 1999

Longrigg, James, 'Anaxagoras', *DSB*, 1, 149–50

———, 'Thales', *DSB*, 13, 295–8

Lowden, John, 'Archimedes into Icon: Forging an Image of Byzantium', In *Icons Word: The Power of Images in Byzantium*, edited by Antony Eastmond and Liz James, Burlington, Vermont, 2003

Lucretius, *De Rerum Natura (On the Nature of the Universe)*, translated by W. H. D. Rouse, London and Cambridge, Mass, 1937

MacLeod, Roy (ed.), *The Library of Alexandria, Centre of Learning in the Ancient World*, London, 2000

Maddison, F., 'Early Astronomical and Mathematical Instruments', *History of Science* 2, 17–50

Mahoney, Michael S., 'Hero of Alexandria: Mathematics', *DSB*, 6, 314–15

Marrou, H. I., *A History of Education in Antiquity*, translated by George Lamb, London, 1956

McDiarmid, J. B., 'Theophrastus', *DSB*, 13, 328–34

———, 'Theophrastus', *DSB*, 328–34

McKeon, J. B., *The Basic Works of Aristotle*, New York, 1942

Merlan, Philip, 'Alexander of Aphrodisias', *DSB*, 1, 117–20

———, 'Ammonius', *DSB*, 1, 137

Milton, John, *Paradise Regained*, edited by Merritt Y. Hughes, New York, c. 1937

Morford, Mark, *The Roman Philosophers: From the Time of Cato the Censor to the Death of Marcus Aurelius*, London, 2001

Minio-Paluello, Lorenzo, 'James of Venice', *DSB*, 7, 65–7

————, 'William of Moerbeke', *DSB*, 9, 434–40

Monfasani, John, *Byzantine Scholars in Renaissance Italy: Cardinal Bessarion and other Emigres; Selected Essays*, Brookfield, Vermont, 1995

————, *Greeks and Latins in Renaissance, Studies in Humanism and Philosophy in the 15th Century*, Brookfield, Vermont, ca. 2004

———— (ed.), *Collectanea Trapezuntiana: texts, documents and bibliography of George of Trebizond, 1396–1486*, Binghamton, New York, 1984

Morrow, Glenn R., 'Proclus', *DSB*, 11, 160–2

Mourelatos, Alexander P. D., 'Empedocles of Acragas', *DSB*, 4, 367–9

Murdoch, John, 'Euclid: The Transmission of the Elements', *DSB*, 4, 437–50

Nasr, Seyyid Hossein, *Science and Civilization in Islam*, Cambridge, Massachusetts, 1968

————, *Islamic Science, An Illustrated History*, Cairo, 1976.

Netz, Reviel and William Noel, *The Archimedes Codex: Revealing the Blueprint of Modern Science*, London, 2007

Neugebauer, Otto, *The Exact Sciences in Antiquity*, 2nd ed., Providence, Rhode Island, 1957

————, *A History of Ancient Mathematical Astronomy*, 3 vols., New York. 1975

Newton, Isaac, *Principia* (*Mathematical Principles of Natural Philosophy*), translated by I. Bernard Cohen and Anne Whitman, Berkeley, 1999

————, *Opticks, or a Treatise on the Reflections, Refractions, Inflections, and Colours of Light*, London, 1952

North, John David, *The Norton History of Astronomy and Cosmology*, New York, 1995

Nutton, Vivian, *Ancient Medicine*, London and New York, 2005

O'Leary, De Lacy, *How Greek Science Passed to the Arabs*, London, 1949

O'Meara, D. J., *Pythagoras Revived: Mathematics and Philosophy in Late Antiquity*, Oxford, 1990

O'Neil, W. M., *Time and the Calendar*, Sydney, 1975

————, *Early Astronomy from Babylonia to Copernicus*, Sydney, 1986

Osborne, Robin, *Greece in the Making, 1200–479 BC*, London, 1996

Owen, G. E. L, M. Balme, Leonard G. Wilson, and L. Minio-Paluello, 'Aristotle', *DSB*, 1, 250–81

Oxford Dictionary of Byzantium, general editor Alexander B. Khazdan, 3 vols., New York, 1991

Pannekoek, Anton, *A History of Astronomy*, New York, 1961

Paschos, E. A. and P. Sotiroudis, *The Schemata of the Stars: Byzantine Astronomy from A. D. 1300*, Singapore, 1998

Pausanias, *Description of Greece*, 2 vols., translated by Peter Levi, Harmondsworth, 1985

Payne-Gaposchkin, Cecelia, *Introduction to Astronomy*, New York, 1954

Peters, C. H. F. and E. B. Knobel, *Ptolemy's Catalogue of Stars: A Revision of the Almagest*, Washington, D. C. 1915

Peters, Francis E., *The Harvest of Hellenism: a history of the Near East from Alexander the Great to the triumph of Christianity*, New York, 1970

Philip, J. A., *Pythagoras and Early Pythagoreanism*, Toronto, 1966

BIBLIOGRAPHY

Pingree, David, 'The Greek Influence on Early Islamic Mathematical Astronomy', *Journal of the American Oriental Society*, 93, no. 1 (1973), 32–43

———, 'Gregory Chioniades and Palaeologan Astronomy', *Dumbarton Oaks Papers* 18 (1964), 135–60

———, 'Classical and Byzantine Astrology in Sassanian Persia', *Dumbarton Oaks Papers* 43 (1989) 227–35

———, 'Leo the Mathematician', *DSB*, 8, 190–2

———, 'Psellus, Michael', *DSB*, 11, 182–6

———, 'Paul of Alexandria', *DSB*, 9, 419

Plato, *The Complete Works of Plato*, edited by John M. Cooper, Indianapolis, Indiana, 1993

Pliny the Elder, *Natural History*, translated by H. Rackham et al, Cambridge, Mass., 1942–63

Plutarch, *Plutarch's Lives*, 10 vols., translated by Bernadotte Perrin, Cambridge, Mass., 1942–9

Price, Derek De Solla, 'An Ancient Greek Computer', *Scientific America* (1959), 60–7

Psellus, Michael, *Chronographia*, translated by F. R. A. Sewter, New Haven, 1953

Ptolemy's *Almagest*, translated and annotated by G. C. Toomer with a foreword by Owen Gingerich, Princeton, 1998

Ragep, F. Jamil, and Sally P. Ragep (eds.) *Tradition, Transmission, Transformation*, Leiden, 1996

Rashdall, Hastings, *The Universities in Europe in the Middle Ages*, 3 vols., London, 1936

Raven, J, E., *Pythagoreans and Eleatics, An account of the interaction between the two opposed schools during the fifth and early fourth centuries B.C.*, Cambridge, 1948

Riddle, John M., 'Dioscorides', *DSB*, 4, 119–23

Rihill, T. E., *Greek Science*, Oxford, 1995

Rivier, André, 'Xenophanes', *DSB*, 14, 536–7

Rosen, Edward, *Three Copernican Theses*, New York, 1959

———, 'Johannes Regiomontanus', *DSB*, 11, 348–52

Rosenthal, Franz, *The Classical Heritage in Islam*, tran. Emile and Jenny Marmorstein, London, 1975,

———, *Science and Medicine in Islam*, Brookfield, Vermont, 1990

———, *Greek Philosophy and the Arabs*, Brookfield, Vermont, 1990

Ross, W. D. (ed.), *The Works of Aristotle*, 3 vols., Oxford, 1908–52

Runciman, Steven, *The Last Byzantine Renaissance*, Cambridge, 1970

———, *Byzantium and the Renaissance*, Tucson, 1970

Sabra, A. I., 'The Appropriation and Subsequent Naturalization of Greek Science in Medieval Islam: A Preliminary Statement', Ragep, F. Jamil, and Sally P. Ragep with Steven Livesey (eds.) *Tradition, Transmission, Transformation*, pp. 3–27

Salmon, Wesley C., *Zeno's Paradoxes*, Indianapolis, 2001

Sambursky, Samuel, *The Physical World of the Greeks*, London, 1956

———, *Physics of the Stoics*, New York, 1959

———, 'John Philoponus', *DSB*, 7, 134–9

Sarton, George, *A History of Science*, 2 vols., Cambridge, Mass., 1952, 1959

———, *The Appreciation of Ancient and Medieval Science During the Renaissance, 1459–1600*, Philadelphia, 1955

———, *The History of Science and the New Humanism*, New York, 1956

———, *Galen of Pergamon*, Lawrence, Kansas, 1957

Sedley, David (ed.), *The Cambridge Companion to Greek and Roman Philosophy*, New York, 2003

Sesiano, Jacques, 'Diophantus of Alexandria', *DSB*, 15, 118–22

Shakespeare, William, *The Complete Works*, edited by Peter Alexander, New York, 1952

Shank, Michael H., 'The Classical Scientific Tradition in Fifteenth-Century

Vienna', Ragep, F. Jamil, and Sally P. Ragep with Steven Livesey (eds.) *Tradition, Transmission, Transformation*, pp. 115–36

Singer, Charles, E. J. Holmyard, and A. R. Hall, *A History of Technology*, 2 vols., Oxford, 1954–1984

Solmsen, F., *Aristotle's System of the Physical World: a comparison with his predecessors*, Ithaca, New York, 1960

Spenser, Edmund, *The Faerie Queene*, 2 vols., New York, 1927

Stahl, William H., 'The Greek Heliocentric Theorem and its Abandonment', *Transactions of the American Philosophical Society* 76 (1945), 121–32

———, 'Aristarchus of Samos', *DSB*, 1, 246–50

———, 'Martianus Capella', *DSB*, 9, 140–1

Steel, Duncan, *Marking Time: The Epic Quest to Invent the Perfect Calendar*, New York, 2000

Steele, John M, *A Brief Introduction to Astronomy in the Middle East*, London, 2008

Strabo, *Geography*, 8 vols., translated by Horace Leonard Jones, Cambridge, Mass., 1982

Sullivan, J. W. N., *Isaac Newton, 1642–1727*, New York, 1928

Taran, Leonardo, 'Anaximander', *DSB*, 1, 150–1

———, 'Anaximenes', *DSB*, 1, 151–2

———, 'Aratus of Soli', *DSB*, 1, 204–5

———, 'Nichomachus of Gerasa', *DSB*, 10, 113–14

———, 'Parmenides of Elea', DSB, 10, 324–5

Taton, René, *History of Science*, 4 vols., translated by A. J. Pomerans, New York, 1964–6

Taylor, Henry Osborn, *Greek Medicine and Biology*, New York, 1963

Theophrastus, *Enquiry into Plants* and *Minor Works on Odours and Weather Signs*, 2 vols., translated by Arthur Hort, Cambridge, Mass., 1916

———, *On the Causes of Plants*, Book I, translated by R. E. Dengler, Philadelphia, 1927

———, *The Characters*, edited and translated by J. M. Edmonds, London and New York, 1929

———, *Metaphysics*, translated by W. D. Ross and F. H. Fobes, Oxford, 1929

———, *On Stones*, translated by E. R. Caley and J. F. C. Richards, Columbus, Ohio, 1956

Thomas, Phillip Drennon, 'Paul of Aegina', *DSB*, 9, 417–19

BIBLIOGRAPHY

Thomson, J. Oliver, *History of Ancient Geography*, New York, 1995

Thorndike, Lynn, *A History of Magic and Experimental Science*, 8 vols, New York, 1923–56

Thucydides, *History of the Peloponnesian War*, translated by Rex Warner, Harmondsworth, 1987

Tivier, Andre, 'Xenophanes', DSB, 14, 536–7

Toomer, G. J., 'Apollonius of Perga', *DSB*, 1, 17–93

———, 'Ptolemy (Claudius Ptolemaeus)', *DSB*, 11, 186–206

———, 'Theon of Alexandria', *DSB*, 321–5

———, Heraclides Ponticus, *DSB*, 15, 202–5

———, 'Hipparchus', *DSB*, 15, 207–24

———, 'Vitruvius Pollio', *DSB*, 15, 514–21

Tuplin, C. J. and T. E. Rihill (ed.), *Science and Mathematics in Ancient Greek Culture*, New York, 2002

Van Helden, Albert, *Measuring the Universe: Cosmic Dimensions from Aristarchus to Halley*, Chicago, 1985

Vasiliev, A. A., *A History of the Byzantine Empire*, 2 vols., Madison, Wisconsin, 1952

Verbeke, G., 'Simplicius', *DSB*, 12, 440–3

Vitruvius, *The Ten Books on Architecture (De Architectura)*, translated by Morris Hicky Morgan, New York, 1966

Vogel, Kurt, 'Byzantine Science', in *Cambridge Medieval History*, new edition, vol. 4, part 2, pp. 264–305

———, 'Diophantus of Alexandria, *DSB*, 4, 110–19

Voltaire, *Letters on England*, translated by Leonard Tancock, Harmondsworth, 1980

Waerden, B. L. van der, *Science Awakening*, translated by Arnold Dresden, Groningen, 1974

Warmington, E. H., 'Posidonius', *DSB*, 11, 103–6

———, 'Strabo', *DSB*, 13, 83–6

Warren, John R., 'Architects to Justinian', *Art and Archaeology Research Papers* (December, 1976), pp. 1–12

Whitfield, Peter, *Landmarks in Western Science: From Prehistory to the Atomic Age*, London, 1991

Wilson, Leonard G., 'Galen: Anatomy and Physiology', *DSB*, 5, 233–7

Wilson, Nigel. 'Archimedes: The Palimpsest and the Tradition', *Byzantinische Zeitschrift* 92, (1999), 89–101

———, *From Byzantium to Italy: Greek Studies in the Italian Renaissance*, London, 1992

Yeats, William Butler, *The Works of W. B. Yeats*, The Wordsworth Poetry Library, Hertfordshire, 1994

Zeller, Eduard, *Outline of the History of Greek Philosophy*, 13th edition, revised by Wilhelm Nestle, London, 1935

INDEX

Academy of Plato 41, 42, 79,
    161, 209
Acropolites, George 174
Aëtius 8, 9, 13, 19, 22, 87, 91
Albertus Magnus, St 169, 181
Alcmaeon 21
Alexander of Aphrodisias 23, 150, 151
Alexandria 77–86, 92, 93, 94, 114, 115,
    119–23, 134–44, 145, 149, 150,
    151, 152, 153, 154, 158, 209
Ammonius of Alexandria 155,
    158, 160
Anaxagoras 5, 33, 34, 35, 40, 44, 45
Anaximander 5, 9, 10
Anaximenes 5, 11, 12
Anthemius of Tralles 161
Apollonius of Perge 85, 103–6, 171,
    191, 201, 203
Aquinas, St Thomas 169, 181, 195
Archimedes 51, 52, 87, 95–102, 103,
    114, 161, 168, 171, 172, 187, 202,
    203, 204, 205, 206, 207, 208, 209
Archytas 23, 41, 42, 50
Argyros, Isaac 178
Aristarchus of Samos 87, 88, 89, 90,
    167, 184, 186, 201, 206
Aristippus, Henricus 171
Aristotle 7, 8, 12, 17, 21, 23, 26, 31, 35,
    36, 37, 38, 54–65, 71, 72, 73, 76,
    77, 78, 145, 147, 150, 151, 158,
    159, 164, 165, 168, 169, 171, 172,
    174, 175, 178, 180, 181, 186, 190,
    195, 209
Athens 5, 33, 39, 40, 41–9, 54–63, 66–71, 145,
    161
Augustine, St 147, 175

Baghdad 163, 164, 165, 166, 167
Bayt al-Hikma (House of Wisdom)
    163, 165
Bessarion, Cardinal 180, 181, 182,
    183, 184
Blemmydes, Nicephorus 174
Boethius 21, 148, 149, 175, 205
Brahe, Tycho 189, 190, 191, 192,
    193, 201
Bruno, Giordano 189
Bryennios, Manuel 176, 177

Callipus 49
Cardano, Geronimo 118
Cassiodorus 149, 205
Chalcidius 48, 148
Chionides, George 176, 177
Chrysippus 75
Chrysococces, George 176, 177, 178
Chrysolaras, Manuel 179, 181
Cicero 11, 145, 17
Cleomedes 174
Constantinople (Byzantium, Istanbul)
    114, 116–19, 153, 156, 161, 166,
    162, 169, 170, 171, 172, 173, 174,

175, 176, 177, 178, 179, 180,
    181, 182
Copernicus, Nicolaus 87, 177, 183, 184,
    185–8, 190, 191, 196, 201, 206
Ctesibius 114, 115, 116

Dedekind. J. W. R. 51
Democritus 35–9, 74, 189, 201
Descartes, René 152, 159, 201
Diogenes Laertius 6, 12, 15, 24, 33, 35,
    38, 55, 66, 71
Diophantus 149, 150, 167, 175, 201
Dioscorides 131–3, 149, 166

Ecphantus 22
Edessa (Urfa) 157
Empedocles 5, 16, 30, 31, 32, 33,
    58, 201
Epicurus 36, 73, 20
Eratosthenes 10, 92, 93, 94, 98, 110
Euclid 5, 43, 51, 72, 78–86, 98, 106,
    110, 135, 154, 164, 165, 166, 167,
    171, 174, 175, 201, 204
Euctemon 49, 50
Eudoxus 50, 51
Eutocius 103, 160, 161, 172, 205

al-Farabi 168
Al-Farghani 165 168
Fermat, Pierre 150

Galen 75, 124–30, 133, 149, 166, 168
Galileo Galilei 191, 192, 193, 194, 195,
    196, 197, 201, 206
Gerard of Cremona 168, 169, 205
Gregoras, Nikephorous 176, 178

Harvey, William 128
Hecataeus 6, 10, 11, 24
Heraclides Ponticus 22, 52, 53, 148, 191
Heraclitus 5, 24, 25, 26, 27
Hero of Alexandria 114, 119–23, 167,
    171, 172, 178, 202, 203, 206
Herodotus 2, 4
Hesiod 4, 5, 24, 27
Hipparchus 106, 107, 108, 109,
    110, 137
Hippocrates of Chios 34, 35
Hippocrates of Kos 44, 125, 149, 166

Hippolytus 6, 20, 37
Homer 3, 27
Hunayn ibn Ishaq 166
Hypatia 154
Hypsicles 85

Iamblichus 18, 148
Ibn Sina 168
Ionia 1–14, 39
Isidorus of Miletus 161

James of Venice 171
John Philoponus 158, 159, 160
Jundashapur 157

Kepler, Johannes 154, 191–195, 206
al-Khwarizmi 163, 164, 168
al-Kindi 165, 168

Lavoisier, Antoine-Laurent de 118
Leo the Mathematician 170, 204
Leonardo of Pisa (Fibonacci) 171
Leucippus 35–8, 74
Library and Museum of Alexandria 77,
    78, 119, 153, 154, 155, 209
Lobachevsky, Nicolai Ivanovich 80
Lucretius 74, 146, 189
Lyceum of Aristotle 57, 66, 70, 71,
    73, 209

Macrobius 148
Magna Graecia 5, 12–14, 27–35
Martianus Capella 148
Meliteniotes, Theodore 178
Metochites, Theodore 176
Meton 49
Miletus 1–3, 6–12, 35, 209

Nasir ad-Din al-Tusi 91, 177, 188,
    205
Newton, Isaac 185, 188, 197, 198, 199,
    200, 201, 202, 206
Nicholas of Cusa 154, 206
Nichomachus 149, 174, 176

Pachymeres, George 175
Panaetius of Rhodes 145
Pappus 78, 85, 96, 104, 141, 151, 152,
    201, 204

Parmenides 5, 16, 27, 28, 29, 30, 35, 36, 45
Pericles 33, 34, 40
Peurbach, Georg 182, 183
Philo of Byzantium 114, 116–19, 121
Philolaus 18, 19, 22, 23, 41, 201
Planudes, Maximos 175, 177
Plato 16, 23, 24, 29, 34, 39, 40–9, 53, 58, 94, 145, 168, 172, 178, 180, 182, 201
Plethon, George Gemistus 178, 180, 181
Pliny the Elder 147
Plotinus 147, 148
Plutarch 23, 33, 41, 42, 43, 96
Porphyry 17, 20
Posidonias 145, 146
Proclus 7, 18, 34, 86, 154, 155, 172
Psellus, Michael 170, 171, 174
Ptolemy (Claudius Ptolmaeus) 106, 110, 134–44, 154, 164, 168, 171, 174, 176, 178, 181, 182, 183, 190, 194, 196, 201, 203
Pythagoras, Pythagoreans 5, 15–23, 24, 27, 41, 46, 52, 58, 82, 185, 186, 187, 191, 199, 201

Qushji, Ali 183, 184
Qusta ibn Luca 91, 167, 168

Regiomontanus, Johannes 182, 183, 184, 06
Reinhold, Erasmus 188
Riemann, G.F.B. 80
Rome 145, 146, 147, 148, 162

Seleucus the Chaldean 88
Seneca 147
Sergius of Reshaina 157
Severus Sebokht 157
Sextus Empiricus 19
Simplicius 8, 30, 50, 52, 158, 159, 172
Snell, Willibrod 144
Socrates 29, 39, 40, 44, 45, 47, 65
Stoics 75, 76
Strabo 15, 111, 112, 113, 181
Strato 70–3

Thabit ibn Qurra 166, 167, 168, 205
Thales 5, 6, 7, 8, 9
Theaetatus 43
Theodorus of Cyrene 43
Theon of Alexandria 141, 153, 154, 167
Theon of Smyrna 21, 94, 109
Theophrastus 55, 66–71, 145, 147
Toledo 168
Trapezuntios, George 180–183

Vitruvius Pollio 100, 114, 115, 116, 146, 147

Weierstrass, Karl 51
Wiles, Andrew 150
William of Moerbeke 172, 205, 206, 209

Xenophanes 5, 12, 13, 14, 17, 24, 27

Zeno of Citium 73, 74, 75, 87
Zeno of Elea 5, 29, 3o, 35, 45